Women Poets on Mentorship

Women Poets on Mentorship
Efforts and Affections

EDITED BY
Arielle Greenberg and Rachel Zucker

UNIVERSITY OF IOWA PRESS
IOWA CITY

University of Iowa Press, Iowa City 52242
Copyright © 2008 by the University of Iowa Press
www.uiowapress.org
Printed in the United States of America
Design by Sara T. Sauers

The University of Iowa Press is a member
of Green Press Initiative and is committed
to preserving natural resources.

Printed on acid-free paper

LCCN: 2007941193
ISBN-13: 978-1-58729-639-0
ISBN-10: 1-58729-639-x

08 09 10 11 12 P 5 4 3 2 1

Poets on p. ii, left to right, top to bottom: Factor,
Fennelly, Field, Ford, Gottlieb, Harvey, Kaschock,
Katz, Lederer, Martínez, Meitner, Moxley,
Nezhukumatathil, Obadike, Pafunda, Prevallet,
Salach, Schiff, Schultz, Sikelianos, Smith, Treadwell,
Williams, Wolff. Photo credits on p. 304.

For the women poets who came before us:
how lucky, how lifesaving to have you all.

CONTENTS

ACKNOWLEDGMENTS

IT WAS IMPORTANT to us that this project be a collaboration, an out-growth of our close friendship, partly because we loved the excuse to be to-gether and partly because it felt in keeping with a female model of cooperative work. But the work of this book stretched far beyond our friendship. We are thankful to all the people who helped make this book possible.

First and foremost we thank the contributors for their essays: it was an honor to work with you. And we thank all the talented poets of our gener-ation: we love reading your work.

The Mindichs and Zuckers lent us their homes so we could get together and work free from distraction. Thank you for these meaningful retreats.

We are both married to exceptional men. Rachel's husband Josh took care of their children, sometimes for days at a time, while we went on our working retreats, and later typed up poems and worked on the index when we couldn't find the time. Arielle's husband Rob cooked meals while we typed and talked, edited and vetted when we had drafts done, and provided child care and support throughout the process.

Annie Finch, D. A. Powell, and David Trinidad suggested possible contributors and subjects. Joy Katz and Catherine Barnett provided superb editorial help. Kevin Prufer and Alicia Ostriker offered supportive and insightful feedback on the manuscript-in-progress. Two private foundations donated funds to support this project. Ken Daley, English Department chair at Columbia College, secured additional financial support for this book as well. The University of Iowa Press, especially our editor Joe Parsons, has given the book the kind of attention and home we wanted most for it.

Lastly, we thank our own mentors—women and men, poets and artists—who by example and influence enticed us into a life of art. For Rachel, these mentors include her mother, storyteller/writer Diane Wolkstein; poets Adrienne Rich, the late James Schuyler, Alice Notley, David Trinidad, Leslie Scalapino, and Anne Carson; poets/teachers Nancy Kricorian, Wayne Koestenbaum, Jorie Graham, Brenda Hillman, Marvin Bell, James Galvin, and Heather McHugh; elementary and high school teachers Larry Sandomir and John Aune; and the late monologist Spalding Gray.

For Arielle, these mentors include Lyn Lifshin, who lived in her hometown and gave her private lessons when she was a young girl; high school English teachers Deborah Kelsh and the late Karen Ludwig; Sonia Sanchez, who gave the first poetry reading Arielle ever saw and at it presented her with an award; Ruth Stone, her college workshop leader, who took her seriously; film scholar Tom Gunning, who introduced her to scholarship; the late Barbara Guest, who gave her a seat in a master class; her female graduate school professors, fiction writer Mary Caponegro and poets Malena Mörling (who taught pregnant) and Mary Karr (who told Arielle to have a child); Kathleen Fraser, who brought her on to the board of How2; David Trinidad, a friend and colleague; C. D. Wright, Anne Carson, and Heather McHugh, whose work has been vital; and poets Jean Valentine and Michael Burkard, whose guidance, poetry, and gracious conduct have been shining examples.

INTRODUCTION

"I HADN'T KNOWN poetry could be like that; I took to it immediately," wrote Elizabeth Bishop about her experience of first reading Marianne Moore. In her essay "Efforts of Affection: A Memoir of Marianne Moore," found in The Collected Prose (1984), Bishop goes on to describe how she later met Moore in person, went with her to the circus, and, at Moore's request, diverted the elephants with stale bread so that Moore could clip a hair off the top of a baby elephant's head.

Bishop's relationship with Moore spanned thirty-five years. The two women shifted between roles of mentor and mentee, expert and apprentice. They were friends, colleagues, and confidantes, sharing drafts of poems and talking about aesthetics, morality, personal ambition, and temperament. Although they didn't always agree, Bishop writes that she never left Moore's home "without feeling happier: uplifted, even inspired, determined to be good, to work harder, not to worry about what other people thought, never to try to publish anything until I thought I'd done my best with it, no matter how many years it took—or never to publish at all."

This relationship, both tender and formal, between two major women poets was exceedingly unusual for Bishop's generation. Bishop had Moore, but whom did Sylvia Plath, Muriel Rukeyser, Adrienne Rich, or Gwendolyn Brooks have? Whom did Amy Lowell, Gertrude Stein, Sara Teasdale, Edna St. Vincent Millay, Louise Bogan, Lorine Niedecker, and Denise Levertov have? These poets were often "invisible even to one another," says Florence Howe, editor of the essential anthology of poetry by women about women, No More Masks (first published in 1973). Those women who *were* published and read were mostly mentored by men, if they were mentored at all. Often they were almost completely isolated.

Things have changed. We may shake our heads sadly at the idea of women writing without the company and advice of other women writers, knowing how dark our own moments of solitude and loneliness feel. But while we all do occasionally experience invisibility or isolation, the true cost of going it alone is hard for young American women writing today to fathom because, in 2008, we have what Adrienne Rich in 1976 considered "the essential condition for all fully realized work": community. We have women whom "we envision as our hearers, our co-creators, our challengers; who will urge us to take our work further, more seriously, than we had dared; on whose work we can build."

In her foreword to The Extraordinary Tide, another excellent anthology of women's poetry (edited by Susan Aizenberg and Erin Belieu, 2001), Eleanor Wilner writes that what the women poets included therein—poets born before the feminist movement of the late 1960s—have in common despite their "heterogeneous backgrounds, aesthetics, concerns and voices" is "the immense silence at [their] backs." Despite that silence, the women of Wilner's generation learned to make noise; they were and are united by their experience of speaking out of that silence. The poets whose essays appear in this anthology are the daughters of that clamor. We are bound together not only by the history of silence experienced by the generations of women poets before us but also by the glorious and recent noisemaking of our teachers, mothers, sisters, aunts, mentors, role models, and peers.

The resulting poetry, the poetry being made by younger American women poets today, bears the stamp of both abstracted literary lineage and the actual, real-life encounters with the older women poets who have shaped and informed us. We have been exposed to the works, many now considered masterpieces, of the women writers of the Beats, the Confessionals, the Black Arts Movement, the New York School, the Black Mountain Movement, the Objectivists, the Language Poets. We have been influenced by the overtly feminist poems and essays of Adrienne Rich, Alicia Ostriker, Audre Lorde, bell hooks, Alice Walker, Gloria Steinem, and other eminent thinkers, who helped define the cultural moment in which we were raised as girls. We have been lifted up by the "extraordinary tide" of older women poets living and working today. We have come to know those in the generation before us who have made various life choices: to become mothers or not; to teach or to work outside of academia; to be an activist or to shield oneself from the world; to focus on the political or the personal, the confessional or the opaque.

In order to document and celebrate the clamor and community of contemporary women's poetry and, in particular, the relationships between these two generations, we invited American women poets born in the 1960s and 1970s, in the middle of the second wave of feminism, to write essays about their living mentors or role models. We asked each to identify the poet she most wanted to write about and were pleased to find almost no overlap, which further proved the wealth of existing mentors. Some of the women our contributors write about here were chosen for their aesthetic contributions to poetry, having caused readers to radically change their own way of writing or thinking. Some were chosen for their personal generosity and kindness or because they were brilliant scholars or great lecturers. There are stories about admiration, jealousy, friendship, loneliness, ambition, vanity, and independence. There are funny essays about eccentric personalities and lighthearted encounters, serious pieces about religious doubt and the work of art-making, and exuberant essays about charismatic teachers and performers. The essays describe how older poets make younger poets feel acknowledged, powerful, eager to keep working.

These essays shed light on how our contributors became poets, where they find inspiration, and how they came to make important poetic and life choices: the essays also describe a new kind of influence, one less hierarchical and less patriarchal than the traditional model. While many of these relationships begin with the classic student-teacher dynamic, the participants often wind up as friends, peers. "Life to him would be Death to me," said Keats of Milton. This is not at all the sentiment these essays describe. The poets here do not lose themselves in the relationship with their mentors. The connection with the mentor or with the mentor's work is often lifesaving for these young women.

We were pleased to discover the ways the myriad aesthetics of one generation have inspired the often hybridized styles of the next. Often defining themselves in between artistic movements, the younger poets mix the evidence of their lineage with the postmodern pastiche of the times, rejecting their aesthetic foremothers even as they embrace them. We sought to publish the essays with poems written by both generations to highlight the poetic moment we are currently experiencing. Some of the steadfast poles of historically divided aesthetic camps have begun to shift and sway; there is no sameness of voice or style here.

The reader may notice that a central theme does emerge in the essays: that of self and selfhood, and of the ways in which the connection between the self and the poem—between identity and form, biography and aesthetic—is at the heart of the mentor-mentee relationship. Many young poets claim that the biggest gift their mentors gave them was the permission to write about the impermissible. Often the taboo subject is girls' and women's bodies, domestic work, or women's rituals and experiences. Our contributors write about being given permission, directly or through their mentor's own poems, to speak about the female experience anew, in ugly ways, in funny ways, in fractured and confessional and abstract and beautiful ways. Matthea Harvey notes that Anna Rabinowitz invented a female poetry ancestor as a project; none of the contributors here had to invent mentors for themselves. The mentor poets are present, connected, even when they are walking alongside the younger poets rather than out in front.

The connections described are urgent: Valerie Martínez, for example, writes, "Joy Harjo's poetry has been a force against my own destruction— my alienation from myself as a girl/woman, as a story, as a historical being," while Miranda Field describes the way in which Fanny Howe's work, in which motherhood is not the subject but the "consciousness" and "medium" of the poems, provided "an entry opening into [her] own" poems after she became a mother for the first time. The presence of a living generation reassures the younger poets that they are not alone, that they are part of a historic lineage and a contemporary community of friendship and experience, or at least an "invisible company" (as Jennifer Moxley writes in her essay on Susan Howe); it also validates the hard truth that the poet's life is frequently one of silence and isolation.

Many of the connections are intellectual: Katie Ford learns how to "inhabit difficulties" as Jorie Graham guides her toward writing from the darkest places of personal and public history and doubt; Katy Lederer "enlists" in the aesthetic academic wars in which Lyn Hejinian played a vital role; Kristin Prevallet defines her own notion of feminist ego through the work of Anne Waldman; Robyn Schiff finds in Gjertrud Schnackenberg a poetic twin whose interest in artifice and the way "received forms and invented procedures exasperate notions of mastery, power, control, and closure" match her own.

Many of the connections are vibrant: Matthea Harvey surveys the flea market in New York City with Anna Rabinowitz; Aimee Nezhukumatathil brings her beloved Naomi Shihab Nye to the college where she teaches; Beth Ann Fennelly writes about the darker and more humorous edges of sexuality after reading Denise Duhamel; Jenny Factor shyly offers a flower and fan letter to Marilyn Hacker.

Many of the connections are complex: Kirsten Kaschock writes, somewhat sorrowfully, about never feeling quite comfortable with a female mentor, despite her passion for poetry by other women. Joy Katz admits a certain shame associated with loving the iconic work of Sharon Olds. Cin Salach writes about the way her relationship with Maureen Seaton evolved from student to friend to lover and back to friend. And Daphne Gottlieb examines what it means to be asked to act as a mentor for younger poets when she herself does not feel ready for the weight of the role.

We invite the reader to uncover other connections across the book. One could choose, for example, to focus on essays that explore mentorship in the academy (in essays by Tracy Smith, Katy Lederer, and Katie Ford, among others) or from a distance (in essays by Robyn Schiff, Jennifer Moxley, and Kristin Prevallet). One could look at the close readings of poems in essays by Kathy Lou Schultz, Eleni Sikelianos, and others. One could read the essays—such as those by Erika Meitner, Mendi Lewis Obadike, and Danielle Pafunda—in which the older poets' personal choices or personalities teach their mentees something about how to live as women writers. Or one could look at essays about poets who define themselves in contrast to their mentors (see the work by Joy Katz and Rebecca Wolff) or who consider their mentors their foremothers (Elizabeth Treadwell, Valerie Martínez, and Crystal Williams). Attentive readers will notice dialogues between the younger poets—dialogues that reach across divides of age, race, ethnicity, sexuality, and aesthetic bents—that are just as compelling as the relationships the younger poets have with the work and lives of their mentors.

Because we asked contributors to choose their own subjects, we could not control which poets of the previous generations would be represented. Although many important poets are absent here, we hope that this anthology, while being the first of its kind, will not be the last, and that future such projects will provide plenty of room for more explorations of the ideas we have begun to document.

As a whole, this book describes a culture of manifold artistic relationships and the clamorous experience of being a young woman poet writing at the beginning of the twenty-first century. Because the poems are always central here, we include a small selection along with the essays. We hope that this anthology will also serve as an introduction to some of the most interesting new voices in American poetry and as a reminder of the wealth and range of women's poetry.

We offer this book as tribute to and celebration of those who have paved our way, those who continue on the path alongside us, and those who are yet to come.

Women Poets on Mentorship

Jenny Factor
on Marilyn Hacker

A wave of chatter subdivides the room.
Are you here on the Bride's side or the Groom's?

I SCRIBBLED THIS couplet on the floor of the Pen and Brush Club in New York City, moments before a poetry reading by Marilyn Hacker and Phyllis Levin. It was a rainy mid-September evening in that hot, clearly lit space. There was indeed an aisle down the center with banks of chairs on either side. We all had on too many layers—it was mosquitoey hot.

Although I first met Marilyn then, I'd known her work for years. Several friends had urged her poetry on me, first during my sexually ambiguous and lush free-verse college days, when I had not responded well to her use of confessional voice and form, then again in my hyperconventional early twenties, when I'd felt threatened by Hacker's overt lesbian and feminist content. Finally, I came to her work in earnest when I began to love another woman writer deeply and unrequitedly. One day she leant me

Hacker's books about lesbian loss and longing with the pointed question, "Is this the way you feel about me?"

During long hours at the dusty local park watching my son, I'd read and reread "Iva's Pantoum," "Gerda in the Eyrie," and *Love, Death, and the Changing of the Seasons* (1995) with personal amazement, my blood humming the answer, "Yes." Hacker, the young mother with rocks in her pockets who appears in Norton's 1994 edition of her *Selected Poems*, could have been me, shoulders streaked with snot, pockets stuffed with popsicle sticks, writing while I chased my son's tricycle. Her coming-out in the middle of a marriage at the age of twenty-seven (with an infant still sleeping in the couple's dresser drawers) seemed to parallel my own evolving and often sordid drama. Her work became my life's sound track, her voice my intimate coconspirator. Her aesthetics lent finesse and prosodic legitimacy to a story that seemed to dip too perilously off my known world's map. Although I still struggled with everything about myself—from my poetic choices to my hair length—I loved Hacker's poems from my stomach to my scalp.

Flash-forward to the Pen and Brush as, sharing a row with strangers, I discreetly looked around. Where were the other lesbians in the audience? I didn't see a single one! In the far back of the room, a nervous woman in a navy pantsuit paced back and forth. The room's sole androgyne, she had giant eyes and striking silver jewelry. Was this Marilyn Hacker? I liked her. I took a breath.

"Phyllis Levin is amazing," I heard from a woman beside me. "I'm taking a class with her at the Ninety-second Street Y."

"Lambda Literary Award. What's that?" one of the men in the row behind me asked, reading the biographies in the program.

Lonely and displaced, a lesbian fan in a room of suave and wholly heterosexual literati, I penned my couplet.

Then, I listened in a sweat. On my lap: my complete collection of Hacker's books; under my seat: a fan's thank-you note I'd penned over my son's nap hour, letting his drowsing dither on as I'd fussed with the words, dreading for him the long wakeful night with a new sitter, dreading even more how I'd feel if my letter was written awkwardly or wrongly. Under my seat was an iris I'd purchased at a small store along the Palisades Interstate Parkway on my way into town. But, unfortunately, examining it in the front seat of my VW before the reading, I'd lost my nerve. The flower seemed too long, and wrongheadedly romantic. So I chopped three or four clumsy inches off the stem with a dull pocketknife before I slammed the car door and stumbled into the Pen and Brush. My palms sweated against my stack of books.

Hacker was wonderful—shy, gracious, and funny, her poems generous, her voice soft-spoken, lilting, and lyrical. You could hear her famously excellent ear for street talk and sibilance, for sound and meter—in the way her voice clung to and released certain words. With just the right collection of phrases, she praised the young and graceful Phyllis Levin. While reading her own work, Hacker dedicated certain verses to good friends and honored a request for "Ballad of Ladies Lost and Found."

After the reading, I approached Marilyn at the signing table, juggling my too-many books, uncertain whether to hide or show my flower. As I got to the front of the line, a Pen and Brush staffer grabbed me by the upper arm. "Excuse me, miss, you must pay for those books before she signs them!" Stuttering with surprise, I jumped, and Marilyn, stammering also, answered: "Those are *her* books. She brought them with her." Emboldened, I handed her my iris along with my letter. She accepted them, but a little warily, then opened each book and signed: "Best Wishes" without jotting down the personalization of my name. I walked away, cursing myself under my breath, feeling exposed, out-of-place, and foolish.

As the room cleared, I saw Hacker leave with a couple of friends. They shared a cab, presumably to dinner. As I walked out into what had become a warm fall drizzle, I imagined her opening my letter, perhaps even laughing at my iris. I had never in my life felt more exposed—a fan who had allowed the intimacy of my reading life to cause me to breach etiquette, an outsider in a big and cultured city. I went home vowing never to do anything so stupidly ingenuous again.

So I was taken by surprise two months later to receive a friendly and belated thank-you note for the flower—with "Marilyn Hacker" printed on a red ribbon return-address label on the upper-left front. Hacker suggested I drop in on her open graduate class at Hofstra University and (I'm sure for the sake of establishing boundaries) added an anecdote about her partner. By and by, I answered the letter and attended several of the Hofstra seminar meetings. A literary friendship started in earnest between us.

Looking back, I see that I had things to offer our dialogue. Although I admired Hacker's formal finesse and suffered a readerly adoration so intense it almost made my tongue numb, I had legitimate qualms and questions about whether I would want to use demiconfessional verse as my own aesthetic. Skilled as a writer myself, I had been the only incoming freshman admitted to Seamus Heaney's master class at Harvard. In short, although I met Hacker during one of the nadirs of my life, I was nevertheless a smart, questioning, skillful, and energetic young writer who had been writing and reading intelligently for many years, able to stand aesthetically on my own two feet. And during what became a working poets' dialogue, my comfort and confidence only grew.

Eventually, Marilyn and I came to read and critique one another's work. I realized that I tended to know, instinctively, how to hear through Marilyn's poem-drafts to her ultimate poem-project, reading with the careful attention of someone who could share an intense and critical personal interest in her words and aesthetic choices. She showed me, in turn, how to sharpen certain tools in my kit and led me to read in an entirely new way poets that I had overlooked, from Gertrude Stein and H. D. to various iterations of Robert Lowell's notebooks, poems in contemporary journals, and beyond. Besides talking about what we read, we'd play poem-games via e-mail sometimes, where draft answered draft. Once, memorably, a single stalled Hacker sonnet turned into a call-and-response cowritten sequence (although we ultimately extracted and completed our sonnets as two solo stand-alone sequences, each of which was subsequently published).

I'll admit that for me, the adoring reader, our early correspondence and friendship was a three-year language flirtation, word-center to word-center with no physical eros attached. Proud of our correspondence, I demanded more from my poems and prose whenever we spoke. I allowed myself to take aesthetic risks and enjoy the safety net of having Marilyn's reactions to them. And I sought to deepen the ties between our projects every few days with humor and questions. As the reader's crush deepened to a shared flirtation in language and language flirtation evolved into a meaningful, collaborative poetic project, everything about our relationship to each other's words and selves changed as well.

In the end, mentorship is most often a misnomer. The chosen communities in which writers grow and work are by nature multigenerational and diverse—dynamic, organic configurations of creative minds who like to use words. Poetry, more than any other medium, changes language, growing and redirecting the stream of what it is possible to say. Sometimes it takes the surprise questions and risks of a mind outside one's own to broaden one's sense of those linguistic possibilities. Marilyn and I did that for one another.

Conversely, one doesn't need to know a poet personally to make oneself a student of her texts and tactics. I had been apprenticed to Marilyn's work long before I met her. Apprenticeships to cold text thrive on the very vacuous infatuations that literary community cannot breathe in. And thank goodness! These apprenticeships, whether to Dante, Milton, or Mary Oliver, allow us a private and probing self-growth that isn't affected by life, circumstance, or social context.

When mentoring works, it meets some primary needs of both parties. The best "student" must be not only doting but also challenging (eager to embark on a complex, delving dialogue about some of the very aspects of craft that the mentor holds most dear). Meanwhile, the established poet may be willing to impart knowledge or, more accurately, restate clearly what she knows in exchange for an invigorating raking-over, especially in the dark zones where she keeps her habits and assumptions. And perhaps she's also electrified a bit by engaging with the vulnerability and enthusiasm of youth, for whom the old questions are still new. The mentor and the mentee, explorers together, are ultimately more interested in the varied terrain than in one another.

There's no doubt that meeting Marilyn and spending time with her allowed me to examine closely that evolving and fluid line between lived life and work. Through e-mails and shared experiences, I saw how a bad night's sleep might become a good line of dactyls and watched closely what she would notice or remember from a night out together at a café. Marilyn has a memory for thingyness: brand names, details, brush-strokes of background characters that I blot out. I tend toward romantic abstractions, jumping willingly and sometimes foolishly into a sweep of pure sound. In short, getting to know Marilyn made it easier to understand that what goes into her acts of making would never go into mine. And that was, indeed, an invaluable gift for me.

But also, by necessity, our very propinquity brought my reader's infatuation phase to an end. Marilyn became real to me as a writer and as a friend. She could no longer be only the intimate voice in my head—so quiet and close it was almost my own. I can sometimes miss the way it was when I was only her reader, and she only my poet, and when her words were larger to me than herself, larger to me than myself.

That clipped iris remains the best symbol of our first meeting. My desire to be seen and understood was too big for its circumstance; ultimately it was no different from the massacred flower—a wilted, leafy erection flopping over in my sweaty palms. A literary crush cannot make a good mentorship any more than a real-life infatuation can make anything but a fatuous and lopsided relationship.

For several crucial years as we got to know one another, Marilyn and I pushed each other's language onto new paths, fueled by our differences and similarities. Our relationship that began in intense vulnerability continues with acts of language transgression and exploration that are effectual and effective, and with a friendship in which I feel personally and poetically at home.

Jenny Factor ✳

from "Extramarital"

Scotch and Soda

The front door slipped from its latch and he
came in—the man you're married to and love.
He knows about this "us," this you-and-me,
and it is for his sake that words like "love"
and "tomorrow" don't flow between us easily
when Ella slips into the groove on the CD
player, your shirt lifts above your head
(my ice settling in my glass, I feel sour beads
of sweat from the summer heat rising
on my skin). Here the truth is surprising
even to me: I don't mind what we *don't*
say, what you *can't* feel. "I love you" is scary.
I mean something lighter. What I want:
Lay with me, wide-eyed, wary.

Rubyfruit

You kissed my mouth as if it were my sex
before you kissed me everywhere, before
that night in Rubyfruit's, my glasses off,
the room elided, darkness stretched, a blur
zip-studded by red pinlights, hemmed and held
a cloth we had no future written on.
Around us, well-dressed women stirred the darkness
as they walked. The bar's cold black streak streamed
past willows, necks swayed in to sup and speak.
I learned the map of textures on your cheek.
Benched near the place where others knit limbs, lives,

my body's affirmation—a surprise—
to our established friendship. You confessed—
amazing humming of my flesh's yes.

Playing Doctor

Yes, my love, I'm yours. I'll give myself
over to your teasing, tender care
to let you open me, deliberate,
your hand, a scientist, whose probing dares
to peel the blossom budded thirty years
in silence. I wake like a newborn, tears
of trust and outrage, wet and cold and bared.
What will be born of us when you have dared
to lift my fetal, embryonic heat
towards your nipples on my floral sheets?
What climax will our drumming raise us towards?
When we make love, new love, what will be made?
In that place, exposed, exhausted, laid,
if I'm with you, I will not feel afraid.

"Now what can we do for my Pretty?" you ask . . .

Sometimes I touch my breasts and think of you.
Sometimes as if my body were your own
private kingdom, I don't want my own
hands to touch myself after you
leave the room. It's like you lock me from myself
by going away. Inside my insides,
I am half-awake, half-opened. From your side
of New York, the Great Woods, you check your shelf
for potions, ivories, hairpieces, sleek combs
to knit my hair around when you return.

Oh mistress, busy worldly woman, turn
the bolt; return to me; set your combed
nape in my lap. Kiss me till the fine
evening turns a deep flush, like your skin, mine.

Adrift

Curled up in my arms like a small boy,
you took my breast into your hungry lips
and met my eye and smiled, nursing child,
and cried into my lap when you had come
too many times for your skin to endure
more touch and cried and cried till you were done
while I said, Si si si . . . as to my son's
despondent nighttime-waking. Dream-wracked, dear,
your rosy body swam through sweetness, tears
on the black sheets of your bed in the ambient light
of two candles. Like a ship sailing to a shore
we've never reached before, we sailed each other
leg over leg, your back washed up against my breasts
till your son's door opened and we dressed.

Safer Sex?

So no more nipples? (post-lactation leak)
and winter comes like sandpaper to lips
who now keep their chaste distance from my lips.
Of course my palm may stroke your nether cheek
as long as I wear gloves for full descent
into the place you want my dig and thrust.
Sex, you call this. I say, lack of trust.
You say I'm inching toward an argument.
I call your latex, Safe Sex for the Heart.

I want to find your mouth on me, the taste
of you, familiar, moving with my tongue.
You've come. Neglected, handled, and unstrung,
I stay in bed and watch you dress in haste.
I've lost more than one sense without your taste.

Confidential P. S.

So now when we make love, what have we made?
Not "life" although our blossoming belies
a simple definition of mere breath
and heartbeat. Surely something is implied
we do not make: not home, not spouse, not child
(though sometimes I am yours or you are mine
in ways that seem to posit us en-womb).
When others speak of loving to create
a life, we know we'll never share a room
for more than hours running. Yes. I mind
this making time by time and lay by lay
a stay against the current of our days.
Real work that moves no rivers. Mother, wife,
we live out elsewhere. Love knitting no life.

Marilyn Hacker ✳

from Love, Death, and the Changing of the Seasons

How can you love me with the things I feel
that scare me crashing on the window glass?
How can you love me when I'm such an ass-
hole (sometimes) I can't take hold of what's really there and use it, let you take the wheel
and put my head back as the truck-stops pass?
Where would we go that morning? Would the grass
beside the highway mount to granite, steel
and rubber take us far enough that I
could pull my ghosts out of my guts and cry
for them, with you behind me, on some high
stone place, where water breaks from underground
arteries with hard breaths, that would sound
like mine, letting them go, saying goodbye?

       ★   ★   ★

You did say, need me less and I'll want you more.
I'm still shellshocked at needing anyone,
used to being used to it on my own.
It won't be me out on the tiles till four-
thirty, while you're in bed, willing the door
open with your need. You wanted her then,
more. Because you need to, I woke alone
in what's not yet our room, strewn, though, with your
guitar, shoes, notebook, socks, trousers enjambed
with mine. Half the world was sleeping it off
in every other bed under my roof.
I wish I had a roof over my bed
to pull down on my head when I feel damned
by wanting you so much it looks like need.

★ ★ ★

Grief, and I want to take it up in you;
joy, and I want to spend it all inside
you; fear, and you are the place I can hide.
Courage is what leaves me brave enough to
turn you around and tell you what to do
to me, after. Rivers, and downstream glide
I; we breathe together. You look, or I'd
get scared, but you're watching while you take me through
the deep part, where I find you, where you need
to know I do know where, know how to drive
the point home. Wit: you get the point and flat
statement of a gift of tongues. I get
up, and you get me down, get lost, you lead
me home, or I take you, and we both arrive.

Beth Ann Fennelly
on Denise Duhamel

STUDIES HAVE SHOWN that, in coed high schools, male students get called on more frequently than females, and teachers are more likely to challenge or prod boys with follow-up questions. That's why single-sex education for women can make a lot of sense. Get the females their own classroom and they will be the ones called on; they will be asked the follow-up questions. When the time comes for student governance, they will be not only class secretary but also vice president and president, and in this way they will gain confidence and leadership skills, someday perhaps moving from president of the class to president of the country.

That's the idea. But the all-girl Catholic boarding school I attended from 1985 to 1989, Woodlands Academy of the Sacred Heart, was no training ground for nascent feminists. We paid more attention to our developing breasts than to our developing sense of self. One might imagine that, in a single-sex environment, students would be free from the pressures of physical attractiveness. On the contrary, I've never been anyplace where beauty mattered so much. Not that this was openly acknowledged: body issues and anything having to do with sex were simply not discussed. Perhaps that's why so many of the girls seemed messed up. Or perhaps it was because they came from families that were very, very rich and very, very troubled. Whatever the cause, at Woodlands you were popular in proportion to your number of eating disorders. If you had bulimia and anorexia, well, you were definitely popular.

I don't recall a lot of learning going on, no intellectual vigor in either students or teachers. The small amount of poetry we were taught was ladylike and pious. The only poem we studied by Emily Dickinson, for example, was "I am nobody! Who are you? / Are you—Nobody—Too?" which is, without a doubt, Dickinson's only cute poem. Her work about ambition—"I play at Riches—to appease / the Clamoring for Gold"—or passion—"I see thee Better—in the Dark"—I didn't even know existed.

My father would only pay for me to go to college if I attended a Catholic school, so, because going ROTC held little appeal, I went to the University of Notre Dame, where one would think I'd get more of the same. After all, it's very traditional, patriarchal, and has a high male-to-female student ratio. But it was at Notre Dame that I had my first good teachers who showed me good poetry. I fell in love with poetry and began writing it in earnest, although I was terrible—timid and imitative.

I discovered the poem that helped me change direction in a workshop led by Sonia Gernes wherein each student was encouraged to bring in a favorite poem from a recent literary journal. Someone brought in "Bulimia" by Denise Duhamel. I was pretty stunned by it. After it was read, I said nothing, just looked around the circle of students to see if anyone shared my reactions. I was excited, embarrassed by my excitement. I'd never heard anyone speak so openly about the body or sex before. Women weren't supposed to have appetites, much less talk about them so nakedly. The frankness of the sexual metaphors and the almost-prose factualness created a tone that was consciously unpretty ("As ingenious as the first / few times she would consciously masturbate, making note of where / her fingers felt best, she devises a way to vomit / that only hurts for a second.") What would they say back at Woodlands? Wasn't this Duhamel person worried about people reading the poem and thinking she was the bulimic? That she masturbated? How could she allow herself to be so vulnerable, so open to scrutiny, so unconcerned about appearances?

Reading "Bulimia" changed my writing because it gave me the courage to be unsavory, if that's what a poem called for. I decided to stop being so self-conscious in my poetry, stop worrying how the "Beth Ann" character came across, stop writing the poetic equivalent of "Do I look fat in these pants?" I began to explore those subjects that weren't discussed where I came from, all of those messy and essential human appetites. It felt naughty, which felt good.

Reading Duhamel's poetry not only challenged me to be less guarded in my subject matter but also gave me permission to be funny, or try and be funny. I realized that I like in a poem what I like in a pal—the ability not to take oneself too seriously. I think humor is a strategy earlier women poets didn't feel so free to use. Perhaps because, for a long time, women poets had to prove they could handle the big subjects as well as the men and so avoided humor that might get them dismissed as a poetaster. If they used humor at all, it was subdued humor and based on intellectual irony. And while Dorothy Parker's humor was both pointed and more caustic, she's regarded as a slight figure in the world of letters, almost as a dabbler in light verse. But now that the generations of women poets before my own have established their seriousness, we're free to establish our playfulness. Now we can investigate the full range of human emotions.

When I was pregnant, I read every parenting book out there—I studied for motherhood like it was a PhD exam—but even so I was unprepared for what it would really be like to become a mother, which is much weirder and wilder and deeper and funnier than hinted at in any book by any pediatrician. I wrote my second book, *Tender Hooks*, because I wanted to figure out what I was experiencing as a new mom. It's full of bodies, full of appetites, because birthing and raising a child are so physical. If it has funny moments, it's because motherhood has funny moments. I wanted to get in the sweetness of having a newborn, sure, but also get in the other stuff, too, because it seems that, until recently, the true complexity of the mother-child relationship has sometimes been left out of our great literature or sentimentalized, which simplifies and therefore lessens our understanding of human nature.

Luckily, I had the courage gained from reading Denise Duhamel to guide me. Her first book of poems, *Smile*, came out in 1993 and included the poem "Bulimia." I bought it with money I made giving blood. I bought the others when they appeared, and I never had to wait long—*The Woman* with *Two Vaginas* came out in 1995, *Girl Soldier* and *How the Sky Fell* in 1996, *Kinky* in 1997, *The Star-Spangled Banner* in 1999, and *Queen for a Day* in 2001. During these years while I was reading her books, we hadn't met. Then a few years back, we had one of those strange and serendipitous path crossings that shrink this wide world of ours to the size of a beach ball. One morning, I opened up my e-mail in-box and discovered a message from Denise Duhamel. It turned out that her husband, the poet Nick Carbó, had been a judge for the State of Illinois Arts Council, to which I'd applied for a grant. She'd read the group of poems in my application after her husband urged her to, and she was writing to tell me how much she liked them. She signed the e-mail—get this—"your fan." Did I save that e-mail? You betcha.

I met Denise at last a few months back. I was anxious about it, because liking someone's poetry doesn't mean you'll like her personality. But I could have rested easy on that account—she's great. And young, which I should mention here, because while others in this book are writing about their poetic mothers, I think Denise is more like a big sister. The kind who's a little kooky, a little brassy, wears fuchsia, tells ribald jokes, and laughs at them. The kind of sister who lets you borrow her glitter nail polish, tells you how it feels to kiss a boy, sneaks you a Pop Tart if you're sent to bed without dinner, who doesn't fit in at Woodlands, who makes you realize that's a good thing, for there is a rich life out there beyond the catwalk of high school, and it can be delicious—here, take a spoon, dig in.

Beth Ann Fennelly *

The Mommy at the Zoo

I used to sleep better I used to
be smarter remember for example words
and remember when I learned them

there was a word for example
for the way a snake loves
a tight place a crevice a chink in rocks

now the word won't answer
though my daughter knocks
the python sleeps tight in his glass hut

the word has slipped
my mind between a rock
and a hard place

Mr. Snake you
you are a . . .
a something-o-phile

O you sneaky . . .
something-o-phile . . .
I rummage

but the word
is nowhere no
where in my diaper bag

among the handiwipes and gummibears
sippiecups of Juicyjuice
crayons slinky and cow-that-goes-moo

before I was a Mommy
say 4 or 5 years or
decades ago I could think in complete

sentences remember all
my favorite words like the one
about loving the tight fit which I did

in the French Quarter
where the hot rain rained down
in the alley beside the bar

where I was bolted against the iron gate
by Tommy's hard cock
hot rain falling on my upswung face

each vertebra fenced
in the tic-tac-toe grid
each vertebra X-ed

on a treasure map
bezel set what a night
for a girl forged of carbon

all bone and saxophone
notes bouncing to her
through the hot drops of rain

who was she
that fresh squeezed girl
just temporarily out of her mind

if it's true as they say
that I am now
that same she

the word I seek
would come slithering
find a chink and wriggle in

like my child up ahead
darting through scissors
of grown up legs

her silhouette
in red exit light
slow down I'm coming wait

wait up

Because People Ask What My Daughter Will Think of My Poems When She's 16

Daughter, the light of
the future is apricot,
and in it you are not
the thigh-child pointing
her earnest index finger
to the yellow balloon clearing
the willows and drifting higher, you're
the balloon. I'm
the grasping hand. Or I'm
the *ooooo* in *balloon*. I'll
meet you there. I'm the brown
hairs, formerly violets, you
didn't water. I'm the hole
in the photos, you're the un-safety
scissors. I'm the lint in the corners
of my purse after you
steal the coins, homemade lunch
you pitch after leaving

my house, buttons you un-do
after I've okayed your blouse. Poems
you burn in the sink. Poems
that had to go and use
your name, never mind
that soon you'd be 16, hate
your name. I'm the resemblance
you deny, fat ass you
hope your boyfriends never
see. I'll meet you
there, that is my promise
and my threat, with this
yellow balloon as my
witness, even if I'm
dead, I'll meet you there.

First Warm Day in a College Town

Today is the day the first bare-chested
runners appear, coursing down College Hill
    as I drive to campus to teach, hard

not to stare because it's only February 15,
    and though I now live in the South,
I spent my girlhood in frigid Illinois

    hunting Easter eggs in snow,
or trick-or-treating in the snow,
    an umbrella protecting my cardboard wings,

so now it's hard not to see these taut colts
    as my reward, these yearlings testing the pasture,
hard as they come toward my Nissan

    not to turn my head as they pound past,
hard not to angle the mirror
    to watch them cruise down my shoulder,

too hard, really, when I await them like crocuses,
    search for their shadows
as others do the groundhog's, and suddenly

    here they are, the boys without shirts,
how fleet of foot, how cute their buns, I have made it
    again, it is spring.

Hard to recall just now
    that these torsos are the torsos
of my students, or my past or future students,

    who every year grow one year younger,
get one year fewer of my funny jokes
    and hip references to *Fletch* and Nirvana,

which means some year if they catch me
    admiring the hair downing their chests,
centering between their goalposts of hipbones,

    then going undercover, their shorts made
from the thin red or blue nylon of flapping
    American flags or the rigid sails of boats,

some year if they catch me they won't
    grin grins which make me, busted,
grin back, hard to know a spring will come

    when I'll have to train my eyes
on the dash, the fuel gauge nearing empty,
    hard to think of that spring, that

distant spring, that very very very
    (please God) distant
spring.

Denise Duhamel ✳

Bulimia

A kiss has nothing to do with sex,
she thinks. Not really. That engulfing, that trying to take
all of another in for nourishment, to become one with her, to become
part of her cells. The way she must have had everything she wanted
in the womb, without asking. Without words,
kisses have barely the slurp-sound of a man entering a woman
or sliding back out—neither movement with even the warning of a bark.
The Greek word "buli," animal hunger.
Petting, those kisses are called, or sometimes necking.
She read this advice in a sex manual once: "Take the man's penis,
slowly at first, like you are licking melting ice cream
from the rim of a cone." But the gagging, the choke—
a hot gulp of tea, a small chicken bone, a wad of gum grown too big.
That wasn't mentioned. It's about what happens in her mouth
past her teeth, where there is no more control, like a waterfall—
or it being too late when the whole wedding cake is gone:

She orders one from a different bakery this time, so no one
will remember her past visits and catch on. She's eating
slowly at first, tonguing icing from the plastic groom's feet, the hem
of the bride's gown, and those toothpick-points that kept them
rooted in pastry. She cuts the top tier into squares,
reception-like. (The thrill she knew of a wedding this past June,
stealing the white dessert into her purse, sucking
the sugary blue gel from a napkin one piece was wrapped in.
She was swallowing paper on her lone car ride home,
through a red light, on her way to another nap
from which she hoped a prince's kiss would wake her.)

The second tier in her hands, by fistfuls, desperate
as the Third World child she saw on tv last week, taking in gruel.
Her head, light like her stomach, is pumped up with air.
She can't stop. She puckers up to the sticky crumbs under her nails.

Then there are the engraved Valentine candies;
CRAZY, DREAM GIRL, ACT NOW, YOU'RE HOT. She rips open the bag,
devouring as many messages as she can at once.
They all taste like chalk. She rocks back and forth.
She has to loosen the string on her sweat pants, part of her trousseau.
The bag of candy is emptied. The paper doily
under the cake's third layer, smooth as a vacuumed ice-skating rink.
What has she done? In the bathroom, like what happened

to the mistakenly flushed-away bracelet, a gift
from her first boyfriend—the gold clasp silently unhooking
as she wiped herself, then, moments too late, noticing
her naked wrist under the running water of the rest room
sink's faucet . . . She's learned it's best to wait ten minutes
to make herself throw up. Digestion begins at this point,
but the food hasn't gotten very far. As ingenious as the first
few times she would consciously masturbate, making note of where
her fingers felt best, she devises a way to vomit
that only hurts for a second.

She takes off her sweatshirt and drapes it over a towel rack.
Then she pokes a Q-Tip on her soft pallet. Keeping in mind
the diagram in her voice class, the cross section
of the mouth showing each part's different function,
the palate—hidden and secret as a clitoris.
The teacher's mentioning of its vulnerability, split-second
and nonchalant like a doctor and his tongue depressor.
It's a fast prayer—she kneels in front of the toilet.
Her back jerks and arches the way it might
if she were moving her body to meet a man's during intercourse.
She wipes what has sprayed back to her chest,
her throat as raw as a rape that's happened to someone else.
She cleans the seat of the bowl with a rag, and cleans
her teeth with a second toothbrush she keeps for this purpose.
Her sweatshirt back on, she gets to the kitchen
to crush the cake box into a plastic garbage bag.
And leaves to dispose of it, not in the trashcan downstairs,
but in a dumpster way on the other side of town.

Miranda Field
on Fanny Howe

A SUMMER OF endless rain—the understory of our garden rots, grows lush and odorous, the grass thick, the bushes full of garden spiders. Their webs glint in the leaves. I write one evening in my room, at summer's end, when the things I'm writing about have disappeared. My assignment is wide open: "What I Did This Summer," and I fill the set number of loose-leaf pages with meticulous descriptions—of raindrops caught in spider-silk nets, patterns of rain on glass. There's no narrative, no "I" in my writing, no acknowledged self in the act of writing, and no attempt to negotiate the otherness of all that lives outside the "I." Only my own implicit, awkward self-estrangement. "A spider moves hungrily toward a fly" is the only volitional movement in the garden I describe. It causes the static details to contract around it.

"Two birds are on the branch of a tree," writes Simone Weil. "One eats the fruit, the other looks at it." These birds, says Weil, are the two parts of the soul. I think they're also two principal operations of writing—

sometimes competing, sometimes antagonistic, almost erotically attached. The eating bird is tethered to the branch. The eating bird is magnetized, fixed in place by its engagement in the gratification of desire. The looking-bird's attention is freer. It has desires but does not lose itself, as its sibling does, in full enmeshment. It possesses perspective.

My first book, *Swallow* (2002), was written at a period in my life when those two parts of the soul had just begun to make their tensions felt in me. *Swallow* is full of memory and projection, saturated in the incessant rain and speech patterns and superstitions of England, the climate I grew up in, the hauntedness of my childhood house, the undergrowth of our anarchic, ungardened garden. I was fixated by the sensuous details and charged spaces of memory. But toward the last stages of putting the book together, I gave birth to my first child, and something both attached to me and far outside myself demanded my full and passionate attention.

This juncture in my life, in which I'd published my first book and entered into motherhood for the first time, in quick succession, was thrilling and terrifying. I stopped writing and blamed the lack of time, the loss of sleep. But that wasn't it. Writing had always been a delicious pursuit for me, and it was gratifying at the most basic, sensual level. But now I had a suddenly compelling drive—a mandate—to meet head on, and converse with, the not-self: the otherness of the world. I had grown up as a writer with the doomed mother-poet biographies of Plath and Sexton always in the back of my mind. Now I needed to hear the voices of mother poets who had survived. I read Sharon Olds's *Wellspring* in the first few days postpartum, and the milk and blood and stitches, the full, frank exploration of birth and mothering in her poems, made me weep. But after I left the birth bed, I began to want a poetry in which motherhood was not so much its subject matter but its growing medium—the unhidden but infrastructural condition of the poet's feeling and speaking mind.

I don't remember how I came by a copy of Fanny Howe's *Selected Poems* (2000), but I do remember the excitement I felt, reading it in the stolen moments while my son slept. In a state of hyperrawness, a sort of spiritual state of emergency, I read Howe's work and felt an entry opening into my own. In this way, in helping me translate this huge change in my life into words, I think Howe became the closest I've ever come to a literary mentor.

The presiding consciousness in Howe's poems—the speaking "I"— seems to be all—or almost all—mother. It undertakes the work, or vocation, of mediating between the two birds of the soul: the instinctively appetitive and the empirical. Each perpetually clamors to be heard—wanting its fair share, or more than its share. "The self is a servant only / to itself," I read, and "soldered to myself / it might be a soldier or a thief / for all I know." The writer-mother senses a particularly urgent need to define herself, even with whole portions of her physical and psychic life designated to another's development. Two drives of nearly equal intensity vie. The doubled soul struggles with its impossible position, its divided loyalties. At times, it steals from itself to feed itself. But at rare moments, a balance is achieved: the self is fed, while the other, the world-outside-the-self is equally attended.

A delicate desentimentalizing instrument, the "I" in Fanny Howe's poems and novels registers impressions, ideas, and observations and synthesizes them, shepherds them, causing them to constellate by a thought process coolly detached, emotionally engaged, and discerning all at once. I think she might have acquired something like the sensory and perceptual equipment of an insect—those compound eyes and microscopic nerves that gather more impressions than can be sequentially arranged. Striving toward a condition of near-invisibility in her poems and novels, yet persistently present, she seems to know the inmost sense perceptions of the fly on the wall—the magnified awareness of a hungering self in an equally hungry world.

I hesitate to claim Howe as an influence in the usual sense of the word. The notion of poetic influence—in its root sense a mechanism of ethereal insemination—shortchanges the work of both "influencer" and "influenced." "The blue-print doesn't exist without someone beaming a light on it," as Howe says, and this requires "a lifetime of excruciating searching." But nevertheless, Howe's eye, her methods, her voice—all instruct me. At times, they transmit to me a kind of music-of-the-inner-ear, a pleasure of almost untranslatable significance. At others, I hear in them a powerful validation of my experience—my experience of imperfect, impassioned, world-hungry motherhood. In Howe's poems, the motherness of the speaking "I" is given as a fundamental, personal, and *a priori* condition—but in this condition it functions as an intellectual lens and as a feeling soul inside a highly charged social matrix. This is in sharp contrast to a half-unconscious view I think I'd absorbed in the culture I grew up in: that the maternal and intellectual, domestic and public, spiritual and material are necessarily divided and best kept that way.

I'm riveted when Howe explodes this view, dissolves these divisions; when she explores—as inseparable quantities—the spiritual and the political, the physical and metaphysical, as well as the complex chemistries of class and personality, race, and psyche. In her poems no aspect of human life is without reverberation, nothing inert; no system, no soul, is entirely self-contained—all is contiguous, all catalyst to everything it contacts.

It's particularly where Howe addresses the phenomenologies of motherhood, eros, community, and domestic work that her writing most moves me. She attends, with clear-eyed, critical, but even-handed and empathic attention, the divinity ("we kissed ourselves and each other, as if each cell was a Cupid"), and she credits in full the bestiality ("But in the zoo an animal / killed his keeper the same night I wanted to kill mine"). She registers imperceptible tremors of labor relations, the rewards and blind thefts of love and work: "I think of the labor theory of value / as meaning nothing for mothers." And she does this with a voice that is both passionate and self-aware, an exquisitely modulated ecstatic/realistic lyric: "I feel the city grow wild with desire fertile / as turned-over sod in the zoo at day's end." If the two birds of the soul eye each other as well as the fruit, and if the fruit both absorbs and reflects it all—all the looking and wanting, the ravishment and reservation—these are the tenuous cantileverings of desire and resistance, subject- and object-hood approached in Howe's poetics. This is her balancing act, her "tumultuous quest for reasonable solutions," and I follow it, rapt.

T. S. Eliot speaks of the "invasion" of the writing self by other writers as an essential formative event. I've been spellbound, held a kind of semivoluntary hostage under the watch and influence of others, found myself speaking in strangers' tongues at times in my writing life. But my attraction to Fanny Howe's work has, I think, taken me to task more significantly than these more usual apprenticeships of voice and style. Her "style" is recessive. Her voice is startlingly real but also nonintrusive. It presents but does not overinterpret, never monopolizes meaning. It is, to me, the ideal (therefore not literal) mother's: a marvel, a miracle of near-egolessness, of consciousness negotiating between involvement and detachment. The observing I/eye looks closely, looks with an intensity filled with mortal appetite, but holds back. Howe's work, adjudicating between desire and perception, attempting a stance of faithfulness toward the phenomenal world, continually reminds me of ways to approach my own. I read her for the pure, breathtakingly beautiful and spare music of her lyric, the exactness of her image-making; but also when I find myself too seduced by, and sealed off inside, my own pleasure-in-language. She reminds me to listen past the perfect cadence—to interrupt beauty, like turning off the music to hear the child crying in the other room, the jackhammers outside.

In Howe's poems, speaker and listener, beholder and beheld—the hunger-bird, primal and self-satisfying, and the bird that senses distance and experiences itself contextually—keep nudging each other and startling each other awake. They make together a tenuous but miraculous equilibrium, a fully dimensional self ideally situated: "under dreamish conditions— / airy and solitary / not here—not there—but always between."

Miranda Field ✳

Animal/Vegetable Fable

The sobbing boy is a length of wire between sky and me.
How should I manage this contraption? Parts of the sobbing break away.
Parts of new growth attach themselves to his established shape.
Once a piece of superstructure is in place—skull or clavicle or scapula—
I can feel its fetal vengeance under any quantity of hair or fat. Dry tracts
    between us,
hazardous, inflammable, fill steadily with water.

★

When I examine him, I forfeit my scientific eye. What is animal—of rat,
of squirrel—snarled in a supernatural thoroughfare? When I touch
   him, vapors
of such artificial apple in his hair! It seems a little twisted, as if some trapper's
twine had . . . as if an "accident" were prearranged . . .

★

Scornful boy and I, dazzled by brachia. A corn maze. A rattle
of leaves, a series of valves, some rain, an almost silent thing, an auditorium
   of whisperings.
   Who goes where?
The spider's web on the chain link fence we're pressed against
   even a little breeze lays bare.

Break

In the middle of the hunt, I must excuse myself, and all through silent
polished halls feel the dog-breath on my sling-back heels. Being flesh,
being mostly hungry, I mostly swallow what is thrown. But am not
glutton, but furnace burning punishments. And know the protocol for
butchery, but cannot call it to my mind. In safety-orange vests my suitors
stand, eyeing my diminishing, my diamonded neck. Offering payment,
but wearied of the work's travails, the intricate entrails tangling. True, I,
too, salivate for blood. In fact, some days I offer listeners lascivious
travelogues: of inroads into bile un-dammed, and fat, and glossy sinew.
And finish dewy. So cast no stones. But where I end up, washing hands
with languorous time-inattentiveness, I hear horns, hooves, hounds. I
stand bleached by gaseous light, and look a gutted thing myself, my
makeup gone, my clothes a net of wind. And say to her who hangs,
maturing, in the mirror, Well. We've been a-hunted. I'm the one. And
other days the other. So what now do we offer?

I Do Not Sleep for Sleep Is Like the Wind and Trees Amazed

I do not sleep for sleep is like the wind and trees amazed
by sleep's persuasive gaze

and self's insistence
signals in a speechless insect's cochlea:

I do not sleep, I do not sleep, but is itself this seed
consumed unseen.

In glistening jelly themes and hollower than Appalachian mines
among pines,

my praise, applause, my anathemes, my subtle worms combine

when moon a world-dividing language sings,
above the hook-and-ladder's dipthonged, crystal, ruby fountain sounds.

Such is my state, my stateless mind
a widowed turtle or green mother in some shady grove,

lost in her native tongue.

Fanny Howe ✳

Angria

When we were a baby
she fingered

my hood

like a fly
on the threads

of the dead

When she was a web
I fingered

her threads
like a spider

in love with a hand

A paper square
and noose-like letters

a floor that's a wall

so when I enter
I crawl

by my fingers and pen

O Angria so burn is the chill
to seek and hit

a place of guilt

where what is hot
is just the busy-work of thought

A grave-eaten parsonage
like its baby's lace cap

smells fertile. At first

the road away
across the heath turns like strings of DNA
But then there are no children

and no instruments
of mercy to help us carry on

Nothing happens that can

Katie Ford
on Jorie Graham

ONE OF MY TEACHERS, Jorie Graham, told us all—her first students at
Harvard after leaving the Iowa Writers' Workshop—that writing poems
would help us go through something we might otherwise choose to go
around. To go through something, however, is not what the mind wants
to do. And so the decision to write poems is the decision, she taught us, to
live inside one's difficulties, to inhabit them, to trespass against the soli-
tudes they wish to keep.

When I first took her poetry course at Harvard, I was a stray from Harvard Divinity School, where I was enrolled in a master's program in theology among Buddhist nuns, protestants, agnostics, Jewish Unitarians,
questioners, academics, Catholic contemplatives, and many others. When
I arrived at divinity school, I was considering ordination. I took Greek and
preaching, read arguments across the ages for and against the physical
resurrection, and sat on the fiberglass floor of the old divinity library, seeing all the floors I could fall through if that glass broke, searching for any

resolution—in writing, in a book—as to why I had become submerged in fundamentalist Christianity years before. I was looking for scholarship, some intellectual explanation, for why Christian conservatism had so ensnared me when I was younger. I wasn't at divinity school to deepen belief but to study its nature in hopes of undoing belief.

I didn't know this was what I was doing at the time. I went everywhere through intuition only; there was no knowledge I could hold onto yet. I was, I can see now, trying to undo what theorist Elaine Scarry calls "the agonizing labor of sustaining belief." Christian dogma was impossible for me to sustain intellectually, emotionally, even physically: the pressure of wrestling with religious doctrine inspired unrelenting bouts of anxiety during those years, making it hard to fly to Boston to begin school, to ride the subway, or even to sit through Jorie's class. I walked to Jorie's first class hoping I could sit through it and not have to leave suddenly, which is what the anxiety sometimes demanded. It was woven so tight, the belief, and although I had rejected it, it still festered in my mind. I wanted to move through it in the way Jorie said poetry would make possible for us.

There was something in her that knew, that had known at least since she wrote *Erosion*, that our histories are not dormant but keep reigniting, which is why her poem, "History," meant so much to me then. History, Graham says, will blaze up again and again, revisiting us, perhaps harming us. It is never static, and it can continue to injure even after our figurative or literal wars are over. This poem, with graphic beauty, evokes a range of specific images from World War II, ending when a tree with a grenade "lodged in the pulp" is brought into the house as firewood, then ignited, "blinding the man, killing / his wife." The poem, a type of urn for holding the remains of the dead, can bear these stories, these lives we seldom live without leaving some ignitable harm in our wake. What has happened in the past does not die as one might hope, without further cost or loss.

I remember standing by my bed in my apartment, on the border between the affluent and run-down streets of Cambridge, reading "History." I could hear two things outside my window: wind chimes drifting up from a backyard on one side of the fence and, on the other, the clients of the methadone clinic, talking through the night until the early morning nurse arrived. I was slowly realizing it wasn't the religious life I wanted, chimes moved by some inexplicable wind, but the life of a poet.

And the poets, it seemed to me, were the ones who knew they were in the straits, who talked to each other until the early morning came, when some door might open.

When I began seriously writing poetry, in the fall of 1999, I couldn't abandon my theology courses altogether—the divinity school was funding me, and I loved studying theology—but I began to see all of my studies as serving my poetry. In other words, I didn't really belong at the divinity school after I began writing. From that time on I was Graham's. How else could I have made a new way for myself? How could religion bear what religion had done? If there was such a way, I couldn't find it. Only poetry seemed to suffice.

At the time, I was reading Julian of Norwich, a medieval mystic who lived in a small brick cell attached to St. Julian's Church in England in the era of Chaucer. Julian was a recluse, but she was expected to speak to visitors who sought her out. Her cell didn't have any windows, so she spoke through a slight gap in the bricks—maybe two or three were missing—having to pitch her voice up and out without even seeing her visitor's eyes. What moved me about Julian's story wasn't her revelations or visions but the structure of her cell: The walls of the cell. The bricks of the wall. The gap in the bricks. The stark fact that there was only one way her voice could get out, a slight gap in the bricks to speak through—an image, for me, of what it is to speak as a poet.

Because it is slight, the space that allows only the most exacting words through. This was the narrow way I wanted: I wanted to find the language that would speak accurately, compellingly, lastingly. Jorie taught us how to move through that eye of the needle, how to pitch our subject matter through that gap, that wall, with no knowledge of who, if anyone, was on the other side.

Her intensity, the rigor of her mind—some students refer to her as a "force of nature"—is what she's known for among her students. And there is a long line of them, of course, writing and publishing poetry today. Perhaps some of them waited outside her door once, sometimes for hours, for a conference. I never thought it was foolish to wait there, in that red upholstered chair by the fake flowers in the entryway to the department. How could it be? When she got there, probably very tired because of all of us, she would sit and read my poems, and it felt as if those poems were the only thing present to her in that moment, and she would take all of her intensity of mind and give it over to the making of poetry. Part of her dedication,

I think, may come from something she said to us during our first class: *You feel lied to*, she said. Her shoulders were bent over the table as if she were cold. *You've been put on the earth and there is no instruction, no guidebook.* That was why we probably felt compelled to write poems, she said. Because we have to write our own lives, our own instruction.

She also talked about how poetry tracks the life of the soul while that other, louder life of ours goes on—the domestic life, our illnesses and work, our car accidents and lonesome subway rides. If you look back on what you've written, she said, you'll read the words of that secret, soulful life, of what was really going on in your life. But first those poems have to be written, revised countless times, then ordered on the arc you hope your collection forms.

After I had worked with Jorie for a year, I spent a summer writing poems, then came back to Harvard. That was when she told me she thought I was close to having a book, and that she wanted me to bring her all my writing—the scraps, the abandoned lines, the drafts—in a cardboard box. I brought the box. After a few weeks we met in her office, and she fanned the stacks of poems (or half-poems) she had weeded out into three arcs across her desk, one for every chapter of the book. The second chapter was nearly done. It was based on the Stations of the Cross liturgy and had been commissioned by the divinity school the year before. But the first chapter, the third—they were rough, they were nothing yet. I needed at least twenty-five more poems to make a book. Somehow I believed her when she said I was close. I remember most of what she said: that the beginning of a book of poetry is the breaking of a long silence. Nothing yet had been spoken by me against or into that silence, so the first words had to be what was urging the voice into speech after all that time. Although we never spoke, until the very end, about the subject matter of my book, she of course knew its stormy, anxious nature, and what she said about the third chapter guided me, and still does, through writing. She said nothing, in the end, could be redemptive. That I couldn't end *Deposition* with rescue, with resurrection of any kind. Nothing could save me, except, she said, the act of transmission itself. *It has to be terrifying. And you can't leave anything out.*

It was September of 2000. She sent me out of her office that day telling me to try to finish the manuscript in three months. By the new year, when publishers are back at their desks. I walked back down Quincy Street toward the apartment where I would finish the book, away from her office, which was always slightly dark, as if there were a continual dusk just outside her window, that time when we know the day is gone but it is not night, it is not. Because we can see just well enough to write through the difficulty, in that dim light that will hold.

Katie Ford ✳

Put Your Hands upon Your Eyes

Tell me how you know the truth, the master says.

I have become forgetful. I should not be trusted.

But tell me how you know.

I listen to something caught in the traplight.
It looks like a dry, fallen oak leaf. Then it is folding
in on itself, then back out,
one coarse moth-wing sloughing onto another.

But do you know the truth? the master asks.

I know what I'm seeing, I've seen it before—

something not quite dying, all night.
Also a hand leads to a body which I cannot see—

And the truth of another? the master says.

—one hand among many, shoved through bars of a cattle car,
a loom of fingers and iron, decaying on the vertical
even as the cloth is made.

But how do you know the truth of another?

I wish what I think they would wish. I wish
God were not inside me.

I wish everything, I wish nothing were hidden from me of day.

And when there is no truth?

I have to hurry. I can't get the water cold enough.
Some of the burns are to the nerve. Whatever they have given her,
it isn't enough. I imagine her skin as a grid of land,
wheat and poppies and charred grass fill whichever square the wind
insists on. *You'll have to get my shoes*, she says. I get them, but I can't tell
where she is putting her weight, so I can't get them on.
She has no sensation in her feet.

How do you know when there is no truth?

There was no emergency in your voice, she says.
You talked to the doctor like there was no emergency,
and that's what I think this is.

Last Breath with Belief in It

They blindfolded her put her in the closet for a month
they didn't want her dead grass pulled out they wanted her to believe

grass thickening a field once or twice dark month they had her
sit with them long wooden table why stray why desire and light came

through the torn robe over her eyes out of which birds were cut out of which
hoods she listened into the night long into the closet she even thought blessing

even thought grace towards her she began to trust they had faith had truth
years pass ocean and winds and moons pass she is cold she pulls she opens

her closet any morning sees the dark corner she could crawl into is it
over now but I beseech thee help her stop believing

help me sometimes I want back in.

It's Late Here How Light Is Late Once You've Fallen

I began to see a gauze over the wheat.
The fields were darker where an owl had flown
against the window of the house. I bent
and put my fingers into its cold down. Hundreds
of tiny spiders unhinged their bodies, bodies
which are their minds, as my body was,
moving like a city wanting to go inside
all the cavities. Moths too,
some were caught and tried to flutter out. I put my hands in
farther. Felt the body of the thing, the owl. At first it seemed
so dead. Then, not at all—either my fingers
pulsing with blood or its breathing. I held
breath too, like a mother bent to the crib. Nothing.
Then maybe something. I looked behind me,
my fingers making out bones, twigs of what was left, glazed
by faint morning stars that pocked the sky when I looked up, stars
in their arc of recovery from being seen
into being hidden again by light. Some of its feathers
were matted. When it had hit the window
the storm layers shook the space between. *Lie still*, I said to you,
I'll go see. But all I really wanted
was to leave that house, your
steady rise and fall of breathing inside it.
Outside, there was no farther in to go. It must have been
a barn owl with its heartish face
and lightly-speckled underneath, its feathers
thin leaves spotted with mold. I pulled out my hands
and spread its wings out full, the soft body
exposed. And that's when I was sure it was dead—
when it let me do that to its body.

Jorie Graham *

History

Into whose ear the deeds are spoken. The only
listener. So I believed
he would remember everything, the murmuring trees,
the sunshine's zealotry, its deep
unevenness. For history
is the opposite
of the eye
for whom, for instance, six million bodies in portions
of hundreds and
the flowerpots broken by a sudden wind stand as
equivalent. What more
is there
than fact? I'll give ten thousand dollars to the man
who proves the holocaust really
occurred said the exhausted solitude
in San Francisco
in 1980. Far in the woods
in a faded photograph
in 1942 the man with his own
genitalia in his mouth and hundreds of
slow holes
a pitchfork has opened
over his face
grows beautiful. The ferns and deepwood
lilies catch
the eye. Three men in ragged uniforms
with guns keep laughing
nervously. They share the day
with him. A bluebird
sings. The feathers of the shade touch every inch
of skin—the hand holding down the delicate gun,
the hands holding down the delicate

hips. And the sky
is visible between the men, between
the trees, a blue spirit
enveloping
anything. Late in the story, in northern Italy,
a man cuts down some trees for winter
fuel. We read this in the evening
news. Watching the fire burn late
one night, watching it change and change, a hand grenade,
lodged in the pulp the young tree
grew around, explodes, blinding the man, killing
his wife. Now who
will tell the children
fairytales? The ones where simple
crumbs over the forest
floor endure
to help us home?

Daphne Gottlieb
on the Circle of Mentorship

IT'S HAPPENED MAYBE a half-dozen times or so now. The e-mail comes in, a day or a week or two weeks after I've performed at a college. A student has looked me up online, found my e-mail address, written to me.

The letters all begin the same way. The students tell me they saw me read at their school, they bought one of my books, and they're writing because they've never told anyone before what happened, they've never written about it before, but after the reading, this came out and they had to send it to me. They think I'll understand when I read it. Would I give them feedback on the attached piece?

And I open their attachments, one hand over my mouth as I read what they sent. They all have this in common: fury. These young women (they are almost all young women) are describing a formative, horrible experience for the first time, confronting the abuse, incest, or rape they endured. I go back and reread their e-mails. While they asked for feedback, what they want to hear is validation. *Did you feel like this?* they are asking.

Do you understand? Am I okay? Will you run away from me now that I've told you? And is this art?

In those moments I feel terrifyingly inadequate. They have mistaken me for someone in command not only of my art but also of my life; they are assuming I believe it is possible to transcend cruelty through making art. They trust me with something huge, something impossible. I want to crawl through the cable modem and wash their faces, pack their lunches, scream Yes! Yes! You are shiny and brave and beautiful! But you've got the wrong girl. I'm not enough to help you. I'm not a good enough artist, not an undamaged enough person. I'm a poet, not a counselor; I still have nightmares and I can't keep stains off my clothes! I'm not old enough, smart enough—I'm not enough—

And then I take a deep breath. I light a cigarette because I'm not smart enough or strong enough to quit yet. And I start an e-mail back. *Dear _____,* is how they always begin, and they're different from there. I never lie to these girls. I say how very grateful I am they trusted me with that piece. That they must be very strong to have survived such an experience. That I can only imagine what it was like to sit down and write about it—especially for the first time—and I hope they have good support systems as they begin working through it. That perhaps they might want to go talk to a professional. That this is dangerous, difficult stuff. That they are brave. For years, I tell them, when I read in public about being raped, it felt like each time I read the piece, I killed the rapist a little more, killed off a little more of what he did to me. We can make art and transcend, I tell them. Getting trauma out of the way, we can make more art, too. Art about joy and struggle and anything else we want. I tell them this is an exciting beginning. That they should keep writing, keep writing, keep writing.

Every time, from when I begin writing until after I've hit "send," something odd happens: I become who they believe I am. For a moment, despite the daily evidence, I believe what I wrote to them: that art is vital, that it connects us in amazing and powerful ways, that reading or hearing a poem can change a life, that writing one might save a life. In this way, the women who write to me help me keep writing, keep writing. Even the worst poem can evolve into something wonderful in revision, but what's not written will never be anything at all. These women remind me that we're all facing that same challenge: to write, to create out of nothingness. They show me something I never understood—how gratifying it is to be asked for help when it's something you can provide.

I always thought asking for advice and help was an imposition. Asking for mentorship means being vulnerable in a very real sense. I would never have written to a stranger whose work I admired and asked for a critique. These young writers who send me e-mail, ask me *How?* and *Can I?*, have far more spine than I did at their age, maybe even more than I have now. But in a practical sense, it was more difficult when I was their age. There was no internet, no easy, immediate way of contacting strangers half a world away and asking for advice. I was too shy to write a letter even if I could have found the right address. When someone I admired was local, if I chanced to be in a room with them, I was too shy to approach them or—lest it seem impertinent—admit I wrote, too (I would never have dishonored their work by calling mine "writing"). I did not understand how some of my peers met and ingratiated themselves to more established writers, got taken under a wing and groomed. They had a confidence I didn't.

Perhaps that's why my mentors have, by and large, been my peers. I have moved forward by looking sideways.

I grew up in upstate New York, and writing was my first love. My first poem was published when I was eight years old. I majored in creative writing in college, wanted very much to make a living as a creative writer. When I was twenty, my father died. I swapped writing for art's sake in order to write for a living, eventually becoming senior and managing editor for a trade magazine. Art seemed superfluous, something with little practical value.

But then, around my second or third year in San Francisco, a friend brought me to a reading. And, as the cliché goes, it changed my life. Kris Kovick curated a series at Red Dora's Bearded Lady Café. Each bill would feature a half-dozen fledgling and more experienced writers, performance artists, and comedians. It was a vital, vibrant scene, a community in which, in the wake of punk rock and riot grrrl, ideas and techniques were exchanged. It felt like anything could happen, and people would help you Do It Yourself. I wasn't mentored by one person. I was mentored by a community. We were pierced, tattooed, shaved, hairy, leftist, ultracaffeinated. Seeing all the young writers get up, shout bile, and purr glitter with all of their hearts made me shriek inside—*I used to do that! I CAN do that!*

I started writing again. Avidly. Feverishly. The first thing I wrote was a love poem to one of the girls I'd seen read. As seduction, it failed (although that poet later did write a poem for me); as a poem, it was an entry to a whole new life. I haven't stopped writing since. I began to read in public thanks to invitations from around the community, from people who saw me at open mics. I had writing dates with my peers, sitting in cafés and scrawling. These readings led to more readings, which led to meeting more writers, many of whom have knowingly or unknowingly nurtured me. I was invited to join a group of queer female writers. I began to curate shows once I knew a lot of writers and performers. I met a freelance editor for a small lesbian press. I began to emulate the confidence and adamancies of the female poetry slammers. I learned to flirt with the audience in the manner of some erotic poets I know. I was inspired to formal verse by other poets still. I have never taken a step forward without sideways glances toward them. These female poets showed me how they made their chapbooks, explained how they got into certain reading series, shared calls for submissions, and helped me book tours.

My mentor has been not one person but a community. And it continues to be, even as there are occasional breakdowns in the system. I've opened up my address book to someone only to find her holding out on me when I need help, say, booking a reading in a particular city. I've had people neglect to pass on calls for submissions for anthologies that would have suited my work because they knew there were only a certain number of pieces that were going to be accepted and they might be jeopardizing their own publication. To a great extent, it's true that there are only so many spaces in anthologies, only so many books of poetry that will be put out this year, only so many paid performance opportunities, but this selfish behavior only reinforces the same kind of old-boy cronyism that feminism should be antithetical to. If we've been excluded as women by certain nepotisms and favoritism, then it is up to us as feminists to create a new, more equitable model in which we are rewarded for merit as well as connections. I can accept losing a reading or a publication in the hopes of fostering a longer-lasting and more powerful alliance. When there's rivalry, I try to let the rarity of the opportunity spur me on to be my best, to make work so good it would be ridiculous to take another piece in its stead. Yeah, it stings, and we get over it. (It helps me keep perspective to remember that this is poetry—what are the stakes, really, beyond ego? The rewards and audience are so small compared with other genres.) And when someone excitedly e-mails or calls to say hey, they got in that book or are reading in that series, it feels terrific. We're walking in lockstep. We're doing it for each other.

But, of course, this would be an entirely useless system if all I did—all we did—was take. And a decade and a half past my early twenties, more and more, I find myself answering the question I once asked: How do you do this? And I do my best to tell them, as someone once told me. Through that exchange, through the art that will come, we are both transformed.

We do it in person, over the phone, and through e-mail. We do it because we're fighting against our acculturation that tells us when we write about our lives, it's trivial. We write out of fury at being relegated to having our lives called "trivial," having our work dubbed "confessional" when we confess to nothing. We testify. We write in love and in rage and in the spirit of sharing the truth. And we help each other get our words out there, because one voice alone won't move the world forward, but nations of women together might.

Daphne Gottlieb ✳

she makes me feel like

a bull in a china shop.
a kid in a candy store.
a canary in a coal mine.
a port in a storm.

a bull in a candy store.
a kid in a china shop.
a canary in a coal storm.
a port in a mine.

a coal in a china kid.
a shop in a storm store.
a bull in a candy ship.
a canary in a port.

a storm in a canary shop.
a store in a china ship.
a bull in a coal storm.
a kid in a mine.

the port gets the coal ship.
the canary gets the china storm.
the kid gets the candy quick.
the bull gets matadored.

Greyhound Rescue

for Maggie Estep

1 SOLITARY JACKSON

Urbanites in the shake and whine of nature: Bees knock at our windows
in the early morning, wolves stalk our bike rides, palmettos snatch at our
knees as geckos shriek away from our rubber soles. This is bad religion.
We've been kidding ourselves. There is nothing restful about nature.
Stripped away from environment, we are so tender. Some nights, without
asphalt to bolster our spines, or a familiar body (pack animals that we
are), perhaps there is nothing inside us at all. And if our cities forget us,
who are we then? We are historic if we depend on corruption to save us:
homes have always been erected where there was wildlife, electric light
buzzes where there was stars. (The stars are still there, if you look. Look.
There.) We depend on corruption. We go to the greyhound track. It's
important. There are too few rules in nature, too few winners. There is
too little that makes sense.

2 CAUSE OF ACTION

Here in the middle of nowhere, I am always learning: from others, from
my own bad behavior, from drawing metaphors not meant to be. I learn
from the program that greyhounds are, by instinct, competitive. They are
easy to train because they want to beat the other hounds out for the rabbit.
They start on circular tracks as pups and later are trained to enter their
starting boxes, muzzled, and chase a "rabbit," a fur proxy. They end up
back where they started. No taste of blood for the hunt, do they even
know when they win?, the oval and around, this makes sense to me. It
sounds a lot like my life. The lights are bright at the track. You put your
money down and walk away with more or less later. Here in the middle of
nowhere, I have a stuffed rabbit on my borrowed bed. I chase myself in
circles nightly, I end up where I started and then I get taken to the track.
The money lost in bets isn't the point. For a few moments, we can win.

3   GETCHA SOME LOVE

It's not that at all. Number two's hind legs look strong but number six is the favorite but the only one I really see, number four, look at number four, with his ears like, well, dogears in a book, folded neatly, his bright eyes, he's ready to go, he's ready to win or—no, he's having fun. He's nuzzling his handler, he's wagging his tail. Number two, ICU Big Baby, has her tail between her legs. Take it Easy is panting. American Justice has a tender paw. It's all about Getcha Some Love, who hoedown stamps his foot and dances for us. He's having a ball. He cocks his head and smiles. Two dollars to win on Getcha Some Love. I'd give it all to that dog. I want to be that dog. At my best, I am that dog.

4   WHY TELL SABINE

I am a writer which means I am a liar which means I want truth in things. Therefore, Getcha Some Love, with odds of 41-to-1 pulled it out, the longshot won.

Does it matter? He came in sixth or last. I am still thinking about that dog. How long do you wait for love? He was born in 2003, so his career may span through 2007, barring injury or something else and then—and then—he will be 42 when his career is up. And then begins the luckiest part of that dog's life: done running in circles, he'll be free to nap, be loved, eat, be loved, amble wherever he wants, eat grass, do whatever it is that you do when you can finally stop running. Humans at 42 are even luckier. 42, I think, must be very good indeed. I will only be 40 when Getcha Some Love comes of age, and I will probably be in California and he in Florida, but maybe we will find each other then. Maybe we all find our way. We follow the rabbit. We run in a pack. We get there. If we're very good, maybe we will be joyous enough to get to 42. It's joy that gets you there, not health or clean living. Don't fool yourself.

5   TOUCH IT UP

The past few nights I've held that stuffed rabbit (you know the one) until we stopped running in circles: mine. Sometimes it takes all night. Sometimes we run all night. I whisper *You've got it, you can stop running, you've got it. You got it.* It makes nighttime safer. Nothing, not even a familiar body, being a pack animal, makes the night entirely safe.

6   BE IN DEMAND

The two forelegs stretch out in front and then tight back in to meet the two back legs that push again back and out punching off as the two front legs reach—to go flat out, to go for broke, to do it for the exhilaration, that's all you get. So maybe it's not so bad, the running. And running well. Show. Place. Win. What else have you got? What else is there? Wouldn't you be ashamed of anything else?

7   BIG DOLL

From the track, even with the lights on, you can see the stars, still. We've been domesticating dogs for thousands of years and still out here, in the quasiwild, there was a wolf here the other day. Two for the quinela. Hell, two for this trifecta. Think it's impossible? Watch. I'll put all my money on it. I'll take the wolf and the stuffed rabbit. 42's already lucky. I may be bad at winning, but I'm never sorry for what I pick. I'll take learning by example. I'll take the show / place / win. I'll take losing and learning.

Mostly, I'll take the number four dog, the one having the party. I'll take the stars. I'll take that rose I've dried and saved. And I give them to you.

8   I'M CUTE THANK U

(The stars: Look! There!) Easily on Rail. Chased Winner. Easily. Chased winner. Good try, Good try, Rough trip, Nosed for Show, No Room Early, Box to Wire, Easily Placed, Showed Despite Block, Won Handily, Won, Won, Won, Good Effort—Up in Time—Win.

speed times distance

She can't figure it out, no matter how hard she tries, in the middle of the park on a beautiful summer afternoon. She walks in six-foot circles in the grass, step, step. She is counting her (body) steps. One, two, three. She counts each time she lifts a foot up and puts it in front of the other, thirteen, fourteen. So it's a pace if it's a step on each foot, but it's just a step when each foot moves. Now, if she had four feet, say, like (the blue flowered dress) her daughter's cat, would she count each step of each foot, or just a complete rotation, foot 1-2-3-4 (that's a step? or four?), or would it be feet one and three (step), two and four (step)? How many steps, how many steps will it take? She sits down in the grass. She pulls on the grass. Ants. There are ants in the grass. She stands up and shakes an ant off her hand and begins (twenty-one) walking in (twentyfourtwentyfive) circles again, she can figure this out, she knows she can so the ants, then, if the ant's six-legged steps are counted as 1-3-5 (step), 2-4-6 (step), it is (thirtyeightthirtynineforty) the same number as counting them as 1-2-3-4-5-6 (step) if you multiply the second by two (marching one by one, two by two) and of course the size of the (body) ant is going to indicate the length of the stride and it looked like it took—maybe, maybe she's been going about this all wrong, trying to figure out how many steps (limp) it will take an ant when actually, there's more than one ant now, and she supposes (onehundredtwelve) that if she was/if she were to figure out the velocity of the ants in the grass, the distance of the starting and ending points, and the time for one ant to reach point b (the mud stain) from point a (her blue flowered dress), she's going in circles, around and around, her daughter's cornsilk hair, the grass, step, step (onesixteen, oneseventeen) (move the body) she would be able to do (her daughter's face) the thing to figure out is not how many steps per ant now but how many (body) ants are crossing, she needs the time and distance and speed and then she could figure out but if she still, if she could (hear the tires squeal around the corner) just sit still, but she can't watch (the driver) as the ants crossed first one by one, now two by two (the mudstained blue flowered dress) across her (limp) daughter's face (please open) and she can't move (the make of the car) can't move the body (twohundredandten) and where (open/open) (blood) where (twohundredandeleven) (still) (limp) is the fucking ambulance?

Matthea Harvey
on Anna Rabinowitz

ANNA IS BENDING over a table with two werewolf heads, partially dissected, crusted with glitter—they're both wearing coarse wigs, and from the brain of the blonde sprouts a miniature landscape of crystals: "I think they're terrific," she says. I'm surprised, but only for a second. Of course she likes them: if you look closely you see how strangely beautiful they are. Anna and I are wandering around Chelsea, looking at art. Outside, Anna puts on her huge Jackie O sunglasses. They have clusters of tiny pink rhinestones on the sides and are the kind of glasses that make me look like an insect.

Anna is always on the lookout, but no single optical instrument can encompass her ways of looking. She's part monocle, part spotlight, and part kaleidoscope—the first because she has an intensity of investigation that makes Hercule Poirot look positively passive; the second because when something new interests her, she shines a light on it so that those around her can see it too; and the third because she is always fracturing, revising, and reconfiguring her version and vision of the world.

I first met Anna five years ago through the tenth anniversary issue of her journal, *American Letters & Commentary*. I found it at Prairie Lights Bookstore in Iowa City, where I was in graduate school, and was fascinated by the work inside. I also felt a slight thrill when I saw that two women edited the magazine: Anna and Jeanne Marie Beaumont. It's less unusual now for literary magazines to be edited by women, but in those days I noticed the magazines I sent work to almost always had men at the top of their mastheads.

The line I remember most clearly from AL&C #10 is "alpenstocking over a neighbor's nettled meadow," from Albert Goldbarth's "Hoverers." Specifically, I liked how "alpenstocking" shimmered between noun and verb. The Susan Rothenberg image on the cover of Anna's first book of poems, *At the Site of Inside Out* (1997), has a similar effect. It shows the outline of a head inside a circle, with a line starting where the eye should be and extending outside the circle. It is an eye, and it is also eyeing. The noun "eye" is indicated by the start of the line, and the act of eyeing is evinced by the continuation of the line outside the circle. I like that the line isn't an arrow, so the image is about both taking in and looking out. Anna references the image in her poem "The Foreplay of Hermeneutics": "Eye, stick out your tongue." This imperative, combining the senses into some strange new being, is signature Anna.

When I moved back to New York in 1999, I met Anna in person. A dear mutual friend, Timothy Donnelly, had told me she was looking for a managing editor for *American Letters & Commentary*. We met at a French bakery in the West Village and talked for two hours among the light green meringues and glistening tarts. Our conversation was rangy—we covered what we were reading, what art we'd seen, politics, and our own poetry without any sense of the cellular walls that sometimes exist between these subjects. When I left, I felt as though my brain had been leaping up into the clouds, falling back down to earth, and leaping up again—my version of Emily Dickinson's "having the top of your head blown off."

Luckily Anna took me on, first as managing editor and later as poetry editor, so we've been having conversations like that for the last five years. Such talks are an integral part of *American Letters & Commentary*—in fact, the forums in each issue are like the dialogues we have as editors. The format is loose. Contributors are sent a list of questions and quotations and asked to respond in their own way. The first forum I was involved with was "Hypertext: Facts, Fictions and the Brave New Word." Then came "Picture This: When Text is Not Enough." After September 11, when we were all trying to understand the role of writing in this newly shaken world, we put together "In Extremis: Seven Essays on Language and the Imagination." In her essay, "After the Fall," Ann Lauterbach wrote, "Prepositions count. The United States has declared war *on* terrorism. This phrase, in which *with* is replaced by *on*, is reminiscent of other wars: the one *on* drugs, the one *on* poverty. These are conceptual wars, front-loaded with their own assent." Craig Dworkin wrote, "Difficult and frightening times may require all the more difficult and extreme poetry: an unyielding writing that will refuse to mitigate a world which we should not find comforting, and from which we should not be distanced." It was a great relief to me to be able to see these people grappling with the same issues.

This year's symposium (the previous year's polar opposite) is a look at the uses of comedy titled "Senses of Humor: Survival, Subversion, or Going for the Jocular." Over the past two years I have become very interested in graphic novels, and with Anna as my model, I have been reading them voraciously. I've found a lot of crossover between the graphic novels and poetry. For instance, in Chris Ware's *Jimmy Corrigan, The Smartest Kid on Earth*, you may see a frame of a bird on a branch four times before the bird finally trills out a note, which is applicable to ideas of repetition and pacing in a poem. I often use Scott McCloud's *Understanding Comics* in my poetry workshops—for instance, we'll use his discussion of the gutter (the blank space between panels) to talk about stanza breaks. This year's forum is an extension of those investigations.

Since I have known Anna, we have each written a second book of poems. Hers, *Darkling* (2001), seems to be a continuation of a poem called "Dislocations" in her first book: "Because I failed / to get the story from my parents if they knew it." The child of Jewish immigrant parents, Anna lost almost everyone in her extended family to the Holocaust. *Darkling* is written to, about, and from a shoebox of photographs and letters her parents left behind when they were sent away. The book evokes rather than tells a story, like one of Eva Hesse's delicate fiberglass constructions. What holds *Darkling*'s fragments together is its acrostic form: the book spells out Thomas Hardy's poem "The Darkling Thrush." Both Hardy's poem and *Darkling* conjure up a narrator looking back on the horrors of the century before him/her, or, in Hardy's words, "the Century's corpse."

But Darkling can't be categorized: it flickers between memory and imagination, between the actual words written in the packet of letters and on the backs of photos and the role of language in creating or destroying history. The poems find no resting place, but Anna's belief in the process of poetry itself is fiercely apparent: "People are afraid to look at each other. / POEMS STARE INTO THEIR EYES."

Like Darkling, my second collection, Sad Little Breathing Machine, is also a book-length project. It contains a number of "introduction poems" that portray humans in conversation with ideas or objects (disease, Eden, the world) conceived of as systems; poems that are run by "engines," or visual diagrams; and fanciful prose poems that take one idea to its most extreme conclusion. Each section is organized around an "Introduction to _____" poem and each type of poem within it is like a vector, a verb, or an eye-beam. The poems address the subject of that first poem, whether the noun is "world" or "narrative" or "Eden," but they come at it with different strategies; lyric dissection, narrative explication, and so forth. Where the poems cross they create a moment of larger meaning. Snow-gust. Alpen-stocking. Eye stick out your tongue.

Anna and I are fellow poets, editors, and art lovers, but we are also incredibly close friends. It is hard to see yourself as someone else sees you, but the glimpses I get of myself through Anna's eyes are filled with faith. She believes in me as a writer, thinker, and, most importantly, as a person. I doubt she knows the spectrum of my love and admiration for her.

I watch her because I look up to her—the way she brings the same enthusiasm and devotion to her family, her friends, and her work, the way she is always looking at the world with bright and interested eyes. She is a model for how I would like to experience life.

This past summer, Anna and I were having a conversation about Rivers and Tides, a documentary about the environmental artist Andy Goldsworthy. In the film, there is a moment when the camera focuses on something ghostly, ethereal, and completely unidentifiable. Whatever it is coheres and fall apart, coheres and falls apart again. When the camera pans back, you see Goldsworthy grabbing mittenfuls of powdery snow and throwing it up in the air. Talking to Anna, I realized that packed snow is everyday language, and snow gusts are poetry. That is the sort of conversation I am shy about having with most people, because the part of me that writes poetry doesn't want to destroy those snow gusts with too much exploration. But Anna's dedicated curiosity has allowed me to slip past some of these boundaries and say things that I need to formulate but might not without her.

In another recent conversation, I was delighted to find that my friend-mentor was busy creating a mentor of her own; in fact, a mentor for all women poets. Anna had been asked to contribute to a forthcoming anthology in which contemporary poets invent a poet, write a poem by that poet, and give an account of the poet's life and work. Anna had just finished creating "Hekenus," an ancient Egyptian poet. The essay states of Anna's invented subject:

> First, her words offered ample evidence that feminism was not simply a 20th-century phenomenon of Western origin; and second, she was a true original, since almost all extant ancient Egyptian texts are believed to have been written by men. Furthermore, the poem I was to translate, predating Christianity by at least 1200 years, seemed to be an account of an Annunciation described by the "chosen" woman herself—a woman who, astonishingly, responds to the offer made to her with a resounding NO.

From the fragments of Hekenus's work that "survived," it is clear that she was incredibly talented and strong-willed and proud. She reminds me of someone—someone who might admire a werewolf head with its mind laid bare, glittering.

Matthea Harvey ✳

Life-Size Is What We Are
(A New History of Photography)

Selflessly the self gave it all away.
Pin all yr hopes, lay all yr love, etc.

Which means the fish that live
in a plastic bag think the edges

of the world pucker. It's one thing to
make an image. It's two things to find one.

Why weren't we mindful of the lady
behind the makeup counter, calling,

"Come here honey, let me give you
some eyes"? The laws were sunsetting.

One puff of smoke rose in the minefield.
People dragged their shadows along.

I'm here to tell you that you're not.
Surprise, darling, surprise.

Sergio Valente, Sergio Valente,
How You Look Tells the World How You Feel

Engine: < : ∅ : □

My "you" came to the city to visit
me: clouds rushed between us

& the sun. The albums were finally full.
Halfheartedly we looked through lenses,

fish-eye & wide, but we'd had enough
likenesses taken. Similes were simply out

of the question. The blind man, regardless,
said, "Please a little light so I can see

my love." (He'd gone through
seven doves without knowing it.) In bed,

the surveyors held their aching heads.
Satellites caught our thoughts & held them.

Then snow fell in between two trains;
then fleas swirled in the hoof-dust; & when

we looked at each other we didn't look
alike. I kissed your magnifying glass

& said, "When the aliens come,
they'll know we're inside our cars."

Save the Originals

For the entrance exam we have to match TV static to a daisy field. After years of practice (books & rocks, near & far), it's a breeze. At orientation, those with fluctuating weight or braces are pulled aside. Not ready. We, who will eventually copy, have chosen one hairstyle & smile & stuck to it—we have the class photos to prove it. Still, we're not allowed near the machines for weeks. The equals sign on the blackboard grows four-boxes-of-chalk thick. Pale sandwiches pile up in our lockers. Then one day we're told to take a left at the water fountain instead of a right, and we're in the copy room. I don't fiddle with the dials; I make a copy. I like him immediately. He looks like me but with darker circles under his my-eyes, a more pronounced scar on his my-cheek. When I look up, I see that Sylvia has made herself three copies at 10%, 35% and 75%. A Sylvia crescendo. I feel a hand on my back & then I don't look at anyone else anymore. For the first few nights, we stay up late. We are each other's perfect hug. He's thoughtful & helpful, my shadow with a shuffle—he plumps the sofa cushions, feeds the goldfish. I can tell from the way he studies Splash and Splish that he thinks Splash is the original and Splish is the copy. How sweet, I think. One day, via the hallway mirror, I watch as he transfers Splash into a jam jar, then lets a golden handful of fish flakes fall gently into the bowl holding Splish. I'm at a distance but I know which is which. The next night my red scarf is missing from the front hall & so is he. My phone rings. The soprano has the flu and the understudy is performing. He's at the opera. We all are.

Anna Rabinowitz ✳

The Foreplay of Hermeneutics

1.
From the top of her head to the black coagulation—
if you think she's floating you're right,
right over slippery scales of graphite.

From the top of her head to the black coagulation—
her throat slit by the hyphenated run.
If you think she's floating you're right,
right over slippery scales of graphite.

From the top of her head to the black coagulation—
her throat slit by the hyphenated run
impossible to subdue once begun.
If you think she's floating you're right,
right over slippery scales of graphite.

2.
Trust me. There's nothing unusual in a lost face.
Dismemberment gets to the parts (heart) of things:
what bleeds, what cannot; what seeps, what clings.

Trust me. There's nothing unusual in a lost face
severed between points, dismantled, erased.
Dismemberment gets to the parts (heart) of things:
what bleeds, what cannot; what seeps, what clings.

Trust me. There's nothing unusual in a lost face
severed between points, dismantled, erased,
flesh bone-dry or cloyingly moist, whatever the case.
Dismemberment gets to the parts (heart) of things:
what bleeds, what cannot; what seeps, what clings.

3.

Look, her lips couple with nuance ardent for things to say,
and under the text of her brow note how the eye,
spangled with lust, resets the margins of desire.

Look, her lips couple with nuance ardent for things to say
about hermeneutics parsed in foreplay
and under the text of her brow note how the eye,
spangled with lust, resets the margins of desire.

Look, her lips couple with nuance ardent for things to say
about hermeneutics parsed in foreplay,
language dandling codes fervently relayed,
and under the text of her brow note how the eye,
spangled with lust, resets the margins of desire.

4.

Adamant colors breathe deep, sustain your duress.
Eye, stick out your tongue. Shake up the old domain.
What is given to understand consorts on new terrain.

Adamant colors breathe deep, sustain your duress,
Fondle nails, ears, sweaty feet, punctuate each caress.
Eye, stick out your tongue. Shake up the old domain.
What is given to understand consorts on new terrain.

Adamant colors breathe deep, sustain your duress,
Fondle nails, ears, sweaty feet, punctuate each caress.
Lick the bottom of the bowl, sweet eye. Yes, oh yes,
Eye, stick out your tongue. Shake up the old domain.
What is given to understand consorts on new terrain.

Kirsten Kaschock
on Being Nonmentored

1

The boneman said he would take the blinded into a darkened room. And put a
hot-herb poultice on their sightless face.—C. D. Wright, *Deepstep Come Shining*

THE BOOKS ON my shelves are reference books. I go to them. I ask them
things. They talk back. I talk back. We have conversations that are better than
conversations I have with people. About art. Talking with people about art is
like talking with them about religion or politics—nerve-twanging. Still,
other people's ideas excite me, especially those I disagree with. I like to tease
out the connections between the idea I hate and the person I love, between
the loved person's hated idea and my own precious one, between good people thinking bad things and my—as yet—inescapable judgments of other
people's ideas. Real people and me: we have a hard time getting to a place
of mutual worship. If something's perfect it doesn't interest me.

Books sit still as you dismember them. Books get naked with little embarrassment. Once you find out the machine inside them, it becomes evident that the stuff you hated is inextricable from the stuff you loved, and you begin to understand them. Aside from family, few real people hang out long enough to go through this process. This makes my finding a mentor unlikely—since, as far as I can tell, a mentor is someone initially drawn to you because of your positioning of self as disciple. I like to position myself as coroner. I cut up work, and it's best to do so coldly, without becoming entrenched in consideration of the victim's family. But that makes me sound psychotic and mentorship sound like a crock. Most educational relationships start out on unequal footing. It's not bad—it's just not me. I undercut the process with analysis, but I'm not a murderer. I wish I were more receptive to living authority sometimes. I didn't have an older sister until I was thirteen. This is true. Real people are complex and fascinating. Real poets are especially complex. I wish I had a boneman I trusted. Sometimes I wish I were blind. To be led could be meaningful: I know this intellectually. At any rate, reference can be a lonely section.

2

inadequately and feeling more and more less so because of not feeling more, but stopped. For I am of course frightened of you, what your bold face will show me of me.—Claudia Rankine, *Plot*

They say it is a good idea to read what's been written. It is good to recognize one's influences, one's lineage—in order to develop a poetics. It is a good idea to subscribe. It is good to go to readings. To do readings. It is a good idea to attend the after-party. But it is not good to get too drunk or sleep with too many visiting poets. Marriage is an OK idea. Support is good. Does your family support your work? Because that can be crucial—support. That's why you need community. Is your work experimental? That's good. Experimental is good . . . experimental like whose? And form. Form is good. But it is not good form to discuss content. Especially if the content is about children. Never fish for community by using content. Not unless you are burdened by a failed relationship, or a surgery. Also, remember: community is comparison. If you must discuss your work, do it by discussing someone else's.

Must community consist only of other poets? Living poets? Other female poets? Can they qualify other than aesthetically? Can I talk with them about my pregnancies? About science fiction? Decay? Can one of us not be better? How about artists—can I talk to artists? Can we talk about genetics? Could I talk to a physicist? Might I allow her to have something meaningful to say? Might I forgo what is good? For awhile? Could bad work? Has anyone tried it? Do you have their e-mail? Can I people my community differently? Could it include dead poets? Might some of them be male? How about male and alive? Can the members shift, moving in and out, unaware? Can anything be truly different from what has come before? Must a community be en/gendered? Must it acknowledge its traditions in the same way earlier poetic communities have done—by categorization, canonization, and exclusion? Can anyone tell me why? No, I don't want to raise my hand. No, I don't want to have to bleed.

it had yes for a skin and a thousand
little hairs for feet
to help it decide
—Brenda Hillman, from "Early Sex," *Loose Sugar*

I've been in school as long as I've been writing. Public school, dancing school, choreographic conferences, grad school, yoga classes, arts camp, intensive language institute, grad school, Lamaze classes, bartending lessons, grad school. I've taught to pay my way through most of my schools. Mostly I've taught dance to teenage girls/women. I've influenced some remarkable individuals, or so they would have me believe. Often they would have me believe this from far away—I've gotten letters. The letters aren't from the people I expected to hear from. They start out, "You may not remember me, I wasn't much of a dancer." And I do remember them. And they weren't. Or they say, "You taught me how it isn't about pretty." And I smile.

Early on, my teacher Bonnie Peckham gave me science, an admiration for the smallest parts of the body, cells. I never went into science. After seventeen years of less effective training, the ballet dancer Françoise Martinet taught me how I should do ballet—how to strive for perfection happily with imperfect tools. I never danced professionally. The poet Mary Karr is braver than I will ever be: I will never be that brave. Perhaps these women were each a kind of mentor, the kind I was prepared to accept. And because I have never been particularly receptive to such intimacy, no one woman ever leaned down and whispered *grow*. Not to my poetry. I don't mind—I forbade it. Does the world need even one more mortality-obsessed gardener-poet invoking the Latin names of backyard blooms? I don't think it does. At least, I never wanted one. I never wanted to be tended. I wanted to be possessed by possessed women.

As I've watched women possessed by their arts, sciences, careers, children, possessed even by their own bodies, I've seen in their disparate, sometimes frightening energies something boundless and life-obsessed. Voyeurism is one of my strengths. Vicarious growth. Empathetic fertility. I am incapable of naming as a source a poet over a choreographer over a scientist over my mother. In the machine, we are all linked.

4

His wings were struggling. They tore against each other on his shoulders like the mindless little animals they were.—Anne Carson, *Autobiography of Red*

The pen grew from my hand at puberty. It was not expected, and it was painful. It was also phallic. I knew enough to know that. Penis envy has long been discredited; still, it would be a lie to say I never identified with Holden Caulfield or Jay Gatsby or Humbert Humbert. I remember my experiences as a boy-man: for years I wanted nothing so much as to trek around the country taking pictures and acid and experiencing life Kerouac-style. I wanted to be hostile and aloof. Or magnanimous and beatific. Demonic or angelic—all mind and/or libido, but somehow always with the clarity of a single identity. I think by desiring what these protagonists desired, even when it was oblivion or violence, I learned things about the kind of person I am not. And one of the kinds of person I am not is male. I am indebted to my past ability to cross-read. One day I want my sons to be able to do the same. I want to write the kinds of poetry that will allow other women's sons into my double nature. And I want my own sons to read writing that is not about them; I want what they read to make them ache to envelop the entire world. Then I want them to learn to accept and love their smaller selves projected within it.

5

The proportions of a body to blue eyes
big as locusts are made frictionless by distance
After the war, the design of refrigerators
became classical in proportion
—Mei-Mei Bersenbrugge, *The Heat Bird*

This is how it would go, I think, if it went:
As an apprentice, you indenture yourself to a master craftsman for a number of years. Apprenticeship is binding. You learn by standing behind the left shoulder of the right-handed expert observing. Watching the woman in action. To see how it's done—one way it's done. You imitate. You draw

graphs. You chart. Design. Redesign. You fall in love. But you cannot match the original at her art. You change the rules, sometimes slightly, sometimes with more panache. You become your own woman slowly and with great perseverance. You fall out of love. You gain respect for her. She gains respect for you. It is all very beautiful, with cello music in the background. You are friends. You are not friends but you e-mail. You have coffee twice a year. You have a bottle of wine once a decade while confessing envy. You follow her work. She blurbs you. You have a dream. It is a dream of the apocalypse. In the dream she is Gepetto and you are the Blue Fairy and you have lost the puppet in a field of young wheat. Nothing could be less radical, more traditional, than this relationship. And I cannot tell a lie: I would like to have had one like it. Instead, I take the strings. With them, some paper, wax, and ink, as alone as I can be surrounded by other people's words, I blindly try to make the stuff pirouette—or better yet, whirl like a dervish.

Kirsten Kaschock ✳

Push

It even smells unclean here, Priya, like a cellar, like week-old bread

I pushed my daughter from the roof of the new schoolhouse
because my daughter persisted in loving whom she should not.
My daughter believed love lasts. I am mourning her. Love
does not last. Her sisters will not be ruined by her heart.
By her reckless insistence. She could not be let to thwart
our futures with kissing and hands beneath the broad fig leaves.
Love does not last. The town came out to see that I performed
what was necessary. They stood below, in a wide semi-circle.
Her body, in dawn-orange silk, became their eye. Her sisters
I made to look. It will be a long time in the town before
another mother must take her daughter's hand and guide
her crying up the narrow stairs that smelled to me like mold,
although my Priya shook her head, and said *no, mama—books*

Old Doll Body

They think mine
a prettypretty blank blank

I could tell them *I am humbly submitting
the same* I could say *here is the same
for your perusal*

Yesterday, it was the same ate through my petticoats
I feared dysplasia, uterine cancer—irrational
fear, another symptom of hysteria

I, in fact, fear I will remain the same
even as I ache to send it out to contests
and for test-drives

The same is in my underwear
—has been since I was made

If they knew the same they'd love it like a root
but would want to get away—if the same
were true for them
day in, day out—their fingers would stop
no *prettypretty holes down there*

They don't know what that's like
everything in and nothing let
inside my forgotten space—cotton

They prize too much response
I prettymuch want it too   rejection, reaction
something that has to do
with something else

keep passing me down they think me
a faithful carrier of the original
embedding   *keep offering the next babygirl*
me   as if I were still just what was given

even dolls evolve so
I give each girl the same
I've given every girl but it is no longer all

I think *this time*
the seams will go but they don't
and I continue with
holding my difference

Assemblage

This is the house Jane built.

Jane begins by standing. Once, this was
Jane finding Jane. Jane avows
a new architecture, its velocity out
rather than up—the foundation in flowers.

First, a field

A making ready. Then, in the foreground—
relevance.
Jane's erection of self: a marker
indicating horizon. Look her body in the middle
of all things is saying what was already here
Not a greedy Jane. A Jane acknowledging.

Meadow first, then—a positioning of Jane
as verticality. As perpendicular to.
Jane, stated.
But also Jane
is temporal
cleft: a Jane streaming out of the field

No longer field, Jane becomes
a thing requiring.

Jane whole unto. Jane isolate.

Order Jane learning is like a god and like a god punitive

Jane seeking to embrace field is straining
Jane, incapable.
—but now I am
in a unique position to feel pain this is distinct
insistent Jane, Jane fraught I have

more space for pain Above the primordial
flowering of was, a shimmer.
In its wake—structure: Jane is.

It is less space.

This is the house Jane built by being the house
Jane built by being. This is not
the good pain—pain
Jane stood to feel *in origin of Jane*

Instead, this is pain of lean-to—
uncontaining. Mere stay against
exposure. This is all is left
a Jane. This is enough.

Joy Katz
on Sharon Olds

WHEN I FIRST started to write, in my late twenties, someone in my community poetry workshop gave me a copy of *Satan Says* (1980). At the time, I was reading Pound's *Cantos*. I had almost no background in literature; I'd studied graphic design in college. I liked the music and surprise in Pound, and I even liked that I didn't understand the poems, the feeling I was working toward something. But reading them was slow going, to say the least. Here came *Satan Says*, with its deceptively plainspoken language about sex and blind girls and Republican living rooms. Sharon Olds was not intellectual. She was accessible, she was sort of grotesque, and she was like me! She wasn't, of course, but as a living woman poet, she was certainly more like me than E. P. was.

I could sense my poetry teacher's skepticism about this discovery. He was steeped in Dickinson, Olson, the modernists. He felt poetry was a complicated music one had to study hard to understand; it wasn't easy, and it shouldn't be accessible to everyone, the way hard bop or modern classical music wasn't accessible to everyone. That made sense, and I wasn't going to stop reading Olson and Dickinson. But I wasn't going to throw over Olds just because she was popular.

Compared with Pound or even H. D., Olds observed the world from someplace closer to where I stood. But beyond this proximity, as a separate phenomenon, there was the painful intimacy. Reading Olds for the first time was like meeting a stranger who immediately tells you about her abortions. But it's hardly necessary to make a metaphor of it—Olds talked about raped girls, vomited buttermilk, the "shame of new breasts." Yet she wasn't shrill. She spoke calmly. Her calm was a beguiling counterpoint to the bloody body imagery, like the wax woman I'd seen in a medical museum in Florence, with long plaited hair, a pearl necklace, a beatific expression, and all of her guts exposed.

A couple of months later, I drove to the James Wright Poetry Festival in Martins Ferry, Ohio, to see Sharon Olds read. There were the wincingly personal images: Olds chasing a lost diaphragm around an apartment floor, a mother's swimsuit with a bit of crusty residue in the crotch. There were brutal juxtapositions: breast milk and rennet, "the comfortable smell of rot," tulip bulbs and rotten chicken parts, and a father's dead body with its "burned bowels." All the while, her voice was measured. At the podium, Olds looked almost fragile.

The poems deployed the same strategy over and over. Each reached a climax somewhere in the last third, and often at the end, so that during the reading, they came in waves you could time, like contractions. I could feel the audience leaning in toward that moment in each poem. After all the explicit description, that was where the speaker made some large declaration about herself. "Like a newborn animal about to be imprinted, I opened my eyes and saw your face." "I am putting my proud American boast right here with the others." "I remember I would kill for you." There was a not-yet-conceived child stretching its arms out "desperately to me." (That seems to me one of the book's most melodramatic moments; it moved me then.) Olds read: "I know love when I see its back."

And the audience said *ohh*. The audience murmured at the end of the poems and often during the reading of them, and I thought, THIS was something. I wanted to mesmerize listeners that way. Poetry, I thought, should make people audibly exhale. It wasn't important to be as famous as Sharon Olds, and I didn't want to write confessional poems. But if I drew close to essential truths, as I thought Olds did, and if I wrote with as much authority, then anyone who heard me or saw a poem of mine in a journal would feel those stirrings, wouldn't they?

Late that night, there was an open-mic reading in the Martins Ferry public library. Sharon Olds sat on the floor, in the front row, and listened with infinite patience to the whole thing. I had brought with me the first poem I'd written that I felt was successful, the first my teacher had praised. In the end, I was afraid to read it in front of a crowd. As she was leaving, I asked Olds if I could give it to her. She thanked me, took it very solemnly, folded it twice, and put it in her jacket pocket. Then she signed my book. I imagined her reading my poem on the plane back to New York, in a window seat, somewhere above the eastern seaboard. She had my name and address—would she contact me? (She wouldn't.)

Sharon Olds's blasphemy appealed. "*Say shit, say death, say fuck the father, / Satan says. Don't you feel a lot better?*" I did. I felt strangely satisfied. I saw that, in poetry, you could say something really ugly against someone. That jived with a feeling I had, even starting out as a writer, that poetry is responsible to all the parts of things—people, events, language. If you want to make a portrait of someone, if you want to begin to make art of any kind, you can't set aside the bad bits, even if they don't wind up in the poem. For poetry to be moral, it has necessarily to be *able* to speak against, even if it's against something or someone one loves. It has to leave room for the chance to say, without irony, "My mother is a pimp."

Satan Says is unafraid of violence, even violent urges in the self. Violence and love—not tenderness, but love—coexist. The woman speaking the poems loves her father. He is also the person who tied her wrists to a chair. The animal love for her own infant comes with a "dream of murder, mutilation, her / old self bleeding in pieces on the butcher paper." Not a nightmare, but a dream: despite the terror, she doesn't overamp the description.

A year or so after meeting Olds, I was working on a poem about a young boy who was molested by his grandfather. I wasn't interested in the narrative. I was interested in the fact that the boy felt pleasure in the act—that sexual longing had no morality in and of itself; it could even spring from immorality. I'm sure I would have written the poem even if I hadn't read *Satan Says*, but Sharon Olds made room for me to write without self-consciousness, without wondering whether such material had a place in poetry.

Inspired by Olds's approachable language and the earnestness, many have written, and write, dreadful stuff. Editors read baskets of work that describes the sad, violent events of people's lives but that has little merit as poetry. Such writing is still praised as "brave." Most is narcissism; much is pornography (as Helen Vendler has called Olds's poems), dependent for its impact on provocative language or images. This is partly why it's embarrassing to talk about being influenced by Sharon Olds. She is like a bride being trailed by thousands of pale, damaged, slightly hysterical bridesmaids. One risks being photographed in the parade.

Yet I don't know any poet who hasn't read Olds. Narrative poets and asyntactical experimentalists and formalists. Men and women both: A man gave me her book. Her readings still attract huge audiences. She gets standing ovations. In 1993, when I met her, Satan Says—her first volume, then thirteen years old—was in its ninth printing. Clearly I owe her a debt, and I'm not alone.

In Satan Says, Olds broke ground by making the body available in a different way than had Plath and Sexton, who stepped away from the body to talk about (or talked about the body via) dolls, allusions, god, angels, mythology, the Resurrection. The gaze in Satan Says hardly leaves the body. When Sharon Olds made those metaphors, she grabbed what was closest, hastily, like a battlefield nurse—household objects, the familiar stuff of fable: breasts like "white wolves' heads" or "hard bags of rock salt," a sick child's face like "the red tinfoil they wrap poinsettia plants in."

Poetry must also allow for woundable feelings, as Carl Phillips has said. This is where I hit a wall with Satan Says. The vulnerable core of the work exists in the distant past. Each poem offers up a fully formed measure of understanding, within its twenty to thirty lines, sprung from this past pain. Her bold, fearless tone, even as I reread the book now, is as alluring as ever. But because the poems offer sealed, complete understandings, the poet-in-the-present—apparently so accessible—becomes curiously inaccessible. I quickly began to appreciate the tentativeness and lack of closure in the poems of Robert Hass, whom I picked up after Olds. These days, I crave the questioning and woundedness in the work of Carl Phillips, D. A. Powell, Miranda Field, and Jean Valentine, all of whom take the body as one of their subjects.

Joy Katz ✳

Big Baby

Scraping sounds, metal straining, and the baby—gainly, smooth-skinned—enters the world with its canyonlike spaces and big things going wrong. And quick big things too: shadows from hopping toads on streets dry as pancakes. Even the raspberries hang heavy-lobed; even the grasshoppers make sturdy sounds of lovers pulling up to long tables. Three balloons on rough waxen cord float upward. Welcome! Take big steps. (The baby brings its feet down with aplomb.) No one is inside my head whispering; people speak clearly into loudspeakers on utility poles. Welcome also to the large-and-quiet world: simple shape of mountain, fat emeralds, carven alphabet block, rhinos moving smoothly on dolleys. In the light and air the shadows of the clouds move bigly over the baby's arms. I speak to it in complete sentences. The baby gains a natural understanding of civics, geologic time, and Canada. Emphasis shifts: the baby will come to accept hormonal changes. Meanwhile it helps itself to large portions and moves about with whales, having learned to swim in wide shallows. I think up terms of endearment that are not diminutive: my bus, my tarmac. What a relief to crush tininess underfoot into an expanse of sand on which you can find pounds and pounds of whelk. To raise up a house of timbers and catch in it bucketfuls of clear soup. To cart the empties to the dump and listen with equal pleasure to Wagner and Dalrymple. To prefer autumn's bigger name, fall, and its battering changes. The baby makes big noises, signifying to me its loud big love.

A Round Porcelain Jam Pot, Painted Orange

with two leaves on its stem (the stem the tip of a porcelain spoon).

Oranges—the real ones, fruit—are dyed that color; a ripe orange
actually is green-tinged.

This napkin printed with a realistic bamboo pattern.

Bamboo shoots look nothing like the parent plant, but more like
acoustical tiles,

which look like themselves. No one likes them. But people with drop
ceilings are happy that upstairs arguments are muffled and sound like
dove-call.

When she cries, the wife looks beautiful. Everyone in our building says
so.

Beneath an acoustical ceiling: a ceiling of pressed tin, painted over many
times, embossed with fleurs-de-lys that have lost the crispness of the
irises they resemble.

Iris! Clear-eyed spear point!

The Victorians covered flowerpots with wax-dipped cotton string
arranged in branching patterns, to simulate coral.

Upstairs, the couple have hung a wreath on their door: huge rustic
crown, hairy with moss and sage, of a scale suitable for a harvest supper
in D. H. Lawrence.

The barns fallen down in Ohio are the most beautiful on earth. They
look like the wreckage of ancient roller coasters, or like old pier pilings.

The fields were once the floors of lakes. Now, in snow, they look like the
ocean floor.

You can buy real trilobites in a store that also sells polished stones, moths mounted and framed, and recordings of surf that will lull you to sleep.

Not because they sound like surf, but because they sound peaceful.

The old Ohio barns have been razed, the barn siding sold to people who pay a premium for reclaimed wood. They build new houses out of it, or cupboards and shelves,

as if the nobler claim on a tree were to hold first editions and pottery (a jam pot shaped like an orange).

Some books aren't books. *Remembrance of Things Past*, hollowed out, holds $200 in small bills. *Alice in Wonderland*, letters from my father and an article about rescue dogs.

Rescue dogs—as if they weren't just plain dogs from the pound but dogs that had been coaxed to leap from burning buildings. Or as if they saved you when you leapt (eight dogs pulling a net taut with their mouths . . .

Just a Second Ago

I had an urge to toss my drink across the visiting poet's shirt.
        Hello. I liked your reading.
Red wine spreading into the whiteness
        It was a wonderful reading
of his shirt. My hand—my glass—
is still full.
                Yes. People starting to drift to the cheese and bread.
At the wedding, the organist stops,
the minister smiles benignantly. She thinks of touching the bride's breast.
        Hello. I liked your wedding.

It's amazing: traffic stays on its side of the road.
What keeps it there really? I trust
no one will stand up and scream when I am a bride.
I don't laugh when I hear someone has died.
You're sitting there quietly right now

very
very quiet.

The slightest noise could cause an avalanche.

It's scary when someone gets pushed onto
        Hello. I liked your reading
the subway tracks.
So scary when someone walks into Wendy's
and shoots the people eating.
                        What I almost did
just a second ago,
while you were crossing the street
while you were finishing your lunch
while you were handing me your terrible secret . . .

Sharon Olds ✳

Satan Says

I am locked in a little cedar box
with a picture of shepherds pasted onto
the central panel between carvings.
The box stands on curved legs.
It has a gold, heart-shaped lock
and no key. I am trying to write my
way out of the closed box
redolent of cedar. Satan
comes to me in the locked box
and says, I'll get you out. Say
My father is a shit. I say
my father is a shit and Satan
laughs and says, *It's opening.*
Say your mother is a pimp.
My mother is a pimp. Something
opens and breaks when I say that.
My spine uncurls in the cedar box
like the pink back of the ballerina pin
with a ruby eye, resting beside me on
satin in the cedar box.
Say shit, say death, say fuck the father,
Satan says, down my ear.
The pain of the locked past buzzes
in the child's box on her bureau, under
the terrible round pond eye
etched around with roses, where
self-loathing gazed at sorrow.
Shit. Death. Fuck the father.
Something opens. Satan says
Don't you feel a lot better?
Light seems to break on the delicate
edelweiss pin, carved in two

colors of wood. I love him too,
you know, I say to Satan dark
in the locked box. I love them but
I'm trying to say what happened to us
in the lost past. *Of course,* he says
and smiles, *of course. Now say: torture.*
I see, through blackness soaked in cedar,
the edge of a large hinge open.
Say: the father's cock, the mother's
cunt, says Satan, *I'll get you out.*
The angle of the hinge widens
until I see the outlines of
the time before I was, when they were
locked in the bed. When I say
the magic words, Cock, Cunt,
Satan softly says, *Come out.*
But the air around the opening
is heavy and thick as hot smoke.
Come in, he says, and I feel his voice
breathing from the opening.
The exit is through Satan's mouth.
Come in my mouth, he says, *you're there*
already, and the huge hinge
begins to close. Oh no, I loved
them, too, I brace
my body tight
in the cedar house.
Satan sucks himself out of the keyhole.
I'm left locked in the box, he seals
the heart-shaped lock with the wax of his tongue.
It's your coffin now, Satan says.
I hardly hear;
I am warming my cold
hands at the dancer's
ruby eye—
the fire, the suddenly discovered knowledge of love.

Katy Lederer
on Lyn Hejinian

ON THE FIRST day of her class—it was my sophomore year of college—I observed her sitting stiffly in a straight-backed wood-and-metal chair, twirling an orange plastic pencil, the kind you can click like a pen, gazing out on all of us, her first class at Berkeley, where, some years later, she would end up a professor with tenure and a half-time load. I want to start the story here because, although I didn't understand it then, Lyn was riding on the crest of an academic wave that would transport her and several other members of the Language movement from marginal positions as adjuncts or working at regular jobs into the heart of the academy, and this trend would affect my relationship to poetry for the next several years. If one can allude to the "Poetry Wars" with a straight face (the idea of poets "selling out"—on either end of the aesthetic spectrum—seems artificial to me now), then I was a casualty. I had no idea that, by taking her class, I was in point of fact enlisting, and that, no matter how aesthetically open or accepting *she* may have been, by dint of becoming her student I'd be taking a side.

But that would come later. Back in 1993 she was simply an intriguing new professor who could speak with a seductive intellectual power even as she kept her features friendly and at ease. She had, I felt, a lovely face: round periwinkle eyes, broad friendly smile. At once feminine and intellectually tough, I thought of Lyn as somehow better than the rest of us: spiritually inured to her particular predicaments (as an outsider poet, a woman, a mother of two), she came across as exceptionally happy, and it was this quality, more than any aesthetic inclination, that drew me to her. I was reading Bloom's *Anxiety of Influence* (1973) at the time, and I immediately placed Lyn in the company of Ashbery and Stevens—two of Bloom's "poets of the air," their intellects burning with ether—while I, who couldn't help myself (oh, how I wanted to be more like them!), was a poet of earth: vegetal, dark, full of longing and anger.

But it is hard for me to write a memoir about Lyn because her entire sensibility, at least by reputation, is anathema to lyric and memoir as I write it. She is, after all, the author of *My Life* (1980), which deconstructed the genre of the memoir before it had really come into its own. I have tended to use the genres of lyric and memoir in order to "make sense" (if not always beauty) of my emotional and intellectual experiences. Lyn, on the other hand, has always come at her writing to make sense of language itself. Her early work in particular is constructed in a gamelike way, complete with rules and strategies that, though they are buttressed on all sides by philosophical ideas (about syntax and meaning and the way that language operates), I have never been able to fully align myself with. I have always wished I could practice my writing as Lyn does—so prolifically methodical, so properly *formal*—but it is impossible for me.

Perhaps, then, this memoir is an accounting of envy. My envy of Lyn's intellectual method, my envy of her taut formal control. Although I am always aware that writing is a comprehensively *emotional* act, an act that, no matter how its practitioners may choose to articulate or calibrate its purposes, is at base an intervention in the world and thus an expression of will, I am also always aware that some writers are more "in control" of their output than others. Lyn has always struck me as a writer of impeccable control, able to begin a project that she works through systematically until it is completed, meticulously tracing her work's implications even as she sets it out in rich, seductive tones. In the classes I took with her in those early years of my writing life, she tended to discuss student work under the assumption that it was conscious, instructive, a product of the intellect; hers was an enlightenment mentality, an aesthetic cleanly minted by the bright white fires of reason. As a young protégée of Lyn and a striving intellectual in my own right (I was an obsessive student of social and aesthetic theory), I was highly attracted to the idea that one could set out projects for oneself, that one could theorize and synthesize—that writing could be so rational, so abundantly under control. But whenever I set about working on such projects, each of which was an almost erotic attempt to emulate my mentor, Lyn, I would feel like a fraud and a failure, veering off in some direction or other—too lyrical or intellectually oddball. It was in my second class working with Lyn, my senior year in college, that I began to think of my repeated and failed attempts to imitate her work as a form of misprision, Harold Bloom's word for the inevitable misreading a poet will do of the work of his or her mentor. After two years of trying to write like Lyn, I became painfully aware that my writing would never be hers, or even be anything like it. A great loneliness suffused this misprision, this difference.

The difference between air and earth, good and evil, light and dark. I think of myself and my writing as earthy; Lyn and her writing are lovely, divine. While I am Manichean, Lyn thrives on ambiguity. Change, for her, is a pleasure; the rejection of closure, a cause. It was as I tried to be Lyn that I discovered the fundamental loneliness of poetic sensibility. There was the loneliness of my parents' divorce, of my much older siblings' departure from the house, of the loss of my mother to the depths of New York. But this was a new kind of loneliness, more hopeless, more impossible. This wasn't the young child suffering at the hands of life's vicissitudes; rather, it was the young adult forced to face her sensibility.

Lyn had taken a road I could not follow. She had set for herself the task of writing through philosophy, of casting sensibility as theory. She was trying to communicate in very different ways, in much more formal ways, it seems to me, than poets had traditionally done. It is incredibly ironic, when I look back on it now, that she was considered scandalous by the poetry establishment. What had always been an *art of the scandal*—lyric poetry, with its rhetorical seductions, its admittance of the dregs of our deepest inner lives to the vaunted white page—was now scoffing at the most proper movement to have come along in decades. Where was the threat in Language Poetry? It was thoughtful and political, even sometimes banal.

Let's write a sentence a day about the sky, thinks Ron Silliman. Let's write in fragments, attempting to ventriloquize the disenfranchised voice, thinks Susan Howe—and the world of lyric poetry is *scandalized*? Proper: this is what Lyn's work was not considered then, in the mid-1990s, and what mine—dark, organic, full of longing and anger—was. It makes no sense to me.

This last year, ten years after that first day of class, on the eve of my thirtieth birthday, I found myself frightened and alone in my room. I was living in Brooklyn, in a rent-controlled apartment at the corner of Henry and Second, sleeping on a single bed I'd bought from a couple with a very young son. I didn't have a job, and I was finishing a full-length memoir about my family. I had never felt easy about the project, but I had figured that a memoir would be as good a way as any for me to support my poetry habit, which had continued during two years of study at the Iowa Writers' Workshop and then through several years of living on no money in New York. I had recently made what amounted to a pilgrimage, at the start of the project, to see Lyn back in Berkeley. I asked her point-blank if it was "OK" for me to write a "mainstream memoir"—you see, I thought that she'd disown me if I did.

"Of course," she replied. "You should write whatever you want or think you need to write."

I was taken aback by her complete disinterest in the matter. I went back two more times in the years it had taken to finish the memoir, each time asking her permission, each time receiving the same vaguely puzzled approval. But now here I was at the end of the line, in my very dark bedroom on a beautiful August morning. I couldn't bear the thought of finally finishing the thing, let alone its publication. Lacing the massive guilt I felt for having written fifty thousand words about my family was the prospect of aesthetic betrayal.

Regardless of the skepticism I felt about the whole notion of an "experimental poetry," I'd been publishing a magazine that, although it had a distinctly lyric bent, was considered avant-garde. At Iowa I was known primarily as an experimentalist, which, in its largest sense, reflected the fact that we were all of us—all young poets in the academy—expected to take a side. Iowa was an interesting place back then. Devoted to no single "school," a hodgepodge of very readily identifiable aesthetic inclinations, it anticipated the direction American poetry and its institutions would take in the next several years. There was the New York School poet, the formal poet, several young Sylvia Plaths, a James Merrill. It was something like a mock United Nations of Poetry, and over two full years of representing a particular faction (I was immediately labeled a Language Poet and expected to explain all things Language when appropriate in workshops), I lost my way. I'd mistaken my identity as a poet—as someone who'd responded to a deep internal call—for this other, far less interesting institutional (or, sometimes vociferously and almost inevitably hypocritically anti-institutional) identity. In retrospect it angers me that what should have been so personal—the painful and frustrating process of breaking away from a mentor and learning to write as oneself—became politicized. From the moment the discourse of poetry is cast into the language of "camps," which is a military metaphor, to break away from the mentor (which under this rubric means ranging away from her "camp") is to give up real strategic ground. If one is allied with an avant-garde or otherwise protean movement, giving up such ground is at best a retreat, at worst a betrayal. This was the destructively cynical line of reasoning I'd caught myself on. Like a well-hooked fish, the more I thrashed, the more aesthetically panicked and trapped I became. I no longer remembered the Lyn I'd met sophomore year, the one who, if I had thought about things more or remembered that time in more accurate detail, would never have judged me for writing a memoir, was truly "experimental" in that she saw all writing as based in experiment. I have never met anyone so eager as Lyn to have her mind completely changed.

And so, as I sat in my dark little room, I decided to write her an e-mail and ask her advice. I told her I was terrified. That I hadn't known what I was getting into, but that now I'd signed this contract, and what was there to do? My family, I told her, was furious with me. The writing, I told her, was not very good. Of course, these were all just excuses. What I really wanted, plain and simple, was to get out if it—to get out of the writing, to get out of the personal risk. As one might expect to feel about any full-length work based on one's life, my feelings about my memoir were ambivalent. After two years of working on the thing, I had lost all perspective. Lyn had always been for me an aesthetic and ethical ballast. Not trusting my own artistic judgment, I looked to her to tell me what was right and wrong, something I knew even then no artist can ever be fairly expected to do for another.

"There is nothing wrong with writing down a life," she replied. "As I think you're aware, I have all my personal letters at the library down in San Diego, and I know how you feel, the idea of people being able to paw through your experience, to know your private life. It can feel awful, but it's truly a generous thing. We need to know of others' lives. If you think, of course, that this will follow you, then don't publish it."

She was equivocal, trying to find the right level with her student who desperately wanted an out.

I'm embarrassed now to admit to the loss of nerve I had then, but the conversation that resulted was one of the most important I have ever had—Lyn on the phone talking all about not just her life but also the ways in which she'd written about it, written through it, and the importance of that. I think of this as the first time—no matter how much I may have adored her, no matter how much I'd looked up to her in all my years of school—that I realized she wasn't by nature a pedagogue. No, she too had a life, had equivocal, hard-earned desires: to write a few really good books. To be happy in her life and in her work. To make, as they say, a contribution to her art. She was, I could see, just a person, a human.

"Influence" originally meant an "emanation from the stars that acts upon one's character and destiny." It's related to astrology, the ways in which the heavens come to shape our very lives. In this it reflects our basic notions of both religion and art: we imagine that our teachers are like angels looking down upon us, their purity and enlightenment guiding our way. And in some sense, this is accurate, a metaphoric portrait of the mentor and her protégée. Yet as the history of literature attests, things are neither so simple nor so poetic: aesthetic grounds shift, sensibilities clash, the mentor and her student grow apart with the passage of time. As in life, even the most intimate spiritual and artistic relationships remain unfixed, and no matter how often I return to that image of Lyn in front of the class with her pencil and generous face—no matter how eagerly I try to embrace a personified version of art, an unstintingly affectionate, welcoming version—I am writing this alone.

Katy Lederer ✳

Dark Ballad

I thought that you had changed me,
but it was only dark. Your shadow creeping
up the wall, the moon in the window,
the subtle dark kneading my feet.

I thought that you had changed me,
but it was just a dream. Atop a pole,
in frigid wind, the moon in the window,
your kiss, which was dutiful, drear.

I thought that you had changed me,
but it was only wind. Your fingers up
the sharded bone, my fretted spine,
all my vertebrae blown, I can't bend.

I thought that you had changed me,
but it was just a trick. You sawing
back and forth above my chest till
I was cut in half, dark magician.

I thought that you had changed me,
but it was only dark. And now I lie
alone at night, my bed as pure and
white as snow, my filthy heart.

Three Poems

BECAUSE OF PASSION OR COINCIDENCE

Because of passion or coincidence, they
must be they. Because of passion
or coincidence, the stricken lovers wept
and said adieu to you and let us do
what we have to do, which is to be
gone. Because of passion or because of
coincidence, the tides were thrift coming,
the sun was thrift shining,
and everything died.

BELIEVE ME

Believe me,
you are lucky, you
have been nothing—.
In intervals you become
a man. You are, for days
and for years, unbearable.

MELANCHOLY

The day has been over for my sake.
These hours fall under the meek yellow shadow of Saturn.
I fell under the sway of the slowest and seventh of planets,
what some say must then be
the distant and dull one.
And how I agree.

Morning Song

You color all. Is this longing?
Or private. Is it private to speak

in the morning, the birdsong
like knives? We sit on this bench

while this wind swirls and billows.
This setting is love, yet we sit on

this bench, yet we listen to birdsong.
This color, your brain, which is bluer

than water. I touch it, your brain,
which is cooler than water. I wonder,

your brain, when it falters will it be
so cold? We buffet one another

with our bodies, with our slackened
hearts. I put myself in it, your body,

which aches. I put myself in it, your
brain, which is cooler than water.

Lyn Hejinian ✳

from "Book Eight"

Chapter 261: Truth

Truth is not a likeness—not of depicted sense
Crystalled, syncretist, scoped, in synthesis, blotted, novice, at nights,
    mixed—I'd need in origin
I'd say in reference
What truths there are in detail have divisions into circumstance
I'll thank the truth
Maximum of distant light and preference for difference rather than
    capaciousness
A true history will enter sleeps, each change taken partly, wishes obliged
And a true person (shouldered, mound) should rise but not
    immortalized
Expanse by mound
Truth after use
Impatience of the usefulness
It's true to experience
Truths in actualities, truths left by practice
The truth to be as we remembered it

Chapter 262: Nature

The light sloped to a season of thinking is also needing
A natural yellow out of shelter and the sky below—though it threatened
    my independence
All of nature's yesterdays return but don't remain
That is the nature of repetition
Nature is description—or rather nature is name
The widest parts of nature are often low
Mud darkens, the mothers are fast, the light rises

The rivers are black
Someone tells a long anecdote binding some condition
Its irrelevance is as inevitable as a fog at noon
The competence of pink shadows, ungeneralized and ungeneralizing—
    the old pause
The city is spread by nature, fits in light
It's light that waits, the reserves of dispersal
In its nature is time to halt it

Valerie Martínez
on Joy Harjo

AS AN ADOLESCENT GIRL, I thought I inhabited a landscape refracted
in another landscape. In the first, I was inarticulate, struck mute. In the
second, I had a language and a story and a history born of legend. This
other place was peopled by young women like and unlike me—reticent
and rebellious, rattled and undaunted, good and beleaguered.

I must have imagined this because I lived as if it were true. There was my
life story—an Hispanic girl born in Santa Fe in 1961, descendant of Spanish
conquistadores, well-taught to speak proper English, follow the rules of the
Catholic Church, and behave modestly at all times. Our particular plot of
land was a one-bath, two-bedroom brown stucco house on San Ildefonso
Road. Like other families, we cultivated turtles and pet dogs and had Ping-
Pong tables and tetherball sets in the backyard. Six siblings laughed and spat
in English. Now and then we'd hear our parents and maternal grandmother
speak Spanish on the kitchen phone to a friend or relative of their generation. We snacked on peanut butter sandwiches, warm tortillas, potato chips,

and *chicharrones*. We ate pecan pie and sweet cow's tongue *empanaditas* during the holidays. Our report cards were filled with Es and Os and As.

Then, as they do, coincidence and bad luck cruised down San Ildefonso Road in the form of a white Chevy and a Shell gas station patch on a shirt pocket. I parked my blue bike and hesitantly approached the man who was asking for directions. In that blue lightning I fell through the roof and floor of my story. Into the other ones.

> There is this edge where shadows
> and bones of some of us walk
> > backwards.
> *Talk backwards. There is this edge*
> call it an ocean of fear of the dark. Or
> name it with other songs. Under our ribs
> our hearts are bloody stars. ("Call It Fear")

Of course, I had not lived in a historical vacuum. The knowledge and force of opportunity, greed, brutal ignorance, and violence are borne on the bones of our ancestors. It was simply that I had not felt them, hadn't known them yet. And then, how much would I have believed, having grown up with the ancestral privileges of Hispanic people in the Southwest? What happened to me, victim of a pedophile when I was seven years old, laid bare the bones. I saw into the other perforated worlds and forever considered myself "other."

And so I turned to secret journals and daydreams and poetry. Better these than the terror of being in one's own body, of being seen to be in it, duped again. And so the poems, from then until now, did not and do not narrate that girl-child's story nor the story of Ping-Pong tables, family dinners, first holy wafers. Impossible. They go through the roof, through the floor, where the metaphors are.

This is why, sixteen years later, Joy Harjo's *She Had Some Horses* (1983) thundered into my life with such remarkable force.

> I release you, my beautiful and terrible
> fear. I release you. You were my beloved
> and hated twin, but now, I don't know you
> as myself . . . ("I Give You Back")

Today, as much as I recognize the presumption and naiveté of a young woman, especially one of Spanish ancestry, identifying with the Native American speaker in the poem, I cannot argue the truth of it. When I first read Joy Harjo's poems, I felt not only my own "true" experience but also the reality of what had happened to her relatives and ancestors. I had been ripped open to the truth of history by terrible circumstance, and Joy Harjo's poems delivered me into the history of my people and their victims, my land and the land of those who mourned its burial by my ancestors' hands.

Perhaps it's surprising that it took so long to be "thundered" in the way She Had Some Horses shook the floor beneath me. Between the ages of seven and nineteen, I had had the usual education in race relations. I was destined by blood and heritage to be an olive-skinned girl in a land where olive meant "Hispanic," oppressor and oppressed. But this incarnation of my "self" remained at a distance, tempered powerfully by a reluctance to "be" in the world at all. To be honest, I was a wounded girl first, a brown girl second. And so I had to be delivered into my woman's body and my complex heritage through the power of Harjo's poetry.

In 1984, about the time a friend gave me a copy of several poems from Joy's first book, I was a year out of college. I had left New Mexico in 1979 and spent four years at Vassar. Like so many young female poets, I was devoted to Emily Dickinson, Anne Sexton, Sylvia Plath, Denise Levertov, and Elizabeth Bishop. I had read and studied the men, of course, and loved Yeats, Thomas, Whitman, Rimbaud, Crane, and Stevens. My first-rate Vassar education left me well versed in British and American literature but ignorant of Native American creation stories, Alvar Nuñez Cabeza de Vaca, Garciloso de la Vega, Phyllis Wheatley, Kate Chopin, Fanny Fern, Zitkala-Sa, and Zora Neale Hurston.

When I read Joy Harjo's "She Had Some Horses," I slipped into a whirlpool of being theretofore unfamiliar to me but immediately more intimate, close than that given to me by the poets I'd read before:

> She had horses who whispered in the dark, who were afraid to
>   speak.
> She had horses who screamed out of fear of the silence, who
> carried knives to protect themselves from ghosts.
> She had horses who waited for destruction.
> She had horses who waited for resurrection.

She had some horses. ("She Had Some Horses")

It was not that the work of so many female poets had not touched me deeply, both poetically and personally. It had. But none of it resonated like this. There was something frighteningly beautiful and personal about Harjo's work, as if I had entered an identity I had unconsciously left behind. I reentered my historical self.

I met Joy Harjo sometime in 1989, five years later. While on the faculty of the University of Arizona's Creative Writing Program, where I was earning my MFA in poetry, Joy had advertised for graduate student volunteers to work on an anthology of Native American women's writing (what eventually became *Reinventing the Enemy's Language*). I wanted to be part of it. I remember being somewhat nervous about knocking on her office door. I had just read her *Secrets from the Center of the World* (1989), a gorgeous book; I was a young poet humbled by the writers I admired.

Secrets had sparked a deep sense of my disconnection from the land of my birth, a hereditary disconnection (as Hispanic families like mine were thoroughly "contemporary") and a personal disconnection (as I had left the West for seven years on the East Coast). If Harjo's influence on me had been primarily personal at first, her ensuing books would join me to myself culturally and through the land. *Secrets* moved me through the stomata of my own world into the land's dreaming eye. Meeting Joy, with this in mind, was no insignificant thing.

Joy welcomed me into her office, humbly deflected my words of praise for her work, and asked me very directly why I wanted to work on an anthology of Native women's writing. I answered, as I remember, quite simply. I could think of no more necessary anthology for myself or for the reading public. The idea of a comprehensive collection of Native women's writing (our plan, at the outset, was to include writers from South and Central America, Mexico, the United States, and Canada) seemed to me the most essential work. We had been deprived of these stories, testimonials, poems, and perspectives for too long. Joy and I went on to talk about ourselves and our families, about our grandmothers, about poetry. A week later she welcomed me and a classmate, Patti Blanco, to the project.

In the following months and years, Joy, Patti, and I enjoyed many hours of small and large talk in Joy's office. We ate together and listened to music. Joy presented us with our astrological charts. And we worked. Hard. A great deal of time was spent in the effort to get submissions from women who lived and worked and wrote apart from the usual literary circles. And when the submissions started to arrive, I received an invaluable apprenticeship in editing. It was a journey that addressed every preconception and assumption I had about poetry. During the editing process, I was challenged by the range of Native women's voices in the submissions we received. There were essays by older women writing their stories for the first time and writers who had no experience with college writing programs, along with poems by women with degrees and honors and all the literary accoutrements. And there were submissions from every kind of writer in between. Our editing sessions, rich and sometimes contentious, opened my mind in a powerful way. I realized that I had particular ideas about what makes for good poetry. I heard myself speaking the literary criteria of my undergraduate professors, and I realized with some discomfort that my bias was based firmly on a modernist, patriarchal approach to the judgment of poetry.

It was not that these criteria (poem as objective-correlative, poem as artifact) were useless or without merit. Much of the work we received fell in line with what is traditionally considered "good" poetry. I simply had not expanded my definition of good poetry to include the range of women's writing that challenged well-worn and traditional ways of valuing literature. In other words, it was through this project that I became part of the postmodern age, wherein the idea of "criteria" became critical and fluid—where "good writing" became the arc between the "good" and "being," "finished" and "finishing," "spoken" and "speaking." This reconception has been transformative and sustaining in terms of the way I read and experience poetry to this day. This was Joy Harjo's doing. In those sessions, she had the ability to articulate, both fiercely and eloquently, the significance of writing that utters itself in languages neglected in the canon of American letters—the various and rich languages of Native women.

Today, Joy's poetry continues to tether me to our indigenous, spirit-and-earthbound ancestors, to my self and my history, to a conception of the universe we cannot have without reading writers like her:

In the last days of the fourth world I wished to make a map for
    those who
would climb through the hole in the sky.

My only tools were the desires of humans as they emerged from
    the killing
fields, from the bedrooms and the kitchens.

For the soul is a wanderer with many hands and feet.
    ("A Map to the Next World")

This way of thinking about existence is unabashedly spiritual: the material and spirit worlds find their integrated reality in language. In Harjo's work, there is always the "beautiful sense of the pattern that was revealed before that first breath." And despite the fact that "this colonized world threatens to destroy the gifts that my people carry into the world," she affirms that "we cannot be destroyed."

Joy Harjo's poetry has been a force against my own destruction—my alienation from myself as a girl-woman, as a story, as a historical being. More important, the poems ward off the destruction of the Muskogee people, of all American Indians, and by extension, of the rest of us. Joy Harjo's writing provides the crucial legend ("Map") that enables our understanding of the gift we are of and in: the charitable earth. This is history, after all, the history of the material universe. Where material rises to "gift" is where the spirit is. And human survival. And grace.

Valerie Martínez ✳

Is All

Between my legs,
all manner of Lamb's Ear,
Cliffrose petals, salt of dirt.

There goes the murmuring,
some word-shine.

Here is a table of tin cups.
You drop in coins, Reader.

You drop.

Pre-teen girls say *like* three dozen times a day.
Hum, says belly, vulva, back of knee.
Chime, like the neighbor's blue-green metal thing.

Deep in, Reader, where sound goes
slow-like, expanding.

Come again?

Salt, tin, metal thing.

Like a refrain, the pelvis all
field, blood, and muscle
hammering.

Ocean Once over This

1.

Here they stand, rotund, and undiluted with grief.
Their hands are violets, invisible.
The velvet of their garments blows
almost imperceptibly over the ground.
Heaven is a room hemmed by wishes,
recently neglected, near enough to perfume the skin

    here,
      in the second realm
     where paradise lingers,
    something on the tongue
      we vaguely know.
  The garden doing its best
    to reach through:
lilac, cherry blossom, cool breeze
      ruining the heat.
  Wishes slip even as we clutch
  and clutch. Even as we grin.

2.

We cannot explain our love of mountains,
clay-red, dotted with piñon, chamisa, yucca.
Perhaps it is the expanse between them,
the sky which fills the space, immense,
the breath opened up like a holy book
blank and ever-blue, on and on

3.

  Now the gangs appropriate
  the Virgin of Guadalupe.

Needled into their arms.
Screened onto cotton.
Scribbled with boxy, tilted
gang tags for protection.

The pallbearers wear her image,
one after the other,
until she blurs under the casket,
the boy with a bullet in his neck.

They feel him passing over.
They choose her because pain
is the passing, reaching through.

They know it.
They know it and know it.

4.

The girl feels her body as nothingness.
Nothingness makes her an angel.
Angels may not be unloved.
Unloved, the body hides itself,
itself—or disappears into air

5.

They surround themselves with creatures terribly injured—a puppy with
four broken legs, crushed by a yellow car. They fill the tub and work his
tiny limbs, numb. He's forgotten they should move, lies with a stick all
day, tail wagging. Lively half-life.

Who could? Why?
Because he's here?
Because half-there?

6.

under the surface

               the sea

echo & blur of voices
every physical thing

               undulating

slowed-down time
blue-green
distant kin

               sing

on the surface

               terror

green veneer
the dark & invisible

               underneath

impending
behemoth

               enormous

7.

The place on the mesa.
The heat and no sleep for two days.
The corn pollen.
The medicine man chanting over her.
The smoke of the pipe in her lungs.
The talisman, feathers, terrible hunger.
The liquid drunk.
It makes her vomit

into the buzzing lack of heat sunset silhouette
the antelope and words so sharp each syllable
is the umbilical thread tugging world to world

8.

It is why the creeping down
is like the bent knees,
crossed legs, forehead
to the ground, hands
pressed together, words
a delirious fever
could be all or one anguish:
devotion, bereft love, deliverance.

9.

I step into the garden (with its hint of bodies)
where the roots spin into trunks and branches,
into yellow blossoms then fruit. Elemental
even as the house upon the ground, hemmed by air.

The layering. The interpenetration.

I say *hint of bodies.*
I say *ocean once over this.*
I say *every creature before us.*
I say *this world and the others*

reaching through

Joy Harjo ✳

She Had Some Horses

She had some horses.

She had horses who were bodies of sand.
She had horses who were maps drawn of blood.
She had horses who were skins of ocean water.
She had horses who were the blue air of sky.
She had horses who were fur and teeth.
She had horses who were clay and would break.
She had horses who were splintered red cliff.

She had some horses.

She had horses with long, pointed breasts.
She had horses with full, brown thighs.
She had horses who laughed too much.
She had horses who threw rocks at glass houses.
She had horses who licked razor blades.

She had some horses.

She had horses who danced in their mothers' arms.
She had horses who thought they were the sun and their
bodies shone and burned like stars.
She had horses who waltzed nightly on the moon.
She had horses who were much too shy, and kept quiet
in stalls of their own making.

She had some horses.

She had horses who liked Creek Stomp Dance songs.
She had horses who cried in their beer.
She had horses who spit at male queens who made

them afraid of themselves.
She had horses who said they weren't afraid.
She had horses who lied.
She had horses who told the truth, who were stripped
bare of their tongues.

She had some horses.

She had horses who called themselves, "horse."
She had horses who called themselves, "spirit," and kept
their voices secret and to themselves.
She had horses who had no names.
She had horses who had books of names.

She had some horses.

She had horses who whispered in the dark, who were afraid to speak.
She had horses who screamed out of fear of the silence, who
carried knives to protect themselves from ghosts.
She had horses who waited for destruction.
She had horses who waited for resurrection.

She had some horses.

She had horses who got down on their knees for any savior.
She had horses who thought their high price had saved them.
She had horses who tried to save her, who climbed in her
bed at night and prayed.

She had some horses.

She had some horses she loved.
She had some horses she hated.

These were the same horses.

Erika Meitner
on Rita Dove

IN THE BEGINNING, her fingernails were enough to convince me that she was cool. With Rita, as with every time we started a semester with a new teacher, our graduate writing workshop examined her with exceptional scrutiny, although we weren't exactly sure what we were looking for. We all knew the quirky things about Rita that we had scavenged from interviews on her Web page—that she wrote from three to six in the morning, that her father had been a chemist, that she wrote standing up at a long-legged desk. But we had real questions: How would she handle X's impenetrable language poetry, Y's ecstatic religious verse, and Z's misogynist statue poems? Would she call us on our bullshit? Would she actually *read* our poems before workshop? Would she notice who was sleeping with whom and who had gone off his antidepressants? Rita's nails spoke volumes about her workshop street cred; they looked like Keith Haring and Paul Klee had gone on a bender, and then given her a manicure. Each nail was carefully filed into a long oval, and painted differently than the one next to it, in a riot of color and abstract detail—swirls and triangles, stripes and dots in metallic hot rod blue, gobstopper pink, rubber duck yellow, and tulip red. These were not grown-up nails. I kept expecting to hear carousel music with a Brazilian backbeat every time Rita waved her hands during that first class meeting.

In 1999, I was living in Brooklyn and teaching English at a public middle school where most of my students were illiterate and borderline violent. It was then that it first dawned on me that I wanted to go back to school for an MFA in poetry. I was burned out from yelling for five hours a day and growing increasingly sure that getting Julio to stop kicking Maritza during third-period Language Arts was probably not the best use of my talent. I had done my undergraduate work in creative writing and English literature at Dartmouth College, and when I consulted my undergraduate mentor, Cleopatra Mathis, about my MFA plans, she advised me wisely in her thick Louisiana drawl to avoid going into debt for a graduate degree in poetry writing. She recommended three schools that had generous funding for their writing students, including the University of Virginia, which ended up accepting me in late spring of that year because the girl ahead of me on the wait list was hiking through Honduras and couldn't be reached by phone.

I didn't know much about Virginia except that, according to the bumper stickers, it was apparently for lovers. I knew even less about the writing program at the university other than the names of the poets who taught there: Charles Wright, Greg Orr, Rita Dove. In retrospect, it was probably shameful that I didn't try to find out as much as possible about who would be guiding me through the next step of my writing future, but I was so distraught about leaving my hip New York neighborhood for a place I imagined to be filled with strip malls and humidity that I didn't have much energy left to ponder the academic part of the scenario.

Rita Dove was the most familiar member of the faculty to me only because I distinctly remembered her from my dog-eared copy of *Contemporary American Poetry*, an updated, fifth edition of the 1971 anthology edited by A. Poulin Jr. that included photos of its poets. Rita was sandwiched between a terrifying picture of James Dickey, who looks as if he is growling, and a forlorn shot of Alan Dugan. Of the fifty-five poets in the book, Rita was one of thirteen women and the only writer to use the word "vagina" in a poem, which was why her work caught my eye in the first place. I had spent a vast portion of my undergraduate writing career getting flak from my classmates for writing poems that included heavy helpings of both sex and genitalia. My work in college, and for a long time afterward, was (and often still is) obsessed with the pleasures and dangers of women's bodies. Rita's poem "After Reading *Mickey in the Night Kitchen* for the Third Time Before Bed" had the bravest and most glorious opening I had ever read: "My daughter spreads her legs / to find her vagina."

After being surrounded by a close-knit community of friends in Brooklyn, the transition to graduate school and the move to a very small town was rough. In New York I went out almost every night and interacted with people constantly during the day in my various career incarnations as corporate computer consultant, teacher, documentary film production assistant, and office temp. When I started at UVA, I lived in an anonymous condo development where I spent so much time alone in my apartment that, some weeks, the only person I spoke to outside of writing workshop was the cashier at the grocery store. I was so homesick for New York that I started to watch television—I hadn't even owned a TV for the six years before grad school—and became addicted to any show that included glimpses of the city: Hot dog carts on *NYPD Blue!* Firefighters with Queens accents on *Third Watch!* A Lower East Side Dumpster on *Law & Order SVU!* I developed raging insomnia and an inexplicable fear of getting lost around Charlottesville while driving. Just the trip to the CVS for toothpaste became a major accomplishment. By spring semester of my first year, I had almost gotten used to the crushing isolation of my new life and the pressure of the fact that my entire sense of self-esteem depended on what everyone thought of my latest workshop poem. I didn't begin to feel a real sense of community at UVA until workshop with Rita kicked into high gear.

Before we started working with her I had asked my friend Kevin, a second-year, what workshop with Rita was like. He told me, with a tinge of awe in his voice, that if you went to see her during office hours about your poem, days before it was going to be workshopped, she could refer to parts of it off the top of her head. She not only read our work but read it repeatedly, and she gave each student at least a half-page of typed comments for each poem handed in. The idea was wonderful but also intimidating—what if she had spent more time reading and commenting on one of my poems than I had actually spent writing it? Guilt inspired me to work harder than I ever had. I wanted my poems to be Rita-worthy.

Rita had all the MFA students over to her house for workshop each week, where she'd seat us at her dining room table and ply us with hot taquitas and colas called Dr. Thunder and Southern Lightning, which she got, she told us, because the names sounded poetic. Her generosity was infectious, and soon we all began trying to out-snack each other every week with ethnic dishes, fresh-plucked fruit, home pickling projects, and elaborate baked goods. Rita's house, for me, became a haven, a sanctuary where we were cared for and fed and where we pushed each other artistically.

At the start of the spring that Rita was my workshop instructor, a very famous male poet came to UVA to be our visiting writer, a weeklong position wherein he was meant to read our poems, mentor us, and offer different insight into our work than our regular instructor might. Our particular poet was quite old and seemed alternately to be either very drunk or trembling uncontrollably from lack of alcohol. When it came time for my one-on-one meeting with him, we sat in an empty office, and he picked up the stapled packet of ten poems I had submitted to him months before. He flipped through the pages. I wondered if he had even read them. He cleared his throat. "None of these are really worth discussing," he said. "So, how would you like to use our time together today?" I was stunned. I stutteringly asked him if there were any he thought might be salvageable; he relented and offered pointers on one of the ten. Later, I relayed the experience to Rita during her office hours, trying hard not to cry. "I am so sorry that happened," she said quietly. She didn't bad-mouth the poet, she didn't act outraged. She asked me a simple question: "Is his project your project?" I thought of the trite, absurdist, novelty verse he had read the evening before. His project was definitely not my project. My poems tended to be rambling narratives that tackled subjects people shy away from: the detritus of the urban industrial landscape, birth control accidents, awkward one-night stands. After spending the year writing and simultaneously worrying obsessively about what my workshop would think about my poems, I felt loosed, as if someone had cut my strings. Whatever my project was, I suddenly realized, not everyone had to like it.

Halfway through spring semester, Rita handed me a sealed manila envelope—one of her famous "wild card" assignments. This was a personalized instruction pack that she presented to each of her students sometime around midterm, which involved writing a poem as a result of strange and very specific directives. The assignment was mandatory and meant to actively push us out of our comfort zones. It had to be turned in to Rita at a particular time, in a sealed envelope. My friend Jen had already warned me that hers involved crafting a poem as if it were a series of notes dropped on the way to her grave. Kevin's mission was to bring a purple object and an orange object outside to write about them. I felt like a CIA operative when I opened my packet, which instructed me to wait until the darkest and creepiest hour of the night, free-write a paragraph on my computer without stopping, print it out, cut it up the middle vertically with scissors, and put it in a drawer for one full day. When I took it out of the drawer, I had to pick a half and form it into a poem without adding any words to the chosen half. I asked Rita later why she had given me that particular assignment. She said it was meant to break me out of the narrative style I had been working in both before and since I had come to UVA. She laughed when she finally looked at the poem that I had made from my half-page. I had somehow still managed to form the disparate fragments into a narrative.

During the silent moments of our workshops, Rita's new house would creak in its joints, moan, and settle into its foundation. Her old house had burned to the ground the year before when it was struck by lightning. She wrote in her poem "House Fire" that "the unspeakable moved through me like a pageant / . . . despair holding me up like a torch." But rather than falling into inconsolable paralysis over the loss of their house and manuscripts, Rita and her husband Fred took up ballroom dancing. The spirit and details of their hobby infuse her most recent book, *American Smooth*.

Every time I've seen Rita over the past six years she's just undertaken something new: target practice at the local shooting range, singing lessons, touring Australia in an RV. As I was finishing up my MFA in the spring of 2001, I found out I had received a fellowship from the University of Wisconsin Institute for Creative Writing to teach and write in Madison for the year. Once again, I had to pack up and move to an unfamiliar place. This time, inspired by Rita, I vowed to take up some sort of new pastime. Madison was the epicenter of all things craft-related; I decided I would learn to throw pots and fantasized about gifting friends with the symmetrical sake sets and smoothly styled bowls I would both design and execute. While working with clay on a wheel was a fantastic idea, my kinesthetic abilities and coordination generally top out somewhere between "flailing" and "spastic," especially when an activity involves using my hands and feet at the same time. Mark, my bearded, gnomelike pottery instructor, turned out lovely vases and platters. I struggled for five weeks just to center my slimy hump of clay on the wheel. I hadn't truly sucked at an activity since archery at camp in 1987. I had forgotten the feeling of frustration and disappointment that left me near tears each time I went home from the pottery studio caked in stiff gray clay.

I was also a poetry instructor that year. I had taught beginning poetry writing UVA, but at the University of Wisconsin I was assigned the intermediate poetry students. My Virginia students had needed instruction in the basics: imagery, metaphor, line breaks, punctuation. For the most part they weren't yet at the phase of breaking out of writing ruts; the strongest of them were just beginning to develop a distinctive personal style in their work. At Wisconsin, for the first time, I struggled to help my students find and hone their individual voices while simultaneously trying to challenge them to move in new directions. It was tempting to avoid pushing them to change their writing: as in my beginning pottery classes, there was more of a chance that their work would be awful during the transitions.

I was grappling with this issue in my own poems, too. Narrative had come easily to me when I was out in the world sleeping with near-strangers, working weird jobs, and generally collecting experiences that might later be processed into poems. After three years of being ensconced in academia and solitude, my work became more internal. My stories of inner-city school kids and bodega dwellers dried up. One of my closest friends committed suicide, and suddenly the chaos of my world was less easily arranged into stories with redemptive endings, or with any endings at all. I tried to write lyric poems—tried to crack myself out of narrative, as Rita had attempted to get me to do the year before—and for that entire long year failed miserably. My Wisconsin work was nonsensical and disjointed, and it lacked music. I didn't know how to go about making poems that hung together without a plotline; I never knew when these new pieces were finished; I couldn't figure out how to work the turns. Rita always told me you had to write the bad poems to get to the good ones. Her philosophy was that the pieces that didn't work were absolutely necessary in ultimately producing the poems that did. So I wrote more bad poems. And every time I pondered giving up on a student, considered taking the path of least resistance and simply praising her work to avoid the hard job of opening her to the new, I channeled Rita. I pretended that I was infinitely patient, wise, and generous with my time. I sent my most difficult poets on field trips to the organic farm or the bowling alley, asked the reductive students to listen to Allen Ginsberg and the expansive one to read Robert Creeley, tricked the absurdist kid into writing something sincere, and assigned the freestyle rappers sonnets.

When people write about their poetic mentors, they often focus on how their work influenced them. As a Pulitzer Prize winner and former U.S. poet laureate, Rita has a formidable body of work. Her poems have wide-ranging styles, often give voice to the voiceless, and manage to imbue personal experiences with a larger sense of history and culture. I've absorbed many lessons from her work, but Rita was a mentor to me in a different way. She taught me that writing and living are the same thing. In order to write, she said, you have to learn how to truly inhabit and push against the world rather than move through it as an afterthought. Poetry isn't something that happens in a vacuum. If you are shuttered to all the world has to offer, your work will be narrow, uninteresting, and lacking a crucial spark. You have to pick yourself up and dance when your house burns, respect your self, and seek out new experiences. Rita reminds me of the quotation I scrawled in a journal once in college, from the Buddhist teacher Chogyam Trungpa: "We must continue to open in the face of tremendous opposition. No one is encouraging us to open and still we must peel away the layers of the heart."

Often when I'm sitting in a conference hotel room in a humorless business suit for an academic job interview, in the hopes of landing a gig teaching poetry, I think of Rita's nails. She never lets society dictate who she is, what she should look like, what her schedule should be, how she writes, or what she writes about. She gives me the courage to wear red stilettos with my suit slacks, to be uncompromising in my interview answers about my projects, to read poems with the word "fuck" in them at job talks, and to feel unapologetic when groggily answering the phone at noon after a night of writing. Most important, she taught me to be relentless in my pursuit of something I've since termed "the delta factor." We each have in us the infinite possibility and capacity for change. We must change to stay alive as artists and as writers.

Erika Meitner ✳

Elegy with No Shoe-Leather Enfolded in a Love Poem

I swear I'm getting softer. I swear
the days are so much longer they've increased

by half. I'd send each hour up a river just to see it
thrash with the salmon, lop your head off if I could

carry it everywhere and you'd remain intact
as the plastic dolls I loved childhood fierce,

whose bitten, thick-skinned cheeks held no marks
the same miraculous way they peel bodies

off the sacked quarterback all fall and he limps
almost-whole from the field towards enormous

sideline boys meant to prevent the pile-up who just
hang their helmets in shame. Our challenges

are proportional, not to our size, but to our ability
to see small, hastily sewn-together animals and not

weep at the crude stitches matted in their fur,
to mask our grief in the square root of a tilted

bus shelter that shields us from dissolving in the rain
like so many packets of artificial sweetener

crammed on a diner counter where someone
always more desperate steals the exhausted tips

of the waitress who's been on her feet longer than
I've been in graduate school. The way she slumps

in an empty booth to count what's left of her change
is the endurance of the long-haul trucker or heat-wave

marathoner when everyone's gone home by the time
she crosses the finish line, which explains how my mother

could sit at the kitchen table after Esther Blitzer's funeral
and tell us, *She rolled my mother out of Auschwitz*

in a wheelbarrow and buried my sister
in the Sussnowiec ghetto, while I squeezed

your hand under the table, which was different
from the way she'd always say *That's life, kid,*

my final year of high school though I never told her
about my Driver's Ed instructor who pressed his foot

over mine on the gas pedal to encourage me to go faster
and closer to the rows of side-street cars, then let me

start to turn accidentally into oncoming traffic once
before he grabbed the wheel and set things straight.

Sex Ed

The back seat of his car glows blue
in the classroom darkness. The filmstrip
is chattering steadily through its loops, teeth
holding it to the light. We're slumped
in our seats, legs stretched in the aisles—
unwieldy, bursting packages of spandex,
watermelon lip gloss, hard-ons,
torn jeans, acne scars, unlaced sneakers.
The guy with the car, bad 70's hair

and a varsity jacket is kissing a girl now,
one hand grasping her waist, the other
roaming her buttoned blouse trying
to convince her to go all the way—
but it feels so good, baby,
how can it be bad?

The film bleeps suddenly, freezes
in mid-convince—the signal
for classroom discussion, all of us sitting
uncomfortably silent, no one wanting
to be the prude or the slut, the scapegoat
for Mrs. Callaghan's lesson on negative
peer pressure or abstinence or whatever
was chalked on the board today
to teach us sex as danger, sex as fear
of consequence, sex as weak-willed passion
gone too far; sex as anything but get-lost-in-it
pleasure, ephemeral treasure-chest
of orgasm, a word Mrs. Callaghan
has managed to avoid all semester—
somehow more uncomfortable
than *menstruation* or *nocturnal emission,*
penetration or *intercourse.*

Who decided to leave the most intricate union
of flesh and emotion to health class, to 30 kids
playing Frisbee with sample diaphragms, batting condoms
from row to row like balloons? We are at risk. We are
self-conscious. We don't need this moral guidance, this
just say no public health awareness training, but sex ed
is not an elective. We have no choice
so we become a captive audience
to latex AIDS prevention, the horrors
of teen pregnancy and early responsibility.

We cart eggs around for a week
and try not to break them.
We take pop quizzes on STD transmission.
We are compulsory in our hormones.
We are standardized in our knowledge.
We work hard on weekends to master
drinking in backyards, smoking blunts in parks,
making out in bathrooms. We get on our knees
to study toilets, torque, touch, taste, zippers,
hangovers, the elaborate instructions that come
in tampon boxes, condom boxes, home
pregnancy test kits. Drugstore clerks
become our examiners, our worst after-school
nightmares in price checks of K-Y jelly or Trojans
camouflaged carefully under *Seventeen* magazines
and double A walkman batteries.
In unofficial night classes we promote
promiscuity, teach each other
gutter words, trade misguided tips
on broken hymens, blue balls, the precise
definition of third base, how to
find a clitoris or get rid of house party
hickeys quickly.

Someone needs to raise their hand immediately
and volunteer to tell the girl in the car
to unbutton her blouse for that guy slowly.
Someone needs to show him how to caress
her eyelids with his thumbs, then run one
over her lips, see if she takes his finger
into her mouth and sucks, then turns her head
to the side so his moist thumb trails her cheek.

Someone needs to remind them, in the silence
of the beep—the longest hanging moment ever—
that we don't need to ask forgiveness for exploring fingers,
roving lips and tangled limbs, for baseball metaphors

and base desires, for holding each other close
in darkness. The force that drives all flesh
exhausts, exalts, raises us up ecstatic.

Homeroom

Yesterday in the mail I got a package
from the Teachers' union: a magnet
to hang on the fridge with their motto—
I Cope—printed in white on a red apple

which is what I've been doing lately.
Sometimes I chant *ung namo*
guru dev namo, feeling stupid, thinking
dignity, serenity, integrity

the way Ellen taught us, twisted in yoga.
Other days it's all I can do to board
the train going in the right direction,
rising mornings above the Gowanus projects

when the subway surfaces into sunlight,
thundering tin cars slicing through my head—
cranes, warehouses, piles of rock shooting past.
The conductor punctuates stops with,

Stand clear the closing doors, and I wonder
what I'll yell today when Curtis punches
Julio with all his might, straddling
his curled-up body because Abel Pena

told him Julio said, *Your dad's a crackhead*,
which he was before he died. But Julio,
he never speaks, which Curtis can't know
because he rarely shows up to class.

And I wonder if this mix of anger
and sadness won't eat me alive by June
since it's only October and the ginkgoes
are just starting to drop their yellow fans,

ginkgo the only piece of information
I remember from sixth grade along with
that Jabberwocky poem. I wonder what
these kids will piece out of this mess I've made—

what old journal entries or ancient assignments
they'll keep. The ginkgo leaves are everywhere
on the way from your house at sunrise
where I've unfurled my body against yours

to rock out this cracked world. With each step
away from you I compress, late to school
in last night's clothes, sloshing coffee, running
past the burnt out bodegas, endless

tire stores, the disapproving stare
of the squat principal. I'm squashed with tension,
wound up, ready to spring. The No. 2 pencil
I need to fill in attendance has been

stolen, Michael Cruz is already at me—
Ms. Meitner, this writing class is bootleg,
a word my kids use for anything cheap,
imitation, though right now I'd kill

for moonshine because Chris Roman has nothing
to write with and Maritza is complaining
her journal is wasted—meaning finished,
not drunk—and I yell, *Silent journal writing*

for ten minutes. Come on kids, you should
know this by now. I wait for my anger

to boil away, stop myself from telling
this turtle-shaped boy with enormous glasses

that he's a bootleg student, stop myself
from losing my temper with Robert Castillo
who didn't do his homework again,
though I won't learn until December

that his mother throws him out of the house
every night from five to ten so she can
work as a prostitute so he really
has nowhere to do it. And when Elias

unscrews his seat and wears it on his head
instead of starting the Do Now on the board,
I make him sit out in the hallway
the same way I will months later though one day

he turns to me and says, *I used to get beat*
with two by fours in the bathtub for
wetting my bed. And Lloyd, who smells rank
this morning, every morning, comes up to me,

puts his red mirrored wraparound sunglasses
over my eyes, shouts, *Yo, look at Ms. Meitner!*
She look mad dope, and I sit down heavily
in my wooden chair with Lloyd's sunglasses on

letting chaos overtake 601 for the morning,
laughing at the kids laughing at me.

Rita Dove *

After Reading Mickey in the Night Kitchen for the Third Time before Bed

   I'm in the milk and the milk's in me! . . . I'm Mickey!

My daughter spreads her legs
to find her vagina:
hairless, this mistaken
bit of nomenclature
is what a stranger cannot touch
without her yelling. She demands
to see mine and momentarily
we're a lopsided star
among the spilled toys,
my prodigious scallops
exposed to her neat cameo.

And yet the same glazed
tunnel, layered sequences.
She is three; that makes this
innocent. *We're pink!*
she shrieks, and bounds off.

Every month she wants
to know where it hurts
and what the wrinkled string means
between my legs. *This is good blood*
I say, but that's wrong, too.
How to tell her that it's what makes us—
black mother, cream child.
That we're in the pink
and the pink's in us.

Jennifer Moxley
on Susan Howe

I BEGAN WRITING poetry in college in the company of a close-knit group of friends. In the spirit of the avant-garde and against the cult of the "isolated genius," we placed community and collaboration at the very core of our aesthetics. It was a playful and contentious way to enter the art of poetry. Because of this introduction, I was spared the crushing loneliness of the writing life for several years. Then I moved from San Diego to Providence, Rhode Island, with my boyfriend Steve. He was going to pursue his PhD in English. I was a college dropout who, uncommitted to any program of study or meaningful vocation, had left my home and family to move 3,000 miles away with the sole goal of trying to be a poet.

Our first three months were idyllic. It was summer, and we used our isolation to get to know the city, to read, browse bookstores, and be together. But everything changed when he started classes. Suddenly I was alone, both literally and culturally. Summer nights we had spent watching movies were now given over to study, and even my typewriter was co-opted in the service of seminar papers. Social gatherings with his new colleagues only made the growing chasm between my vocabulary and his feel that much more acute.

The collaborative and social nature of the poetry scene I had left behind seemed far away indeed. That moment was over. My primary network had become dispersed and, in many ways, was foundering. Nobody was writing or sharing work. All were trying to figure out their postcollege lives. The only thing I was sure of was that mine would be with Steve—a decision that, as is not uncommon for women, effectively separated me from everyone else. Now I faced the difficulty of writing poems not into a circle of opinionated friends but into the silence of an imagined audience. I soon discovered it felt like writing poems to no audience at all.

Although I know neither the origin nor vintage of it, we had around the apartment a photocopy of the Montemora Foundation edition of Susan Howe's *Pythagorean Silence*, originally published in 1982. One evening I sat down and read it. I was comforted to find my recent feelings of isolation and separation skillfully mirrored in Howe's words. The company of shared emotion that her poem provided helped me to think about how I was going to face my art in this new situation, without guarantee of readers or a receptive community.

A book-length work divided into three sections, *Pythagorean Silence* begins with a daughter going to meet her father the day of the bombing of Pearl Harbor. The scene is twilight in the snow, the words they exchange are spoken in whispers. The dim light, the frozen landscape, the whispers, and the knowledge that the father will be going to war combine to create a startlingly desolate atmosphere. These words fall in a thin strand down the page: "(her cry / silences / whole / vocabularies / of *names* / for / *things*." In that silencing cry Howe turned the isolation of writing into the power of renaming. It struck me as an imperative, but also a warning. The moment a woman decides to rename, she steps away from the comforts of the known. I had done the latter but had not yet faced the former. The imperative was to combine what my absent family and friends had given me with something completely new and entirely my own. Or, as Howe's poem puts it: "Body and Soul / will we ever leave childhood together."

The scholarly life is a lonely one, and Howe's poem underlines its seductions as well as its terrors: "But I am wandering off into irrational / magnitudes / Earth has turned away from the sun / and it is night." She alludes to literary images of separation and loneliness: Penelope awaiting her husband's return, her eyes growing dim looking at the sea: "what ships I have seen // Sails filling   or falling / horizons wandering"; Yeats's missing child, stolen away from his family by fairies; Pound's "River Merchant's Wife," who desires her dust to be mingled with that of her absent beloved "forever and for / ever."

Howe deftly intertwines memories of her father with literary references until the poems themselves become her personal history. Grief for her father and grief for Lear are one and the same. The mastery of Howe's intermixing lies in her formal technique. By writing the poem in the *way* she did, she reinvigorated the heavily codified and tired poetic tropes of both literary reference and personal confession. Combining the allegorical gestures of a long poem like *The Waste Land* with the intimate lyric unities of a poem such as Wallace Stevens's "The World as Meditation," Howe creates a book-length occluded narrative in which words tentatively move in and out of phrases, momentarily join to make frail meanings, and at times are utterly separate both from themselves and others:

He plodded away through drifts of i
ce

Reading Howe's poem at that moment in my life taught me to feel, in the company of a book, the comfort I had theretofore only felt in the company of other people. I began to connect my personal experiences to the ideational life I lived in books—a connection I had always been afraid to make, but without which I never would have become a serious poet. Soon after reading *Pythagorean Silence* I wrote this in my journal: "I've come to poetry again, as if by grace, and am all the more contented for it. Strangely enough it is now that I've decided to do research, to study other poets and read their works, their poetics. To try and understand my writing and its motivation. The result so far has been coming out as a very different poetry from anything I've done before." A few days after writing this entry I went to special collections in Brown's Hay Library and had all of Howe's published books called up from the depths of that cavernous building. I sat in the stodgy reading room diligently studying, cover to cover, the whole of this living poet's work. In truth I only comprehended half of what I read. But Howe's artfulness kept me fully engaged. I was addicted to the thought provoked by her work, and I read her enigmatic small-press pages with a certain desperation, for I was as impatient to grow artistically as I was certain I would have but one chance to prove myself a poet.

That fall Howe's books became my guides to the poetic art. From them I learned the value of words in isolation and, by extension, isolation itself. Looking back it seems clear that her comfort with literary culture, as well as with the New England landscape that permeates the geography of her poems, also taught me a language with which to navigate my California self through the foreignness of the East Coast Ivy League.

Evenings I began to steal typewriter time. I would sit with a sense of inquiry and purpose, totally alone in thought, as if suddenly I was no longer trying to pull something out of me but rather, with a redirected intellect, to *find* something "out there" in this new company of words that Howe's work had led me to. I began to write like a reader, searching for answers to impossible questions. Curiously, this shift in motivation effectively erased the "problem" of audience. Since I was no longer writing to anyone, it didn't matter whether anyone was there.

In my new poems I imitated Howe's formal device of building the framework of an occluded narrative around isolated clusters of words. Inspired by her engagement with the past, I took my vocabulary and questions from the histories I was reading: *To the Finland Station*, *The Waning of the Middle Ages*, *The Second Sex*, and so on. Despite her formidable influence, my poems remained mine in what they could and could not see. In truth, outside of "history" as a broad category, I shared no obsessions with my invisible teacher. I didn't particularly care for Dickinson, barely knew Melville, and felt what might be described as hostile toward the work of Charles Olson. But the fact that my interests rarely mirrored hers was of little or no importance: from her dedication to her obsessions, I learned to value my own, and that *my interest alone* was justification enough.

After an e-mail conversation about my influences, Canadian poet Pete Smith wrote in a review of my 1998 chapbook *Wrong Life* that Susan Howe was an early mentor to me. This is not true, or at least not in the strict sense of the word "mentor," for I never studied with Howe. However, by the end of that lonely fall—the isolation of which, in retrospect, strikes me as enviable—I did muster the courage to write her. It was my first-ever attempt to contact an older poet. I confessed my love for *Pythagorean Silence* and asked her advice as to what I might read. She replied three weeks later.

How well I remember the excitement I felt upon seeing that envelope on the step! Steve had a friend over, and I, loath to share my secret joy, hid the missive until I could read it in private.

Generously claiming that my letter had bolstered her "strength to go on," Howe confessed a profound feeling of isolation, not unlike the one I had sensed within her poems. She was kind and forthright, suggesting several books she thought I might like: H. D.'s *Tribute to Freud*, Jackson Bate's biography of Keats, Duncan, Nietzsche, Virginia Woolf—some of which were new to me, others quite familiar. But considering I was a young writer trying to make the difficult transition from dilettantism to serious commitment, the most important thing she wrote was the following: "I know what loneliness can do and how moving can be a terrible disruption . . . so all there is to say from me is just go and get some writing about writing by writers you admire. Make word lists—do anything but don't stop." Don't stop. Crucial words to send a young poet who fears that whether or not she stops or chooses to keep on writing makes, as far as the world is concerned, precious little difference.

CODA

I was not mentored by Susan Howe, but I *was* mentored by her writing, and through this "invisible company" I learned a great deal. I suppose I could have had a similar "library apprenticeship" with any number of dead women writers, but I have no doubt the fact that Howe was living and trying to make sense of being a woman poet at the same time that I was greatly increased the meaningfulness of her advice. I replied to her letter, perhaps too quickly or with too much enthusiasm. I never heard from her again. The thrill of engaging an older poet as countless male writers had done was followed by disappointment and self-doubt when the correspondence did not "take." I was hurt at the time, but thinking about it now, I'm thankful that Howe refused my overture. The message I gleaned from her reticence has been crucial to sustaining my artistic life: to survive you must insist on your own vision in defiance of both the style *and* the silence of others. An important lesson for any writer, but particularly for a woman.

Jennifer Moxley ✳

localized

deployment, a novel place

torsospeakers lay flat, a
traverse ignored, detected in

her book,

(her book) credit (debt)

planted on the screen
the ennui of obligation

as birth, you go your

signage, I'll hunch

enter slowly the master narrative

hoary spread

reconnaissance (home)

the minor, grafitti

in

Atlantis

—Fall 1989

admitting
space,
in that "humanity" takes liberties
the crowded annals place
the faded statute
in males, to not agree
goes in holes, the defeat by books
to disagree in space is a bold white move
a race implied endless, sightless female, my photographic history
there is memory of what isn't and not silence,
we're never quiet only graspless,
only inconvenient, wileyness wills, grab hold or be kept
violated.
I know and therefore am ceaseless not imaginary,
ready for demanding
the annotated vanishing

—Fall 1989

Mother Night

Right before the darkness turned around
and began to head in the other direction
I had a dream that you and I were decorating
the Christmas tree and I asked you,
as we hung the aging trinkets—the crippled
pine-cone elf, the dry construction-paper Santa,
the several odd souvenirs from cultures
both Christian and un-Christian,
bought by my well-meaning parents
in homage to that naive dream
formerly known as the "family of man"—
"How much goodwill would it take
on this cold mid-winter's eve,

to renew the genuine warmth
we used to feel towards one another?
How many prayers of peace,
or mummer's carols, how many joyous songs,
with saturnine themes and themes solemn too,
how many earnest petitions?"
After untangling the string of mini-lights
with uncustomary ease, we passed
the neat lasso of green wire around
the sticky sap and slightly prickly needles.
With a confidence not unbecoming,
you looked me in the eyes and said:
"For you I guarantee that, by the end
of the season, sympathy and tender care
shall outreach judgment and critique.
Two late-century soldiers will meet
in the desert, lay down their arms and embrace,
Martin Luther, out walking at midnight
will be awestruck by the elegant stars
peeking luminous through the German trees,
holly & ivy will grow up through the snow—
the burning bush, the drops of blood—
and Father Christmas, astride a goat,
Kristkinder, christ child, abolitionist,
a jovial elf, slender pipe in hand,
will rouse the Union soldiers to their
grim task again, and then, in homage
to these, and other half-reasoned-out rituals,
you and I shall go hand in hand,
and hang a sprig of sage-colored mistletoe
on the arc of the new bassinet."
    Delirious I awoke from these words,
got out of bed, and tip-toed to the living room
to sneak a peek at the tree. There was thin silence
and the smell of pine. In the uncanny snowlight
the enchantment of the expectant scene
was no less powerful than when, as a child,

I had been entranced by the magical appearance
of the festive packages under the tree.
"Time of the wheel." *Yuletide,*
the old solar tricks and the hopes
of what the New Year might hold in store:
dreams fulfilled and heavenly peace or,
it struck me, as a *tractor-trailer* passed
and shook the darkened house, perhaps
we're on the eve of some fortune
less propitious. On this cheerless
point of suspicion, the folk personages
on the Christmas tree, with their frozen smiles
and arthritic postures, seemed, as they bobbed
their heads up and down, to agree with me.

—*Winter 2002*

Susan Howe ✳

from "Pythagorean Silence"

5.

I thought I did not live in night

for the future   I used to say
lighting the light

farewell to star   and star
As if light spreading

from some sounding center   might
measure even how

familiar
in the forest   losing the trees

Shadows   only shadows
met my gaze   Mediator

I lay down and conceived   Love
(my dear Imaginary)   Maze-believer

I remember   you were called
sure-footed

and yet off the path   (Where
are you) warmed and warming   Body

turned and turning   Soul
identical soul   abandoned

to Sleep   (where
are you crying)

crying for a mother's help   (fell

forests or plant forests)   Dreams
wheel their pale course

We write in sand
three thousand proverbs and songs

bottom is there   but depth
conceals it   Dreams wander

through the body of a parent
Rub hands together   stressing how

we are made of earth   inevitable
our death   Wisdom

a sorry thing   dream in a Dream
remembering a dream

mimic presentation stained with mortality

Aimee Nezhukumatathil
on Naomi Shihab Nye

TEN YEARS AGO I was studying for a midterm in my major, chemistry, at Ohio State University, and some nincompoop down the hall was cooking macaroni. Burning it, actually. Macaroni and cheese is one of my favorite comfort foods, although at the time I had never cooked it myself. My Filipina mother favored healthier meals of sweet chicken adobo or fish with rice and vegetables. It was always rice and vegetables, no matter how many times I pleaded for mac 'n' cheese, a corn dog—anything that was fast and filling, like the food the other girls from the tennis team had at their homes.

The dorm study lounge had an old crusty stove. Looking up to see if anyone was going to claim the charred food, I noticed a green handout on the study table next to me. The smell of burnt cheese made it impossible for me to concentrate, and my contact lenses had dried out from reading and rereading questions like *What is the molarity of 5.30 g of Na$_2$CO$_3$ dissolved in 400.0 mL solution?* I got up and took a look at the paper, probably left or forgotten by the quiet, cute English major who always played his guitar on the steps of our dorm and who had been studying next to me just a few moments before. It was a poem. A poem about mint. And green ice. And grandfathers. I read "Mint Snowball" by Naomi Shihab Nye and suddenly found that the molarity of sugar solutions didn't seem so pressing—chemistry midterm in six and a half hours be damned.

The way my high school teachers taught female poets like Plath and Dickinson made it seem like you had to be pretty miserable to be a poet. But here was a woman's voice so filled with joy, so filled with exuberance in savoring each minty bite of this frozen dessert that I had never tasted but now felt like I had. Sylvia and Emily are among the group of poets I turn to again and again now, but I simply was in more of a *Naomi* state of mind those early college years. My new friends had me howling with laughter every day in the dorm cafeterias—all our overflowing bowls of Lucky Charms for dinner, jumping inside the elevator to try and catch that moment when we would be levitated midlift, giggling about the burly football players in our enormous lectures, doing the wave with over a hundred thousand screaming fans in Ohio Stadium. Every day was filled with my own tiny moments of wonderment and surprise, and yet for the first time in my life, I was sick with longing for the company of my younger sister, my parents.

Boil water. Add macaroni. Cook till tender, drain. Add milk, butter, cheese. When other students were experimenting with drinking or drugs in college, I experimented with forbidden foods. At the local pharmacy/mini-mart around the corner, I bought my first blue-and-yellow box. I made my own macaroni for the first time in the dorm, away from my mother's ever-watchful eyes. Soon, there were Macaroni Mondays, Exam Week Macaroni, and The Big Game Macaroni. It's only thanks to the small body frames of my parents ("the thin mint gene," my roommate used to say) that I escaped the Freshman Fifteen. I couldn't and still can't get enough of it. Perhaps this is why mac 'n' cheese sends me back into a reverie, recalling the idyllic autumns of my college years, that sizzle I felt when I first read a poem by Nye.

It's worth noting that the poem that triggered my march to the campus library the next day to find more of her work led me to *Mint Snowball* (2001), a slim volume not of poems but of what Naomi herself called "simple paragraphs rather than *prose poems*, though a few might sneak into the prose poem category were they traveling on their own. The paragraph, standing by itself, has a lovely pocket-sized quality. It garnished the page, as mint garnishes a plate. Many people say (foolishly, of course), they *don't like poetry*, but I've never heard anyone say they don't like paragraphs. It would be like disliking five-minute increments on the clock." This little paragraph was a form that rang true for me. Into it Naomi slipped nostalgia, longing, loss. She created, in "Mint Snowball," a shimmering outcrop of images: "glistening, dangling spokes of ice," "little chips of ice on the tongue, their cool slide down." But the lines that stood out to me were the ones about the speaker imagining her mother as a young girl: "the spin of [her] on the high stool and her whole life in front of her, something fine and fragrant still to happen."

This was the first time I had ever read a poet speak lovingly of a parental figure. No angst, no anger for past wrongdoings—and it was this tone, this tenderness I felt I could embrace, not only in poems but also in letters to my parents to share my latest discoveries: *Bill Clinton is coming to campus! Gyro sandwiches for sale on the corner at midnight!* Here, finally, was a way to write about feeling displaced on the largest campus in North America, about having moved six times growing up, about not wanting to study medicine like my mother, about not knowing what I wanted to do anymore, only that I could no longer write drawn-out lab reports on blue graph paper. I would never calculate the rate of sugar dissolving in a heated flask. I would never again click a striker to light a Bunsen burner and never worry about setting my eyebrows on fire like the guy two rows over from me in lab. The only thing I knew for sure was that I had to write.

For years in my predominantly white, upper-middle-class high school, in Beavercreek, Ohio, any semblance of celebrating or even *acknowledging* my background was, well—it was just never discussed. I never wanted to be seen as an Other, yet I felt I had so much to say, so much recording I needed to do. Writing about my various definitions of the word *home*, my family, the wild and wonderful foods and landscapes I grew up with—this was a way, I know now, of telling my folks that I'm not embarrassed after all about their accents, my strict upbringing, having to bring weird food like shrimp curry to class potlucks, having hulva instead of cake at birthday parties, about the constant reminders to "be a lady, be a lady." It was as if writing about feeling displaced all my life was a way to feel, finally, placed.

What draws me now to a Nye poem is the element of surprise in each line and her sheer love for her poems' characters. Even when she writes about a heartbreaking abuse situation ("What Has Been Done to Women"), the speaker's compassion and the pathos of the situation are apparent right from the opening lines:

> Yesterday you cried in the car when you said soldiers in that war asked if women were fair game and the leaders said, "Yes, fair game, do anything you want to them." My own throat filled up when you said the woman you are loving now asks you please say more nice things to her.

But instead of lingering on this situation, she whirls us away later in the same paragraph to the small joy and wonderment of passing a rest stop that has trees planted from all of the fifty states. This delightfully odd swirl of compassion and appreciation of the world around her, often blending the ugly with the beautiful, is what still hooks me, makes me want to dog-ear hundreds of Nye's poems to return to and savor. Her poems are comfort food for me, a place and space where I feel both independent and at home, reassured by the company of a writer's voice that clicks and laughs in syncopation with my own. In Nye's books, my hunger for family, my hunger for wanting to share overlooked quiet moments—here in the folded pages of her collections, I am sated.

I still love cereal (this year's favorite is Special K with strawberries), and that's what I was eating when I got the call: *Hello, Aimee? This is Naomi!* I almost choked. I had become an assistant professor at SUNY Fredonia and was allowed to invite one poet a year to campus. There was no question who it would be. But how to explain what that call meant to me? Naomi's voice was exuberant, as I had expected, but deeper, milkier, nuttier, like a coconut. And she spoke quickly. We made airport and hotel arrangements in five minutes. On the hour's ride from the airport to Fredonia, Naomi found out I was a guest lecturer in my colleague's multicultural literature class and would be discussing her book *Words Under the Words*. She insisted on attending, to listen in. That wasn't in her contract. I had envisioned dropping her off at our local bakeshop to write or read. Try the Fredonia Fries! The Chocolate Death Muffins! Do anything but watch me teach *you*!

Naomi wouldn't have it any other way. We walked into the classroom and I could see the startled faces of the students, most of whom only vaguely knew me as "Professor Nez" around campus. They reached frantically for their Nye books and flipped them over to check the author photo. Could it be? Was that *her*? Their professor didn't tell them they'd have the visiting poet *herself* come to class! The students sat straighter, pushed back their ball caps and bangs. When Naomi took a seat to my right, I turned away from the class to the chalkboard to write some notes and to say a silent prayer, *Please don't make me sound like a Valley Girl. Please don't make me screw this up.*

Then I began talking about the very poems I had loved since I was in college. Every so often Naomi would chime in, "Beautiful! I never thought of that! So good you pointed that out!" She slapped her desk with the palm of her hand in ecstatic agreement when a student answered a question. I sighed with relief: so many times I've said to students, *When we read a poem by ourselves, we don't have the benefit of the poet sitting there, able to chime in with footnotes about each image. The poem better be able to stand on its own.* Now we had the poet in the very same room with us. She was asking us what we thought—and agreeing with us! She teased even the shy ones to speak with her head-nodding, her smiles. She poked fun at the talkative ones. The class was rapt, clutching her book and scribbling marginalia. And that day, this professor became a student, wanting to take notes in a marbled composition book all over again.

That night, a night of freezing rain, Naomi drew a crowd of over three hundred at her reading. Only after a full day of sitting in on my lecture, guest-teaching a graduate poetry workshop, and signing each and every person's book (which took over forty-five minutes) did she declare she was tired. "Little sister, let's skip the bar. Let's go for some ice cream!" From the blog on my Web site:

> How much light and empathy and beauty she brought into this town. Afterward, we had ice cream in Dunkirk's local *Big Dipper* parlor at about 10pm, even though it was below freezing. The high school girls who worked there kept asking each of us if we wanted to purchase a ticket for a bike raffle. We couldn't bear to tell them we'd been asked several times already. One girl would come out of the back storeroom and ask us, then go back inside when we told her

we'd pass. Another girl came out from the back entrance and asked us about tickets and disappeared when we also told her no. Still another girl from behind the counter asked us a third time, and still, even after such a long day and almost an hour of signing books—Naomi was so patient and cheerful, laughing, *I'm sorry. I can't ride it all the way to Texas if I win.*

She visited Fredonia just as our country had begun its war on Iraq in the spring of 2003. I knew many students might take offense at her writing, even students who had been in classes wherein I shared poems of hers that humanized Iraqis ("Ducks") and talked about how one can still love this country and support troops but not support a given *reason* for war. But, like the speaker of her poems, Naomi's compassion, grace, and ability to connect with people from all walks of life shone through, especially when she read a new essay she wrote on the country's joy at finding Elizabeth Smart, the young girl abducted from her home in Utah in late 2002, and connected the kidnapping to the fact that children in Afghanistan and Iraq would still be missing at year's end. The crowd was silent; some were trying to hide tears. But a few poems later she had them laughing again.

Aimee Nezhukumatathil ✳

One Bite

Miracle fruit changes the tongue. One bite,
and for hours all you eat is sweet. Placed
alone on a saucer, it quivers like it's cold
from the ceramic, even in this Florida heat.

Small as a coffee bean, red as jam—
I can't believe. The man who sold
it to my father on Interstate 542 had one
tooth, one sandal, and called me

"Duttah, Duttah." I wanted to ask what
is that, but the red buds teased me
into our car and away from his fruit stand.
One bite. And if you eat it whole, it softens

and swells your teeth like a mouthful
of mallow. So how long before you lose
a sandal and still walk? How long
before you lose the sweetness?

The Woman Who Turned Down a Date with a Cherry Farmer

Fredonia, NY

Of course I regret it. I mean there I was under umbrellas of fruit
so red they had to be borne of Summer, and no other season.
Flip-flops and fishhooks. Ice cubes made of lemonade and sprigs
of mint to slip in blue glasses of tea. I was dusty, my ponytail
all askew and the tips of my fingers ran, of course, red

from the fruitwounds of cherries I plunked into my bucket
and still—he must have seen some small bit of loveliness
in walking his orchard with me. He pointed out which trees
were sweetest, which ones bore double seeds—puffing out
the flesh and oh the surprise on your tongue with two tiny stones

(a twin spit), making a small gun of your mouth. Did I mention
my favorite color is red? His jeans were worn and twisty
around the tops of his boot; his hands thick but careful,
nimble enough to pull fruit from his trees without tearing
the thin skin; the cherry dust and fingerprints on his eyeglasses.

I just know when he stuffed his hands in his pockets, said
Okay. Couldn't hurt to try? and shuffled back to his roadside stand
to arrange his jelly jars and stacks of buckets, I had made
a terrible mistake. I just know my summer would've been
full of pies, tartlets, turnovers—so much jubilee.

Crow Joy

Almost all of the gold leaf on the Kremlin domes was scratched off years
ago from the fleet of crows converging at the top. Contrary to popular
belief, they were not stealing the shiny flakes for their nests, as they
would a lovely kerchief pinned too loose on a clothesline, or withered
breadfruit left too long in sun. A closer look revealed their game of
sliding down those onion domes, their claws scraping the roofskin raw.
In sunlight, crow wings flash a wild blue, as blue as the nose of a jolly
mandrill. Half a world away, a family of these monkeys dips their fingers
into a stream for the first time—their black fingernails dulled square for
scratching stems to drink, their noses wet, warm. A shopkeeper near the
Lobnoye Mesto, The Place of Skulls, once recorded distressed crow calls to
scare the birds from their play. But the top was too high or the tape too
quiet—the birds' feet already too gilded to ever want to step foot on this
earth again.

Naomi Shihab Nye ✳

Mint Snowball

My great-grandfather on my mother's side ran a drugstore in a small town in central Illinois. He sold pills and rubbing alcohol from behind the big cash register and creamy ice cream from the soda fountain. My mother remembers the counter's long polished sweep, its shining face. She twirled on the stools. Dreamy fans. Wide summer afternoons. Clink of nickels in anybody's hand. He sold milkshakes, cherry cokes, old-fashioned sandwiches. What did an old-fashioned sandwich look like? Dark wooden shelves. Silver spigots on chocolate dispensers.

My great-grandfather had one specialty: a Mint Snowball which he invented. Some people drove all the way in from Decatur just to taste it. First he stirred fresh mint leaves with sugar and secret ingredients in a small pot on the stove for a very long time. He concocted a flamboyant elixir of mint. Its scent clung to his fingers even after he washed his hands. Then he shaved ice into tiny particles and served it mounded in a glass dish. Permeated with mint syrup. Scoops of rich vanilla ice cream to each side. My mother took a bite of minty ice and ice cream mixed together. The Mint Snowball tasted like winter. She closed her eyes to see the Swiss village my great-grandfather's parents came from. Snow frosting the roofs. Glistening, dangling spokes of ice.

Before my great-grandfather died, he sold the recipe for the mint syrup to someone in town for $100. This hurt my grandfather's feelings. My grandfather thought he should have inherited it to carry on the tradition. As far as the family knew, the person who bought the recipe never used it. At least not in public. My mother had watched her grandfather make the syrup so often she thought she could replicate it. But what did he have in those little unmarked bottles? She experimented. Once she came close. She wrote down what she did. Now she has lost the paper.

Perhaps the clue to my entire personality connects to the lost Mint Snowball. I have always felt out-of-step with my environment, disjointed in the modern world. The crisp flush of cities makes me weep. Strip centers, poodle grooming and take-out Thai. I am angry over lost department stores, wistful for something I have never tasted or seen.

Although I know how to do everything one needs to know—change airplanes, find my exit off the interstate, charge gas, send a fax—there is something missing. Perhaps the stoop of my great-grandfather over the pan, the slow patient swish of his spoon. The spin of my mother on the high stool with her whole life in front of her, something fine and fragrant still to happen. When I breathe a handful of mint, even pathetic sprigs from my sunbaked Texas earth, I close my eyes. Little chips of ice on the tongue, their cool slide down. Can we follow the long river of the word "refreshment" back to its spring? Is there another land for me? Can I find any lasting solace in the color green?

Mendi Lewis Obadike
on Toi Derricotte

WHEN I MET Toi Derricotte in 2000, I had already seen her give a public reading. I didn't get to know her, however, until I went to Cave Canem, the workshop for black poets that she and Cornelius Eady cofounded. At the time, I'd been writing for several years, had published some poems, and had been workshopping with local groups in North Carolina—including Four Bean Stew and Carolina African American Writers' Collective. I had also been creating conceptual works in Internet art, audio art, and performance with my husband Keith Obadike. The way our local scene was invigorated by those who had been to Cave Canem (Evie Shockley and Lenard Moore) drew me to the workshop.

My experience at Cave Canem was supportive and challenging. Each day we workshopped with a different faculty poet; each night we went to readings before writing our poems for the next day. My very first workshop was with Toi Derricotte. Lucille Clifton—with whom I had already had the privilege of studying—happened to be sitting in. Before discussing poems,

Clifton and Derricotte interviewed each of us about our voices; then we talked about what it was to be a poet, to claim a poetic voice.

Derricotte came to the table that day with a handful of white clovers. She told us a story about the jokes people in her family had made about her inability to sing as a child. Thinking about the ways in which she'd learned how not to be heard, Derricotte announced that she had started singing. This singing seemed to be an act of defiance, but she said it was mostly a reminder she had given herself to honor her own voice even when others did not. She gave us each a flower and asked us to keep it by our desks as we wrote to remind us to cherish our voices.

Later that week at the faculty reading, instead of reading her poems, she sang them. It seemed to be an improvisation, and Derricotte's voice was haunting; these were not poems that seemed to lend themselves to song. They did not rhyme and they were not light in subject matter. They were narrative poems, and the speakers were vulnerable: they were children, victims of abuse, or both.

I was already familiar with most of the poems but had not experienced them with the intensity that Derricotte's singing/reading style gave. When was the last time a poetry reading had ever made me feel out of control in this way? On the page, I'd been able to meditate on Derricotte's ideas and her craft. When spoken aloud, the poems had drawn me to empathize with the speaker. But sung, the poems evoked two entirely unexpected responses. First, Derricotte's beautiful, haunting singing voice represented for me the innocence and despair of the speakers in the poems. Secondly, because Derricotte had made us aware that singing was a way of cherishing her own voice, I saw the act of *singing* the story as a triumphant one. The singing voice was a voice of despair and of victory at the same time.

Because of these experiences, Toi Derricotte came immediately to mind when I was asked to consider what it has meant to become and develop as a poet with feminist poet role models. She is significant in my process because of the way the unspeakable and the invisible function in her work.

As a conceptual artist, I don't always think of the results of my writing as *poetry*. They sometimes become something else: net.art, sound art, conceptual art. In net.art, for example, I often use hypertext to highlight parts of a narrative that, when isolated, tell a story quite different from the story from which they are lifted. For example, in my work "Keeping Up Appearances," readers first see what appears to be a poem:

i used to work for this fellow.

he was a pretty nice guy.   i knew him from the
church.

he was from a powerful family.

so anyway,
                                        he showed me the ropes
at work. he was a mentor to me.

At first glance, this text seems to be a banal story about getting a job
and having a cordial co-worker. If readers move their cursors over the
white space, however, a racially charged story of sexual harassment
emerges that, even from the beginning, reads a bit differently:

i used to work for this fellow. under him. with him, you know.

he was a pretty nice guy. he was white, but i knew him from the
church. this won't make sense if you're thinking of my church
home. there were no white people where i worshipped. we worked
together at the board of the worldwide church. (the only place
where we integrate.)

he was from a powerful family. he was also married to this sister.
we were supposed to think he was therefore on our side or, you
know, at least interesting.

so anyway, (it's best not to dwell on white people's miscalculations
in public, even in invisible parentheticals) he showed me the ropes
at work. he was a mentor to me. the only thing was, showing me
the ropes often meant we had to be off somewhere alone together.

the strangest things would happen in these moments, the first of which was when he reached inside my blouse to adjust my bra strap.[1]

My point with this kind of work is not just to lead the reader to read between the lines; I also want to tell a story and simultaneously represent my resistance to telling the story. This form also makes clear how a reader could miss the story without realizing it if she doesn't go to where the story lives.

Consider where the story lives in Derricotte's poem "Grace Paley Reading." This poem describes a poetry reading at which Grace Paley is the featured speaker. When it is time for the reading to start, Paley is missing and no one knows where she is. Derricotte, sent to look for her, finds Paley backing out of the bathroom, wiping up her own footprints. Paley explains that the bathroom had been clean when she entered and she wanted to leave it clean in case someone came to check on the cleaning lady.

When I first read this poem, I thought about Paley's consideration for the person who cleans the bathroom—a person who is not present but whose proof of existence Paley finds in the absence of mess. After months of rereading this poem, I have also begun to think about what is happening on the literal level: a woman poet is erasing her footsteps instead of taking her place at the microphone. I love this poem because it gets at something often overlooked. It helped shift my focus in my latest work; rather than working from sadness over how things I care about go unnoticed, I'm working from the empowering aspects of witnessing and documenting the erasure.

The story I tell in "Keeping Up Appearances" is connected to Derricotte's practice on a number of levels. Both works document silences. My narrative tells the story of a woman's willing refusal to talk about an event, and it tells the story while refusing to reveal the parts of the narrative that make the event. Derricotte's narrative tells the story of a woman's willing refusal to take the microphone while refusing to leave evidence of her presence elsewhere. But because her poem also includes the element of witnessing, I have learned from Derricotte not only *that* we can be silent and invisible but also how to recognize and give voice to that silence and invisibility and how to change our relationships to those moments. Anyone familiar with her books—from *The Empress of the Death House* to *Tender* and

The Black Notebooks—will know that she has a fierce commitment to exposing the painful truths. In her workshop spaces, too, the tenacity with which she forces herself to confront the silences in her own work is evident and infectious. I have watched her wrestle with the ways issues of racism, classism, and sexism operate on a personal level.

What I cherish most about Toi Derricotte's presence in poetry is her ability to face the difficult with patience and grace. Even when she doesn't know if her audiences will be ready to deal with the truths she exposes, she tells them. In so doing, she teaches us how to *get* ready for each other's truths and for our own. Though many of us respond to Derricotte's charge to confront silences and fears in our work by composing autobiographical works, those who have been in her presence also respond in other ways. Sometimes the responses to her work have to do with having the courage to try to tell new stories or to tell them in new forms. In other moments the responses to her work are uncharted because she pushes us, as she pushes herself, to be challenged and changed on the inside.

NOTE

1. "Keeping Up Appearances," a hypertextimonial, is viewable online at http://blacknetart.com/keepingupappearances.html. At first glance, the viewer can only see the text that appears in black. As one moves the cursor over the white space, the text underneath the space appears. The text shown here in gray appears in pink on the screen, but only when the cursor is over it.

Mendi Lewis Obadike ✳

A Free Thing

on Toi Derricotte, doing

Floating things are said to haunt
on account of ghosts aren't bound by gravity.

They don't respect what humans build. Anything
that wafts or comes through walls reminds us.

This woman speaks and her voice hovers,
a free thing, over us.

Tender, but frightening. Airy, but exacting. It says,
I'm small, but fills up space.

It says, I'm afraid, and breaks through skin. You don't
want this, it says, then does what it came to do.

Get accustomed to this terror. See if you survive
the sweet song that follows.

Even the Magnolia

Even the magnolia, trapped
in the jaws of frost, catches
snowflakes on his tongue.
Whether numbed or bitten,
he knows the sting of winter
unlocks a green door. Even
the magnolia, like a once-lost
foreigner, trusts the seasons

of his second home, fears
daybreak in his first.

Keeping Up Appearances

i used to work for this fellow. under him. with him, you know.

he was a pretty nice guy. he was white, but i knew him from the church.
this won't make sense if you're thinking of my church home. there were
no white people where i worshipped. we worked together at the board of
the worldwide church. (the only place where we integrate.)

he was from a powerful family. he was also married to this sister. we
were supposed to think he was therefore on our side or, you know, at
least interesting.

so anyway, (it's best not to dwell on white people's miscalculations in
public, even in invisible parentheticals) he showed me the ropes at
work. he was a mentor to me. the only thing was, showing me the ropes
often meant we had to be off somewhere alone together. the strangest
things would happen in these moments, the first of which was when he
reached inside my blouse to adjust my bra strap. he walked away, leaving
me standing in the middle of the office floor, thinking about the two
separate occasions in which a male had, without invitation, reached for
my bra. the first time, the other kid and i were both around twelve years
old. it was a little strange, but i was okay with it. he was a friend. this
time, it felt creepy. on the one hand, there was the age difference. this
guy was at least twenty years older than me. on the other hand, he was a
peer.

i was, after all, eighteen. an adult now. maybe it's just like that when
you're an adult.

but then he turned around and came towards me: "oh, don't think
anything of that," he said. "i have a wife and kid, i would never . . ." i

don't remember whether he let it trail off like that or i just stopped listening.

i never said anything to him about this. but of course i thought something of it. standing there, head pounding. there was the attempt to pull my thoughts together. looking at the faces of people now walking by or moving around in nearby rooms. busy in their cubicles. busy in the copy room. there was the desire to keep this from happening again, but bigger than that was the desire for this to be nothing.

this is a series of things i told myself i had forgotten: there was the chance he really meant nothing by it, wasn't there? and if i just made sure my bra strap didn't show again, there would be nothing to question, right? i could tell him about my discomfort and he could get better (and keep explaining how he meant nothing by it) or get worse. or i could act like it was nothing and things could get better (because nothing had happened) or get worse. worst case scenario: i could say stop and he could show himself to be as evil as i feared him to be. best case scenario: i could say nothing and nothing (else) would happen. i was an optimist.

in front of the closet the next morning, there was the hunt for something sufficiently unremarkable. a shirt that covered, fully, the shoulders and neck, but not a form-fitting shirt. a blouse. a bra with tight straps that didn't move.

i don't have to tell you that things got worse. you already know, don't you? i don't have to say anything, most likely, anything at all about those jokes or the other times he took liberties with a strap or hem. (how it was. the way muscles in the backs of other white men would tighten, as he did these things only in their presence. how their lips pursed, the wheeze of air escaping through their nostrils. the desire to accept friendship. the desire to see acts of aggression as something else. the theories that develop. if you don't acknowledge the bad feeling, it means the thing isn't what it feels like. the thing. all this had to be worked out in silence, in the head. words, you see, betray themselves.) but maybe you don't know how things can look better as they are getting worse.

he praised my work to my real boss all the time. i wanted things to be right and so, between wrong touches and wrong words, i held my breath. simultaneously added up every undesirable act and erased it from my short term memory. optimism has a way of dimming when you look some people directly in the eye. the longer things went on like this, the more important it became to keep up appearances. if you were to look in on us, at a meeting or in his office, you would often see us laughing together. somehow, i kept thinking, i'm going to get out of here before i feel forced to confront him. if this is happening because he wants to hurt me, i don't want to know. he became smarmy. i became small. something i still wonder: how small could i have gotten before i felt forced to confront him?

he praised me and praised me. i didn't drink, smoke, eat meat, or take caffeine. i didn't seem to have, he kept saying, any vices. he held me up against his step-daughter, who was unwed and a new mother, my age. her baby was much lighter than she was. when she came to visit the office, he insulted her the entire time. after each insult, she would smile a resigned smile, shrug, and look to me . . .

Toi Derricotte ✳

Grace Paley Reading

Finally, the audience gets
restless, & they send me
to hunt for Grace. I find her
backing out of the bathroom, bending
over, wiping up her footprints
as she goes with a little
sheet of toilet paper, explaining,
"In some places, after the lady mops,
the bosses come to check on her.
I just don't want them to think
she didn't do her job."

Danielle Pafunda
on Susan Wheeler

Wherein I count my blessings and pronouns

IF I WERE to pretend for a moment that parity is as relevant to fair distri-
bution of rights and resources as most talking heads profess, and that liberal policy feminism could uproot centuries of cultural inscription, then I
might run the numbers. I might note that in my academic career, I have
been instructed by an equal number of men and women.[1] Were I to break
it down more specifically, I might note that the women were younger over-
all than the men, and that while a sizeable portion of the men were gay, very
few of the women were. I might note how few of either came from a
working-class background or how many of both were white, and I would
likely discover the ratio of men to women in academia is not actually so
well balanced. And when I examined my writing workshops in isolation, I
would notice a glaring disparity. Eight men, three women.

Does a woman poet need a woman teacher? An author's gender obviously informs his or her writing and may manifest itself in any number of

ways (content, form, diction, etc.). But does the gender identification of the author *predetermine* any element of his or her work? I consistently warn my creative writing students not to assume the speaker of a poem is performing gender in the same way as the author, even as speaker and author so often do occupy the same point on the gender spectrum. Judith Butler and company tell us that the expression of gender is always a performance. So why do readers resist an unexpected performance? Is it the influence of the New Sincerity? Or are we so thoroughly inscribed by gender, we can't get a bead on it? Thus, I must interrogate my own assumptions and allegiances.

I would not begin to discount the men who have taught my workshops, advised me, and, in at least one case, mentored me. They all took my ambitions seriously. Which is not to say my experience was always ideal. A high school English teacher applauded my work for its "sex appeal" (share with me a retrospective shudder), and one college professor insisted an anorexic persona was too angry a voice. Others encouraged me to further detail first sexual encounters or praised my objectification of my own small breasts (without noting the irony therein). Such suggestions betrayed expectations of how women should write and what was the most publishable work. Maybe these men were aware of their biases. Still, I felt I was missing out on some crucial instruction. I do not mean to suggest that all (white, middle-class) women poets necessarily experience the role of woman poet in the same way or that we have some natural tendency to bond (though we may have an artificial one).

I did not choose to discuss Susan Wheeler as an apt mentor for me because our chromosomes pronounce female or because we were both offered Sylvia Plath and Anne Sexton at a young age. I gravitate toward a woman mentor for the same reason I chose a woman doctor: the inside scoop, the greater likelihood of affinity. Science, art, men on the street, and magazine covers critique my doctor's body as they do mine. As an adolescent, my doctor was misinformed, as I was, about the intricacies of reproduction and the links between libido and biology. My doctor had been told, as I was, that birth control pills have no side effects and that her autoimmune disorder was a hysterical hallucination. When she became a doctor, she had to demonstrate a competency and intelligence at least equal to those of her male colleagues every day. I go to her because she understands what I am up against on both a physical and a psychic level.

Does a woman poet need a woman reader? Every scholar/writer is trained to recognize the various manifestations of the *masculine subject* written by men—Don Juan, Christ-like, cuckold, Raskolnikov—and of the *feminine subject* written by men (although we may more often call these *object*): consumptive courtesan, Medea, Ophelia, adulteress. Until recently literature professors have doubted the necessity or possibility of teaching the various manifestations of the *feminine subject as written by women*.[2] Poetry is a relatively small and exceedingly self-conscious field, so despite the fact that women have only recently been critically recognized in it, tactics and types we might call feminine have rapidly emerged. Consider, for instance, Plath's interrogation of the voyeuristic in "Lady Lazarus" or Sexton's dissatisfied "The Farmer's Wife." Consider Gwendolyn Brooks's "The Mother," whose rhetoric evokes in the reader the same conflicting allegiances that we might suppose a woman who chooses to abort her child navigates. These women tell the story from inside out.

Or we might simply list the feminist appropriations of traditional masculine form, for example Notley's epic *Descent of Allette*, wherein Notley picks up where Elizabeth Barrett Browning left off—a hell-bent Aurora Leigh. I am skeptical of the rhetoric about women's literature, of the work by critics like Cixous, who demands that women invent a wholly new kind of writing for themselves, or Wittig, who seeks to abolish gender categories altogether, and I am wary of the ways in which a feminine tradition can become a static field. Yet it would be a mistake to read the feminine subjects above as isolated anomalies. If Dickinson, Stein, Moore, and others are read as anomalies rather than as a source of lineage, their echoes may go unnoticed in the work of women poets today. We can expect that many careful readers will identify a feminine lineage whether or not they are taught to. Unfortunately, the same readers may develop reductive expectations about women's writing, that is, speakers must be jilted wives, trod-upon mothers, or ecofeminists. Further, while most readers accept the terrain of the inhabited male body (at least that terrain most often on display—"my erection," "my calloused hands"), not as many accept the terrain of the inhabited female body ("my uterus," "my clitoris"). Ideas of the vagina dentata and the hysterical womb, which we might like to think of as anachronistic, are not necessarily so.

Wherein mentee and mentor first meet

In fall 2001, my New School MFA class began workshop with Susan Wheeler (the previous instructors were men—both white; one gay, one hetero—and the students were two-thirds women, for those keeping count). Curious to meet her, we entertained not a few rumors. She was a ball-breaker. She wore leather pants. Was she? Did she? While an undergraduate at Bard College, I had read through every back issue of *Best American Poetry* in our library. I came across Susan's poem "He or She That's Got the Limb That's Got Me Out on It," which influenced my choice of programs more than my application essay might have suggested. The narrative seems familiar—young girls, a boat, an invitation, a flirtation, a threat—but the events do not add up as such. Things twist, and not just at the level of the line. In his afterword to Wheeler's *Smokes* (1998), Robert Hass identifies this poem, the first in the book, as a parody of Frost but also "as a kind of homage." I had found an example of how a woman poet might play with and against convention, how she might laud what she loved in the writing of "great men" and at the same time reconstruct their methods. In my essay, I diplomatically expressed my enthusiasm for Susan's work and left out my more radical aspirations. I was wary of showing my feminist cards before I had established myself as a "serious poet."

It is not that I wished to ingest and reproduce the systems of Susan's poetry. They suggested a phenomenal and foreign-to-me understanding of the elasticity of diction and form, of the folds and rents in the space-time continuum of language. Still, if Susan could make language do *that*, maybe I could get it to communicate the instability I felt as a subject and a body, the lack of coherent narrative in my own life experiences. And I felt this would all be easier if Susan liked me. With men instructors, I could write off their dislike, citing some old-school sexist tendency. If a woman didn't like me, I imagined she had a good reason, a substantial reason. I clearly bought into the popular psychology suggesting women value interpersonal warmth and community building (and while we may bake whole-grain muffins for our neighbors, don cozy sweaters, and participate in the refurbishment of the local community center, we obviously cannot attribute inexhaustible fair-mindedness to all women always). I wanted Susan to see that I was not just another quirky girl poet stinking of old lovers and sporting theatrical hairdos. But a poet cannot up and claim a mentor. The relationship must be somehow reciprocal.

Does a poet need a mentor, anyhow? I picture a radically oversimplified not-so-distant past. A gruffly avuncular older man claps a wiry younger man on the back. The younger man reminds the older of himself as a boy; the younger sees the older in a station to which he would like to ascend. Camaraderie, but not without undercurrents of intimidation and jealousy. A pretty bit of reductive hoo-ha.

Mentor: explains how he/she succeeded in the field and how you might accomplish same. Mentor: praises your work (to others!). Mentor: writes blurb for your first book. Mentor: trusts you to look after his/her mail and plants while he/she teaches in Europe, brings you a rare edition and a bottle of Czech liquor. Mentor: cuffs you on the / squeezes your shoulder and buys you a beer / brings you a cup of chamomile tea.

What if your mentor doesn't bring you tea or explain how she got from Minnesota to *Bag 'o' Diamonds*? What if she does blurb your first book but doesn't leave her houseplants in your care? What if she doesn't invite you for coffee but throws a group brunch and invites you? What if, on your wedding day, she sends you all her four-leaf clovers? What if you wouldn't call her crying about a bad review or a bad breakup, but you would publicly perform a role in a play she had written that required you to appear unwashed and unrefined, and you would do so gladly?

Wherein I question the woman question

I will not pretend to know what goes on between men poets, or, in fact, between poets in general. My empirical data is limited. But there are times I experience myself as the silhouette of a woman writing in a genre that has only very recently made room for the likes of her. Most of my classmates have been women, most of the books on my shelf are by women, I go to lunch with other women poets, and despite all this, at the faculty level we are three-to-eight.[3] Spectacle or not, the picture can appear pretty grim. In 1980, a rough-hewn clay sign hung on my bedroom wall. *Anything boys can do, girls can do better.* I was surprised to find not everyone has such a sign.

I cannot recall discussing with Susan the peculiarities of being a *woman poet* or the burden of the term. Her poems and essays do not gloss over or sidestep gender, but neither do they focus on it. I rarely saw her in skirts, although I am pretty sure she shaves her legs. Her hair is shoulder-length, she wears a minimum of makeup, and I have never seen her flirt. Her husband is a soft-spoken, charming scientist, their relationship appears loving and equitable, and their flatware is gorgeous. In our (mis)reading of that old adage "the personal is political," this is the sort of diurnal information we seek when attempting to determine whether or not another woman is a good feminist, a potential sister. But Susan is not so easy to suss out. She seems to me no more confessional as a person than she does as a poet. Maybe the teacher/student divide has her checking her tongue, or maybe her skeletons are long buried and not hanging alongside her fabled leather pants. Thus, Susan—who has asked me to complete difficult poetic tasks as though it were a given I would, recommended the books that pushed me further, critiqued the poems, not their content, reminded me not to fix what ain't broke, and always seems so sure that the first book, the second book, and so forth, are just a matter of time—fits my hopes for a mentor.

We children of the 1970s prize the sacrifices our mothers made for us and recount the battles they fought for us. But what if one's own mother is not particularly laudable? I once received a C on a college paper wherein in I was meant to narrate my presumably empowering relationship with my mother. When I failed to characterize it as such, my professor told me I had presented my mother incorrectly. I invented a new, better mother and received an A. But of course, I was lying in this representation: my mother is not, was not an ideal role model, and I am not alone among my generation in that. I have heard enough horror stories from women my age to confirm that second-wave mothers were in many ways as conflicted about and critical of their daughters as the mothers against whom they initially rebelled.

The contemporary ideal of mother as bastion, bosom, and breadwinner deserves a thorough critique. In the aftermath of the 2004 presidential campaign, one can safely say that the American nuclear family is undead. While both parents may work and do the dishes, and children of either gender may attend soccer practice, we have hardly halted the zombie of mommy-daddy-sister-brother. None of us is safe from the prescribed-gender-role household or from the continued conflation of paternity/maternity with authority/benevolence. Women are still raised to mother, only now this condition bleeds into the workplace.

Wherein I attempt to locate and leave the ghetto of women's writing

I am loath to sentimentalize or romanticize anyone, particularly a poet whom I so greatly admire. If I describe Susan as compassionate, confident, brilliant, and so on, this is indeed how I view her, but do I not sound like a lovesick schoolgirl? If I say she has been an inspiration to me, a role model, do I tread too near mother-talk? Think: the James Lipton–esque interviewer asks, "who has been your greatest influence?" and the successful career woman answers firmly, "my mother." Echoing the good daughter's praise of her unimpeachable mother leads us directly into the ghetto of women's writing. Here, women sing of those martyred women who have gone before. Here, women edit out the fathers and cast themselves in the image of the mothers, whose flaws have also been edited or justified. And all these mothers look frighteningly alike. The ghetto, while not without its charms, is vast and sticky. Even well-intentioned men (instructors, editors, colleagues, lovers) tuck us back into the ghetto when they praise us for combining fragility and chutzpah, when they select out of a submission batch the poem that most exposes our tits, and when they offer us a visa to the boys' club. But their ghettoization feels inconsequential, nonbinding. Where one man reader finds vulnerability, another finds sarcasm. What one reads as tits, another reads as fish scales. I bank on this. What I fear more is self-ghettoization. In her essay "Confessions of a Postmodern Poetess" in the anthology By Herself: Women Reclaim Poetry (2000), Annie Finch asks, "[W]hat image of poetic endeavor is now most universally despised? . . . The woman with three names who muses piously on love, flowers, and the deaths of mothers and babies? That's clearly it."

I am no enemy of love or flowers, and many of us have lost our mothers, our babies. These things exist and would worm their way into our poems even if we made an effort to keep them out. It is no sin to write about them, but it is a betrayal to normalize them, wear them as a badge of femininity, or speak about them for other women. For those of us who grew up under the rickety aegis of late second-wave feminism, it is not so easy to embrace the agreed-upon terms of modern womanhood. If one's mentor came of age during the second wave, what side of feminism/postmodernism will she land on? For me, Susan exists outside of the ghetto. I call her unapologetic, but this term has me treading water with the bad guys. For what should she apologize?

I am grateful to have had an instructor who enjoys teaching, takes it seriously, encourages students to explore their trajectories, and suffers none of the "kids today . . ." mentality of many a midcareer poet. I am grateful to have had a reader who embraces the incoherence of the "I" and its refusal to perform consistently. In my own classes, I attempt to project similar high-but-reasonable expectations while maintaining an awareness of the innumerable trajectories on which my students could be. While a mentor traditionally watches over the mentee, she may also provide a focal point. Susan's mentorship is that which helps me orient myself in some otherwise unmapped terrain. I can see her in the distance and know I can aim for somewhere close by.

NOTES

1. Throughout, I will employ *men* and *women* rather than *male* or *female* to keep the discussion from staggering into the biological.

2. "Discussing the job candidate's research interests, one of the two male scholars said, with some disbelief, 'You're interested in American women writers? But there aren't any'. . ." ("Preface." *The Aunt Lute Anthology of U.S. Women Writers Volume One*. Hogeland, Lisa Maria and Klages, Mary, Eds. San Francisco: Aunt Lute Books, 2000. xxiii–xxxi.).

3. Based on my own spurious calculations in the second paragraph of this essay.

Danielle Pafunda ✳

Wherein a Surrogate Covers a Debt

I grew fat for this animal, and still
it does not come near. I pasted
to the concrete barriers innumerable
squares of reflective paper.

None were actually square as such.

In my pillow, I hid the forked talon
from the fowl and in my hemlines
I secured the plaster teeth nicked
from the instructional wherein they

grew from the gums, sunk back,

grew again.

For this animal, I rubbed my skin
with oleo and wore a gown of egg white.
The midwife imposed a thermometer
and materialized in the fragment hour.

Where does it sting? she asked me.

And I answered her in my deck.

Wherein the Surrogates Discover the Flight

With grim and matted skirts, I thought of the parrot,
whom they called a *bird*, and from him wrest
their language. He told a joke in two parts:
First, he trilled and told it *telephone for Betty Anne.*
Second, he trilled and *phone for Bird.*

His demand to *locomote.* His desire to go *nigh-night.*
Once you give out grammar, they said. And nursling
was no different. In my claw, I made safe the packet
thick with lanolin. Soon my breast would trill. Soon
my shift aside, my tandem would expire.

In the cupboard they kept a projection, a gray
with orange noosing. It did not meet my expectation.
Where was the brigade of foliage? Where was the clip
from which a bullet shot beneath his wing would stun,
the chitterlings sick with laughter?

Wherein a Surrogate Begins

For some time, they had been using my abdomen as a receptacle
to chronicle the violations. Those which were mine, but also
the others'. I held an encyclopedic pose. And I petitioned
for an official collection. An inventory. I held a rat, amputated
from the paws. A pleated wool skirt, each felting pleat rimmed
with a rigid mold. Etc. I labeled each with a three by five card,
in architect's script, a strip of cellophane tape black at the edges.

I had been napping. They took from the peg the key and digit.
My skin rolled back, my snap. Window, they said.
Slide, they said. And the package was secured to my rib
with a length of cable and a clove hitch.
                                    I held a rat, a skirt, a temple
pressed and indented, a draught of drain opener, a wire that could easily
cut meat and bone, etc.

It was not as they wished when my enzyme sank. My wheeze
in the hall disrupted the others. What pins and brads I could dislodge
I did. When the procedure failed, they sent the midwife, whose manual
was the thickness of thumb, the rule. She noted the condition.

I should clarify. The first.

Susan Wheeler ✳

Fractured Fairy Tale

So activate then. Beforehand the birds
settle in for a roost, and the shiny clock hands
start to rattle. The frog prince bewails
his casaba schnozz. De-activate's more like it.

Several men rest their rakes at their crotches and begin to talk.
They are having an ur-argument. They are arguing over
pure and impure analyticity, or error theory or a nonfactualist
theory about ethics. It might be the Chinese Room Argument.
The light through the elms reminds them of dinner.
The hunger reminds them of loss.

Doze Doll Does Wiz Biz—a century that, her sleeping,
a stenotic century self-circling, noodling its tunes, drug
by the scuff of its kitchen to stand, squinting, at thing
coherent, drooping from clouds, bungeeing to boot.

Kristin Prevallet
on Anne Waldman

I GREW UP in a house that was built in 1958 and is located in southwest Denver. It is a little square brick house sitting in the middle of a block surrounded by other little square brick houses, situated in a vast neighborhood that stretches over one hundred blocks, each block containing a variety of little square brick houses. My mother bought the house in 1968, two years after I was born and a year after she and my father were divorced.

In 1968 there were not many women buying their own properties, and there certainly weren't many women intent on learning how to be handy. Gradually throughout the 1970s my mother set about fixing everything that went wrong in the house, from replacing the plumbing to pruning the trees to laying new shingles. When something was broken she didn't just fix it—she rigged it, finagled it, bent it, soldered it, taped it, stenciled it, rewired it. Professional handymen call this jury-rigging, but to my mother, the experts were called and the instructions were read only when all else failed.

In January 1972, Ms. magazine published its first issue. It was (and remains) a publication focused on the right of women to assert themselves, to perceive their roles as caretakers and housewives as hard work, to rebel against the limitations set by domineering husbands and patriarchal power structures in general. These early issues of Ms. were a revelation to many women, and my mother was one of them. She stored all her issues in an oversized Wheaties box that she had covered with red contact paper and decorated with big black stencil letters reading "Ms."

One summer day in 1976 my mother decided to reshingle the roof. She put on her jeans and a torn T-shirt and dragged me to the hardware store, where I remember feeling very out of place. There were no women, and certainly no children, anywhere to be seen. My mother impressed the salesman with her vocabulary: shingles, felt underlayment, rafter, fascia, joist. Knowing these words was what forced him to take her seriously. When we got home she organized the materials and climbed up onto the roof. My job was to throw away the debris as she tossed it down. To the people driving by, we may as well have been sitting on an elephant. They slowed down, pointed, and made faces. Some yelled insults: "Get back in the house!" "Where's your skirt?" My mother didn't seem bothered. She just ignored them or, to my utter embarrassment, smiled and waved.

Houses are structures designed by architects and city planners and built by contractors and carpenters. A house is one part of other larger social structures that feminists in the 1970s called "patriarchal." A house represents a long lineage of houses designed and built to sustain family units, which in turn are designed to hold together in order to uphold a social order. Historically, men are the designers and the framers of houses; women are sustained and protected by them. I grew up in a house that was constantly being modified by a mother who insisted on inserting herself as creator, maker, transformer. She insisted on constructing the symbolism of the house by playing both matriarchal and patriarchal roles. She insisted that there was no tool built by any man that she couldn't figure out how to use. Chain saws, circular saws, sanders, drills, and ratchets—I associate these tools with my mother.

Language is a power tool that can be used to oppress, to liberate, to articulate, to silence. Historically, according to feminist theorists, women were excluded from the process of making meaning. In other words, they were on the receiving end of the conversation. In *Stealing the Language: The*

Emergence of Women's Poetry in America (1987) Alicia Ostriker writes that, throughout literary history, women writers were "imprisoned in an 'oppressor's language' which denies them access to authoritative expression." Of course this doesn't mean women weren't writing, but it does mean that their writing, their ideas and opinions, were not perceived as valid. Feminist scholars developed ways of reading the work done by women writers, showing how their language, sense of narrative, character, and plot were distinct from that of the work by their male contemporaries. I happened to grow up in a household with a mother who was constantly battling with the social order: she dressed like a man, talked back to televised football games, hacked away at the prescribed order of her house and replaced it piece by piece. When I first read feminist theory in college, the texts were the articulation of an ideology that I had lived with in practice.

Women writers set about redesigning the house of language from the inside out—fixing the plumbing using their own logic about how water might run through the pipes; fixing the roof with their own intuitive sense of how shingles keep out the rain; reconnecting lengths of wire via their own mental circuitry; attaching disparate pieces together with a unique understanding of how thread and tape and solder work to connect fragments.

There are hazards, of course, to the act of defying the social order by fiddling with its controls, to changing the circuitry from within the patriarchally defined motherboard. One of the books I read when I was beginning to conceive of myself as a writer and trying to figure out whether or not I was a "woman" writer was Toril Moi's *Sexual/Textual Politics: Feminist Literary Theory* (1987). She paraphrases Julia Kristeva's concept of the "spasmodic force" that rises from deep within the subconscious of the woman writer: "But if these unconscious pulsations were to take over the subject entirely, the subject would fall back into . . . imaginary chaos and develop some form of mental illness. The subject whose language lets such forces disrupt the symbolic order, in other words, is also the subject who runs the greater risk of lapsing into madness." In the margin of the book, I wrote "Is this madness a necessary and useful process to becoming a writer?" Otherwise stated, does the house have to be completely destroyed and rebuilt from the ground up?

It's interesting how these early ideas affected me as a writer, although I can't say how much I'm connected to them anymore. The "patriarchal order" so important for me to combat as a young woman has now been re-placed with a much more sinister order—this being the (dis)order that has erupted now that the logic of patriarchy has gone completely mad. The symbolic order, it would seem, has fallen into absolute disarray—and messing with language as a means of disrupting the signs doesn't seem relevant to me in a culture where the signs are already so scrambled. Mad-ness isn't my objective living in a country that has gone so wrong. I now see that there are degrees of patriarchy—it's not one all-encompassing and oppressive system. Patriarchy has many manifestations, and dealing with it in the abstract is an intellectual exercise not overly effective in effort to change the system. I now see the system as something that is within me, and I see my relationship to language as the most immediate way to shape it, move it, change it. I write through the urgency of changing language into form. Anne Waldman's work speaks to this calling.

All this makes it sound as if I have always been intellectually focused, but in spite of having a radical feminist mother, it took me a long time to have the desire to be articulate. Being slightly clueless was my own private rebellion against my mother. If she was strong, creative, confident, I was going to be inhibited, cautious, conformist. She teased me saying that while I dreamed of marrying Superman, she dreamed of becoming Super-man. It wasn't until after she died that I understood what it meant for a woman to become a Superman. It meant she had harnessed the power of constructing her ego so as to intentionally mess with social expectations. (I use the word "construct" in the most practical sense—she really did build herself, like a house, from the ground up, brick by brick.) With her potbelly, huge arms, super short hair, tube socks, and lumberjack shirts she cut quite a frame—and there is no doubt but that in 1976 this woman was informing the rest of the world that she was a force to be reckoned with. It took me a long time to realize that writers and Superman have a lot in common, that to become a writer, I would have to dream my mother's dreams and aspire to her perpetual sense of self-creation as a means of survival.

Ownership, possession, appropriation, balls. At some point a person who wants to be a writer must feel entitled to play around with language and trust her ideas. Feminism was a crucial movement because it sent the mes-sage that women needed to take control, to seize the power and possibilities of language. I don't think I would be a writer today had I not, at some point, decided I had the right. I've read many women writers who say that at some point in their lives they had to give themselves permission to write.

For me, it happened when I took a class that Robert Creeley was teaching on Charles Olson at SUNY Buffalo. I was still practicing my speaking voice, still mustering the courage to overtalk like the rest of the poetics graduate students in class. The idea of claiming Creeley and Olson as my teachers was intimidating. To do it, I had to believe they were speaking and writing directly to me. This meant listening and reading not as a passive receiver but as an active participant: asking them questions, provoking them, sitting down with Olson as my mental teacher at the proverbial kitchen table and sharing a glass of milk. This is an approach to poetry that allows a person to discover within it a life of the mind.

A conversation spontaneously erupted in the class one day. Here is where our little brick house and the feminist theories that frame it becomes the story of how Anne Waldman became a major influence on my writing mind. One day, Creeley asked the class whether there was anyone alive today undertaking the writing of an epic as ambitious as Olson's *Maximus Poems*. I raised my hand and enthusiastically said, Anne Waldman's *IOVIS*! Creeley was generous in his response, as he always was in class. But essentially he disagreed. Too much ego, he replied.

It was a shock to me to think that Olson's ego, so present in the pages of *Maximus*, was somehow more authentic than the ego of Anne Waldman, also very present in her epic poem *Iovis: All Is Full of Jove* (1993). Why is the masculine ego an explorable space and the feminine ego a restricted one?

I decided to write a letter to Anne Waldman—I don't think I had ever been brave enough to write a letter to a writer I admired. And to my amazement, Anne published this letter in *IovisII* in all its raw, emotional, unedited, ranty glory. It made me proud and embarrassed simultaneously. I was aware of myself trying hard to be a writer and engage passionately and intentionally with an idea. Yet I was terrified of my words and mistrustful of my perspective. What if I had it wrong? What if I was misunderstood? I wrote: "I am very confused about this whole ego thing because I am being confronted with the problem—to be forward or to hang back— to perform or to whisper—to vanish or to shine forth—and of course it seems that the answer is obvious—and yet it is confusing." She wrote back, essentially saying, "you must do it all!" Someday I will find the letter and publish it in my own epic.

Although parts of my letter still make me cringe, looking back over it I can see that working through "the ego thing" has been one of my primary challenges as a writer. Gradually I began to test out my writerly ego, my voice, my language . . . lashing out, getting irate, even didactic. I've since toned down, realizing that being too reactionary was not good either for my own internal sense of self or for keeping friends. Anne Waldman has been my guide through this process. Her own writing is a synthesis of masculine and feminine mind energies that zip across the page like an electrical transformer. From Waldman I have learned measure and tone; I have learned that conviction, if coming from an inner source of generosity, does not have to be dismissive. And there is the wonderful model of *IOVIS* that literally allowed Waldman to claim male forces (Jove, Olson, Williams, Cage, Pound, Buddha) as her own and then to rechannel them to create radical change. Waldman describes the poem: "The Iovis project has an exalted tone and purpose: total assault on and transmutation of patriarchy—through imagination, compassion, and magic. . . . As reclaimed tantric female epic it challenges assumptions of form, intervenes and torques narrative, disgorges themes, and shunts war again and again. It names and calls out enemy, weaponry, swagger."

Waldman's writing does not distinguish between the political, the personal, and the poetic. It incorporates all of the elements of the busy, conflicted worlds of mother, teacher, shaman, diva, activist, and truth teller. Her work both on and off the stage/page is in a constant state of flux. Her glorious ego, her humble self, pours over; she is generous in creating space for conversation between people, in absorbing the facts and shaping them into her own narrative. Hers is the constant and urgent challenge of creating a life of the mind situated to oppose male dominance (of the Ashcroft kind) by harnessing it and then directing it back at the powers-that-be-absolute. Her Medusian logic is not madness but activity, a positive, generative force unleashed to provoke change in the larger social order. As her perpetual student, I find my own mind is ablaze with possibility.

My own poetics have developed out of Anne's insistence that poetry can enlarge its own circular logic, radiating outward to the space where the personal and political intersect. This involves perceiving myself as a woman and a writer whose life choices are affected by, and in many ways determined by, the events of the world, the wider environmental field, the perpetuation of injustice that cannot be ignored, the genealogy of oppression that gets passed down through generations. I am a wife and a mother battling with the conventions that try to dictate how I should behave in these roles.

I think of my poetics as a synthesis of the visual, the verbal, the spiritual, the material, the spatial, the economic, the domestic, the extraterrestrial, the psychological, and the planetary. Through my poetic construction business, the form the poem takes on the page is inextricably linked with the content. And this content is in a perpetual state of rearrangement and repair, shared and redistributed among other poems. The graphic design of the page is the intersection of numerous sources of language, ideas, and emotions. I'm not aiming to write a perfect poem, only to keep the building process going.

Last week, Anne and I took part in a spontaneous "Poets for Peace" reading on the steps of the New York Public Library. With my baby in her sling, I shouted out Kenneth Rexroth's poem "Thou Shalt Not Kill" at the top of my lungs: "They are murdering all the young men. / For half a century now, / every day, / They have hunted down and killed them. / They are killing them now, / At this minute, all over the world" (from his book *Swords that Shall Not Strike: Poems of Protest and Rebellion*, 1999). I startled the passersby on Fifth Avenue and even startled myself. As I was leaving, someone said, "you should take that baby home." I just smiled at him and waved. I bet my mother would have done the same.

Kristin Prevallet ✳

Apostroph

in the shadow of Whitman's "Apostroph"

O daughter! O me!
O international agencies!
O mountain lilacs of my mountainous youth!
O cosmic strings! O cheap labor!
O urban sprawl! O chaos of dictators!
O hopeless future! O soulmate!
O internal source! O longevity!
O fear! O God *in absentia*! O moral norm.
O poets! O goateed carpenters! O street slumberers!
O ignorance! The cold sparrow's window song! Even in winter, she
    wakes up early.
O, as I walk riverside, I see the darkening clouds—the devilish shapes,
    pink and gray, through the sunset . . .
O I saw and still see, triggered thunder; O soldiers! See how they control
    even the sky!
O animal warning, unheeded! (Silence them, before they learn to speak!)
O cynicism! Middle ground! (O if the whole world knows injustice, why
    don't they rebel?)
O I believe there is nothing pure about America and her freedom!
O impostors! Interlopers! Invaders! Thieves! How mighty the fanatics
    have become!
O you who dare to represent us and them!
O self-adorned king! O southern trees bearing noose marks, still!
O to occupy through grace! O generosity!
O all of us, separable—time, time, time!
O CURSE HE THAT WOULD DISSEVER THIS UNION FOR ANY REASON
    WHATEVER!
O evil, o slaughter, o giant wave!
O torture exported to the highest bidder!
O fear shapers, O bomb threats! O celebrated terrorist!

O suburbs, O the slum! The citizens are shopping their minds away.

O utopia where everyone gets stared at equally!

O fake Louis Vuitton! Fake pashima! Did he who made the lamb, make thee?

O child's hand in Indochina!

O images of future centuries! O dreams of a better world!

O strength and luck, don't leave me now!

O hour of my need!

O workmen building the structures which sustain me!

O immigrant laborers nailing boards for 15 hours straight!

O subway drivers! Cab drivers! We travel together every day!

O I will make the encyclopedia of all your lost and forgotten glimpses!

O internal conflict! I love and I hate you, always!

O storage of childhood junk! O inseparable toy bunny!

O sun, o moon! Move along, you know nothing different.

O brooder! O I must start building my own life, before we all die!

O biodiversity! O organic farmers! I won't speak for you, but I'll buy your apples.

O poisonous river, my neighbor!

O rigged contests, O privatization! I can't save you, I'm not your poet!

O goodbye past decades! Feminists! Nuns! Public mourners!

O courage of rainbow people!

O vast preparations for emancipation! Black and white! O diversity, they now call you dogma.

O how long does it take for a message to reach the future! What will they say when they see what we have become!

O clairvoyants! O teachers! To separate morality from judgment.

O reality! Filter down, filter down, to all red states!

O Birthday! O Jesus! O humble adoration, unlegislated faith.

O conviction! Infect troops of poets! Artists! Singers!

O depression! O unproductive passionate intensity!

O songs of freedom! Songs of contractor, middleman, manager, sergeant!

O arrogance! O freedom! What's being done in your name, to your seekers?

O ecstatic liars!

O me, I, they! Preparing for what? Afraid of what?

O insurgency! O dark ages! O phoenix inspire oppressors and oppressed to raise above their worst inclinations!

O brilliant, burning, amazing youth!

O visionary slogan-makers, still writing dissent on subway walls!

O prophets! You started writing self-help books and lost what was most inarticulate about your vision!

O unspoken! O cosmic and biological marriage! O consciousness! O quark!

O America, you have been dissevered!

O Whitman, who never saw it coming!

O my soul! O powerless speech!

O infant, speck on the century!

O states! Cities! Buying conformity over human rights! I can't love you as you self-destruct.

O death wish! Why else would they vote for terminators!

O new history! Forge inarticulatable humanity! Scratches! Scratches! Push forward into speech!

O muted poets! O you sitting there! What are you hearing in this broad dribble?

O height I seek! O infinity in an empty bowl!

O nameless force! Threatening apocalypse by making it happen!

O sculpted history! They pull a lever and you quake!

O unseasonably warm sea, glaciers drop like fallen towers!

O poets, the sick fish and the floating limbs! All counting on you!

Anne Waldman ✳

from Iovis: All Is Full of Jove

DEAR CREELEY
Later to think of him, a father
all the other young women but me
become his daughters
What doth a daughter do?
How doth a daughter woo?
How does she counter weaponry?
Rule about the house
on a mind of a teen
his clothes, how they smell
musty of south Jersey

           or

                spermy

        with battle

            to mount a tank
              artillery,

                     pull down

              artillery,

                     pull down

& I wanted you as a thief in the night, & I wanted you
to promulgate my cult & I wanted you as breakdown, as private life
& I wanted you, parent of revolution, & I wanted you to make
the land carry more sheep for the wool trade, and I wanted you,
a talisman, & I wanted you, arboreal mixed up with city
& I wanted you at the front, as someone who might walk to the

edge of town, & I wanted you up to my neck, & I wanted you
as partner to my friend's existence, and I wanted you changed
by daylight, and I wanted you as I need books, & I wanted you

I wanted you, history doesn't count, & I wanted you as spleen
to a carefree nature, & I wanted you in the sense of opposite,
& I wanted you the cows can come home, we were in the country,
I wanted you, & I wanted you speaking as we were children again,
& I wanted you to sneak up on me like children, & I wanted
the clothes you wear, I wanted to wear them, I wanted you
in hot pursuit, wanted you the column could wait, &
I wanted you writing the story of Athena, of black Athena, and I
wanted you to be law abiding just once & I wanted you early
I wanted you late, I wanted you the others can wait, they
wait if I want you & only you I want
I wanted you at the beginning of civilization, I wanted you
the clocks can run down, I want you on the way outside, I want
you resting on my laurels, I wanted you forbidden to "panegyric"
to "ode" to "sonnet," I wanted you formless, I wanted you &
the page is the only place I know for this, I wanted you the
night of the day the manuscript came back, I wanted you settled
in a home, I wanted you cherished by the landlord, I wanted
the textures of illuminated manuscripts in our love

& I wanted you in agreement that women invented the alphabet,
& I wanted you to close down please the laboratory for me,
& I wanted you as water flows downhill, I wanted you over
my head, on top of me, I wanted you under me, & I wanted
you sitting in front of books as you always do, the rest can
wait, I wanted you to give something away the day I noticed
wanting you, I desired the table of contents to include you,
I desired the year of our lord to slow down

                              (I went out seeking these things
                                  to remind me of you)

Cin Salach
on Maureen Seaton

I say:
In the darkness we are all holy.
—Maureen Seaton, *Furious Cooking*

THE FACT THAT I was a girl was something I never really bothered with before I met Maureen Seaton. In fact, it was something I mostly avoided. I nurtured a more androgynous appeal. Boyish girl-next-door. Ally Sheedy in *The Breakfast Club*. Everyone assumed I was a lesbian, even my husband. The only one without a clue was me.

I first met Maureen through a book of her poetry recommended by former students of hers who had started a writing group I had just been invited to join. This was in Chicago, where I had been performing my own work for a little over a decade as part of the performance/slam scene. I had become disillusioned with everything poetry. I hadn't heard or read or written anything that moved me in a very long time until someone put

Furious Cooking in my hands. I read the first poem and felt my skin shift over my bones.

I heard Maureen was giving a summer workshop in town and inquired about signing up, nervous, excited. One afternoon I came home to a message on my machine saying I indeed had a place in her workshop and that she was an admirer of my work as well. I replayed the message and jumped around my room. How could *she* possibly know who *I* was? What I didn't know was that, around the same time I got a copy of her book, a mutual friend had given her a copy of mine.

I had been a closet poet until I was twenty-four, at which point I walked into the Green Mill Lounge in uptown Chicago one Sunday night and witnessed poetry happening in a way I could not take my eyes off of. It was the fall of 1986. The Green Mill Poetry Slam instantly became my church, my grad school, my comfort zone. After my first open mic experience, I felt poetry align my heart with my body, and in the spring of 1987, I quit my full-time copywriting job, went freelance, and began to live life centered on poetry. I was dating a saxophonist at the time who put to music a poem I wrote called "The Loofah Method" and slipped it into the tape player at a party as a surprise for me. When people started dancing to it (this was the '80s, so it was all synthesizer and samplers), someone asked if we could perform it live. Someone else said "yes" and offered to add visuals to the background "if we wanted," and just like that I was the cofounder of *The Loofah Method*, a poetry-driven multimedia performance group. For the next ten years we collaborated on live shows, poetry videos, and theater events until our lovely but increasingly high-tech and dysfunctional group needed a break. The timing was perfect. I was tired of creating poetry that way and wanted to begin a relationship with the page. My first book, *Looking for a Soft Place to Land*, was published by Fiction Collective 2 in 1996.

The workshop I took with Maureen happened in the summer of 1998. The first thing she asked for was our astrological signs. I was surprised and secretly delighted. I would have been content to hide behind the other participants. I felt a little intimidated because many of them were in graduate programs, but Maureen pulled me into the center immediately. "You're the Aries," she said. "You go first!" And so I did. The ice was broken, and I felt instantly comfortable, open, and, most important, able.

I doubt Maureen knew how crucial that moment was. I didn't until long after the workshop was over. But I believe her extraordinary instinct for who needs what and how much and when is part of her brilliance as a teacher. I'm sure it's part of her brilliance as a mother, too. She is committed to who she is teaching/nurturing and willing to do what it takes to make it possible for that person to grow.

What I learned from being around her is that this kind of nurturing takes a particular combination of patience, generosity, and creativity. I had never been around energy like that before, and although it was quite subtle, it went to work on me immediately. My poetry seemed to expand overnight. I was enjoying writing, enjoying my writing, and enjoying the world according to poetry on a whole new level.

There was one thing that surprised me about my writing during the workshop: the word "lesbian" suddenly started appearing in many of my poems. I was married at the time and not really thinking about not being married. The poems weren't about me being a lesbian, but still, I was curious. Who was this lesbian that kept popping up? Did I know her? Was she the same woman in each poem? It didn't matter. She thrilled me. Maybe she was sending me secret messages via poetry? Maybe she was a poet herself? That idea thrilled me even more. A lesbian poet sending me secret messages via my own poems. I couldn't imagine anything cooler.

Maureen's workshop began about six months after I read *Furious Cooking*. By that time, I was no longer disillusioned with poetry. In fact, I was completely focused and invested. A few months prior, I had participated in the Northern Arizona Book Festival in Flagstaff with Tia Chucha Press, the publishers of my book. Besides being asked to perform at the festival, I was also invited to work with some of the kids on the neighboring reservation. This gave me the opportunity not only to meet poets I admired, like Joy Harjo and Quincy Troupe, but also to co-teach workshops with them for the "rez" kids and youth at risk. It was the first time I was asked to be a teacher and it was intimate, empowering. Experiencing firsthand how poetry connects all of us to all of us was both humbling and energizing. I left Flagstaff knowing I needed to be more poet and less copywriter.

The last night of the workshop our group went out to dinner. What I really wanted to do was ask Maureen if she would have a cup of coffee with me and talk about poetry. The festival in Flagstaff had woken something in me that felt urgent, and Maureen seemed like she could offer guidance. Poetry always seemed to be at the top of her list of priorities, and that was how I wanted to shape my life. So I asked. And she said yes.

We met the following week for dinner. We talked about MFA programs and making it in the world as a poet, and I eventually got up the nerve to ask her if she thought I had what it took. Of course in my gut I knew the answer. I don't know if we ever dare ask such intimate questions without already having the answer tucked away somewhere. But hearing her say it was important. She seemed so much more real to me at that time in my life than . . . me. And she was gentle. And smart. And present. I remember early in our relationship commenting that "everything seems louder with you" and she smiled, knowing exactly what I meant. The truth was that I was more present, too. That first dinner was the beginning of a self-awareness and acceptance I was so ready for, and I was so hungry for someone to show me the way. Looking back now, I see my poetry heart so clearly on my sleeve. But I learned quickly that my poetry heart was safe with her.

We began exchanging e-mail, meeting for coffee and walks, and it soon became obvious there was more between us than just an admiration of poetry. We spent weeks auditioning different names for it. The first one we tried was "crush." The second was "love," into which we easily fell, spending the next couple of years growing a relationship that embraced many roles. During that time I came out, got divorced, and stepped more fully into my poetic skin then I ever thought possible. Maureen and I worked our way through so much. As a daughter, she was tending and grieving her dying mother; as a mother, she was tending her daughters' full and complex lives; as a poet, she was creating what would eventually become her fourth book; and as a lover and partner, she was accompanying me on my new journey.

By being exactly who she is, Maureen showed me what it means to take yourself seriously as a poet. Do you know she unplugs her phone when she's writing? I didn't even know that was legal! Of course it's more than that. It's that her compassion, creativity, enthusiasm, and love all come from the same place as mother/teacher/ poet/woman—they all feed from the same river, so they all affect each other. Her priorities change only slightly according to her schedule. During the school year they are (1) woman, (2) mother, (3) teacher, (4) poet. During the summer they are (1) woman, (2) mother, (3) poet, (4) teacher. She shapes her life around her writing, her relationships around her writing, and both of those around her daughters. The fierceness and consistency of her mothering inspires me. Her daughters come first. No questions asked. It's a warrior spirit that feeds both her writing and her relationships equally. As a woman who wants to be a mother someday, I craved a model for that behavior. As a partner, I was offered a sense of protection that I had lacked in my life. I wrapped it around myself like a blanket.

The fact that Maureen was a page poet who loved performance and I was a performance poet who loved the page gave us an admiration and respect for each other that put us on a more level playing field and allowed our relationship to go beyond that of mentor and mentee. That wonderfully balanced philosophy of "we are all each other's teacher and we are all each other's student" was very present for us, although my hyped-up poet's heart always believed I had far more to learn from her than she ever could from me, even when she insisted it was the other way around. Our official student/teacher status lasted only six weeks, but it was impossible for those roles not to spill into other parts of our relationship. Sometimes it was hard to just be partners—hard for me to see myself that way, and hard for her to wait for me to step into the role of an equal. That was what eventually led to our breakup.

We spent hundreds of hours—I am not exaggerating—talking, trying to work our way through as many layers of relationship falling away as we could, but eventually the only thing we could do was undo us. Maureen made the call. I wasn't ready for it. I didn't believe it. I was stubborn and naïve and inconsolable. It was sad and strange for a long time, but when I woke up it was spring and I began to let that in.

Cin Salach and *Maureen Seaton* ✳

evolution three

This is how we fall the first time, not by accident, this
Sliding into explicable chaos, the witty lovers

leap into the hallelujah chorus
make up adverbs as they sexily play

questionable singing voices humming along with god
the way the Holy Ghost slips between the mouths of lesbians

earth quaking—spewing gardens, gravity, dessert.
how everyone twinkles then becomes flesh.

We feel the spin of creation, watch our feet devour the ground
Presto. Suddenly young suddenly young suddenly

in a beloved dance we were born dancing, we move
heavy like a hat of fur like a hand on the angel bone

our holy selves into unquestionable positions, into doorways
our swirling DNA, our cute tongues torquing

like a trickle into gushing, we come to be again and again
we come again and again, nipple to sticky nipple

vibration to sound. This is how we see when there's too much light
foundling, believer, the arc of womb and clavicle

to tell our story—the one about the beetle landing
beneath autumn hair or the woman called fire

on a windowsill, opening the smooth shell of the universe
about to leap from the fourth story, the one

like a dream eyeing inevitable sleep.
from which some suicides survive.

evolution *six*

In a crouch of sun beside great lake water
We breaststroke through pools of foamy light

in a popmail kind of way dot com—
words vaporizing like communion wafers—

honey, we henna-write on bellies, fingertips,
we communicate via memory, skin's secret satellite

and once just once we floated away completely—
(when our perpetual ocean comes, we are already gone)

Albuquerque, seed pearl, Helene Cixous.
you don't need a raft in the desert.

We are rollercoaster princesses, tornado ladies
We are neon dreamers screaming "look mom no hands!"

because we like bluster and the wind is red
licorice-whipped, like our lips after licking all the sugar off,

like a pig's eye or some say (as if amazed) like
like the farmer-in-the-dell, red-lipped and love-whipped too,

the way God might look again someday—
after taking a wife who makes hay hi-ho-holy again—

Virgo mother reducing paperback pulp to poems
rewrites genesis to read: in the beginning it was dark and we liked it that way

ink beneath fingernails, blood on the tip of a tongue
our pens indistinguishable from our churches.

In every stanza, she is the one who blesses everything.
When she spills the wine, it goes everywhere.

evolution *eight*

Into preherstoric laky unlit caves, our
Loamy wombs open and empty,

breakfast seductively burnt and devoured
we swallow apples and rocks whole,

we follow the stone's throw, seep into mud mud
delicious ying arcs through air, snaps and falls into

mud. Where shall we go from here, luscious?
bed. Two Eves skinny-dipping in a swamp of breath and sex—

You don't need a rope when you're swimming in sand.
you don't need Adam when you're swimming in Eve.

And sometimes we hold each other for life.
And sometimes we drown each other in life,

Dear life. The way the lake is molten at sunset and changed
always in over our heads by the end of the day, transposed

into an ocean, into a wide and trackless fabulous place.
into an abandoned body of storms and smells

Everything seems holy again, even God, who
making the world flesh, making the sky come,

(and this is crucial) liked it that way,
so order is irrelevant, evolution random,

our chaos as sexy as shirt-free mornings.
our heat as interchangeable as our clothes.

When there's nothing left to drink, she drinks the sea.
When the sky empties, she's speechless.

evolution *ten*

We stitch the dark back together again,
We beg the light to *leave us alone please,*

follow each other into every hollow shell's home,
bring each other over a thousand salty thresholds a second,

supple seapods, the real ones found beneath the ocean.
swimming in and out of the ocean's open doorway.

Who are you? (Gurgle) Who am I? (Glug)
There are apples in pears in you in me

Or: There are Adams in Eves in Adams in Eves.
(Have you ever asked for your penis back then changed your mind)

The way gender flips and flops,
One holy on top, one kneeling under,

intransitive verbs butching and femming
abandoning language to melt in the sun—

into a syntax that fits us perfectly—
we feast, famished, food everywhere, our crumbs tumbling

tumbling down.
to the ground to the ground.

We are good at this, this tricky noise and flux,
exquisite singing voices screaming oh god oh god,

guilty as a seabred siren a-hoying toward the land.
welcome as a night hawk on Wilson.

Kissable as a baby fish mouth.
She is.

evolution *twelve*

Let us incubate, isolate, dilate, cool—
Then let us add fire to the fuel, the way sun blisters light under our skin

the way the mermaid meets the seaweedy crone
face first, splash swoon surrender, wet green-gold then

blue-black like that. Mercurial.
orange-red. Like the weather buried inside us.

A pomegranate with its starfish center slashed.
One seedy death after another.

Have you ever wanted two
More than yourself

lovers at the same time, perfect image/mirage
your history of sex frozen in a mirror, your future

a stutter of wind and possibility.
a small silver key ready to open.

And is this what you prayed for
It is

while in you a small voice broke
like a thousand wine glasses, singing

for the stillborn kitten
go to sleep go to sleep

buried in a child's garden on Wrightwood.
you are.

She is mapping her resurrection.
Awake.

Robyn Schiff
on Gjertrud Schnackenberg

I WAS BETWEEN books and in a hurry when I slipped Gjertrud Schnack-enberg's volume *Supernatural Love: Poems 1976–1992* (2000) into my bag to read on the subway ride to the Frick Art Reference Library. Today the cover gapes, there's a red stain along the bottom edge from being carried around in a purse with an open lipstick, and because the spine is cracked at favorite poems, randomly opened, the book always reveals the last, breathtaking section of "Kremlin of Smoke," the first page of "Angels Grieving Over the Dead Christ," where silkworms are "smuggled / Into Constantinople in the head of a walking stick," or the dire dream of "the ruler's brother" in the long poem "Imaginary Prisons." There's also a bookmark from the Frick tucked inside that reminds me of my first encounter with Schnackenberg's labyrinthine syntax. Her book was new to me then. Settling in for the trip uptown, I chose "Imaginary Prisons" from the table of contents.

I was going to the Frick that day to research Sèvres porcelain, a porcelain house that with Madame de Pompadour's support, cornered the decorative arts market in France through the mid- and late eighteenth century. The mantelpieces, coffee tables, and dinner tables of the aristocracy in Versailles and beyond were crowded with an unprecedented accumulation of porcelain figurines, vases, and tableware, all with the distinct sweeps and flourishes we've come to associate with the decadence that precipitated the revolution. The early history of European porcelain, which led to this fever in the mid-eighteenth century, is the history of failed attempts of the Europeans to achieve the same white translucency of imported Chinese porcelain. In the 1760s, kaolin, the missing secret ingredient, was finally unearthed from the very soil of France.

The Frick Collection, a museum in New York City that houses mostly European art from the Renaissance to the late nineteenth century, exhibits several pieces of Sèvres porcelain. Teacups and soup tureens painted with tiny flowers and gruesome hunting scenes decorate the antique sideboards as if they were abandoned midmeal. Henry Clay Frick, who acquired his art with wealth he amassed as a steel magnate during the grand age of steel, arranged for his mansion and the artwork inside to become a public museum after his death in 1919. Today the collection is curated in such a manner as to seem not curated at all, but pushed against the walls to make room for guests at a Gilded Age ball. The hostess who poured the tea from the eighteenth-century tea service was probably led to the guillotine; the guest who thanked her and accepted the cup, balanced on its saucer, was probably also led to the guillotine; and the teacups themselves survived centuries of war without a chip. Or, just as likely, the teacups were expertly restored to seem immortal.

I was planning a poem about the porcelain flowers with which Madame de Pompadour replaced the real flowers of Louis XV's garden. At the time, the king's passion for Madame de Pompadour was cooling into friendship. While the new arrangement would prove more influential for France as the king grew to rely upon her as an advisor instead of as a mistress, Madame de Pompadour must have been heartbroken when Madame du Barry replaced her in the king's bed. Apparently the porcelain flowers were so masterfully fabricated he didn't notice the difference, and neither did the bees that landed on them all morning long.

Art history is full of tales of trompe l'oeil deceptions, some of them apocryphal. Zeuxis's grapes; the audience that ran screaming in 1895 when the Lumière brothers showed their film of an oncoming train. We love to tell ourselves stories about how authentic we can make things appear. American poetry is likewise fascinated by claims of authenticity: think of Whitman eschewing received form so his barbaric yawp could rush forth unbridled. The covert replacement of natural flowers with porcelain that appear on the one hand more permanent, on the other more fragile, resonates with my preoccupation with poetic artifice. My perception of what is natural becomes even muddier when I consider that the genuine article—the king's garden—was a rigidly designed bed of transplanted imports. Maybe these porcelain flowers, with their beginnings as kaolin deposits deep in French soil, are the more natural. How did Madame de Pompadour's elaborate practical joke belie the anguish of her changing status at court and, moreover, the collective paranoia of the French aristocracy generation just before revolution?

I think of Madame de Pompadour leading Louis XV through the lanes. Is she thrilled or desolate when he takes the garden for a garden?

Anticipating my research at the Frick, I had not only porcelain and artifice but also empire on my mind when I encountered the character identified as "the ruler's brother" deep in Schnackenberg's poem "Imaginary Prisons," a version of the Sleeping Beauty legend. The poem tells the story of a fairy-tale people cursed by their king to literally live without a point, lest Beauty's finger suffer its prophesized prick, and cursed by Fate, which sees to it that Beauty's finger is pricked despite all human efforts to prevent the calamity. Schnackenberg depicts a tableau of sleeping subjects, revealing the villagers in suspended states of anxiety by narrating their dreams: aching expressions of powerlessness against the absolute, against the state, and against one's own mind. I was shocked by her description of "the ruler's brother," discovering in the swirl of one of Schnackenberg's maddeningly long sentences that he had developed a "theory // In which the world is made of porcelain, / But porcelain that cannot crack or shatter." Here was a character so aware of his own precariousness that his insistence on reading fragility as strength tragically acknowledged defeat. He and the Madame Pompadour of my nascent poem shared the same dream. The ruler's brother attempts to shore himself against mental fracture by envisioning a world that, while molded from a fragile material, is actually invulnerable to breakage. When the porcelain platter he meditates on to confirm his unassailability cracks, he must reverse his vision and find a way to prove that the laws "breaking //

The tragic glaze apart come to appear / To be the laws by which it's held together."

If Madame de Pompadour hadn't stopped at the garden wall. If she had gone on to commission a porcelain walkway, porcelain front steps, a porcelain hallway to a porcelain bed.

Writing in form is recasting the world in porcelain. Received forms and invented procedures exasperate notions of mastery, power, control, and closure. Choosing when and where not to draw attention to the artifice of form has dramatic effects.

When Madame de Pompadour finally asked the king to meet her in the porcelain garden, he sat down beside her on their bench as usual. When he failed to notice that the flowers, just beginning to bloom, were not real, she cracked one under her heel.

Most of Schnackenberg's poems evince formal principles that aren't particularly popular today: her use of rhyme, iambic pentameter, stanzas with fixed numbers of lines, and lines that tend toward the symmetrical make her something of a curiosity in the age of free verse. There is such a stigma against formalism in contemporary poetry that I'm almost tempted to say that she is an excellent poet *despite* her use of form. But it would be a mistake to read her bracing imagery—imagery that displays an intelligence as visionary and scrupulous as any in the history of American poetry—as distinct from the formal strategies that pace its revelations. That would be like reading Whitman or Creeley without noticing the length of their lines. While misgivings toward formalism probably spring from a healthy suspicion of the authority of tradition, contemporary formalism at its most exciting explores power dynamics as potently as poems that forgo traditional prosody.

The energy of Schnackenberg's poetry derives from the tension between her overflowing, unwieldy sentences and her tidy metrics and lineation. In a way, her adherence to form is one voice, her extreme syntax and absurdly long sentences another. Her work enacts the conflict between structure and disorder.

Schnackenberg's poems have inspired me to consider the multivocality that formalism can express. Following suit, I have tried to use inherited form to foreground the activity of making and to explore the utter sadness, the futility, of asserting presence—the constant announcement of the self as a maker—in this manner.

I wonder if "the ruler's brother" is a stand-in for the poet. Indeed, as a quasi-formalist under Schnackenberg's influence, I've sought to use form to simultaneously express wilderness and cultivation. It strikes me that composure is not composure without the acknowledgment that the forces one maintains one's composure against make a good case for discomposure. The fragile web of laws holding the tragic poem together come to appear to be the laws by which it breaks apart. The serpentine syntax that maneuvers through Schnackenberg's forms participates in the tragedy: the overwhelming length of her sentences hinders access to her ideas. Reading them, one is attuned to the difficulties of expression, the terrifying proximity of clarity and convolution. Reading Schnackenberg, I have come to consider the sentence unit as a poem in miniature. In my writing, I try to explore the drama of a long sentence as if each is a gothic mansion with infinite possibilities for clausal trap doors, sonic haunting, and disorientation.

Instead of researching Madame de Pompadour's porcelain garden that day, I found a seat in the Frick's reading room and lost myself in *Supernatural Love* until closing time. Way leads to way, and although I've yet to make it back to either the Frick or the poem about Madame de Pompadour that I hoped would find inspiration there, in absorbing aspects of Schnackenberg's poetics, I've come to associate my own use of form with broken French porcelain flowers. In that sense, I'm writing my Madame de Pompadour poem every time I write. Reading Schnackenberg and writing with her book nearby help me see the relationship between writing and observing. Quite literally, in the composition of a long sentence, the very distance between subject and predicate is a slowing of the gaze, an effort to literally keep the conclusion in mystery. As the details of my poems often reside in history, maneuvers derived from inherited forms seem to me to be the appropriate manner of stalking them right now. Schnackenberg is also a poet who delves deeply into historic moments—Chopin's Poland, the palimpsest of past residents occupying a single home, the tragedy of Mandelstam—and thus her project particularly fires my own. Although the balance between control and abandon that Schnackenberg achieves in her work tends to play out in my own as comic melodrama, I am not parodying it. I think there are two kinds of formalists in contemporary poetry: those who are silent when they crush the porcelain flower and those who laugh, like mourners who can't compose themselves at funerals.

I've never met Gjertrud Schnackenberg and haven't had the privilege of studying under her. In a sense, making a claim for Schnackenberg as a personal model in this collection of essays is a claim for distance as a value, the way distance is a value in a poem through sentence length, narrative digression, or alarming juxtaposition. As a reader and writer who readily embraces digression, distraction, delay, dwelling, free association, speaking parenthetically, and changing the subject, I am interested in the byways of influence. In the largest poem, contemporary poetics itself, if a porcelain plate breaks in Schnackenberg's poem, how can it appear in mine unscathed?

Robyn Schiff ✳

Colt Rapid Fire Revolver

The wedding cake of Elizabeth Hart (Colt since
noon) was trimmed with sugar pistols
with revolving sweet-tooth chambers with gears
that rotate one position over like a
dancer down a dance line
prompted by an aisle that parts in music
to switch partners while a

fly drawn to the sugar places a stringy foot
on the trigger. Dysentery.
There must be a gallery with bull's-eyes
blown through sugar faces spun on the same scale
and a wife at a sewing
bee bridging a scarf like a ray of house-
fly regurgitation

between her sticky knitting needles who admits
that when her husband said he'd be
at the gallery she assumed he meant
to see pictures she was too innocent to
see. She imagined him hat
in hand leaning toward a battle scene and
deep in the grainy wound

in the painting's newly dead, indeed a bullet
too deep to see gleams beyond the
vanishing point in both his vision as
he aims and fires in target practice and hers
as she conjures past a line
she would never cross on foot following
the caravan of her

thinking in tedious steps over internal
prairie until it overcomes
the body of her youngest catching
a fly off an ox's tail while the
oxen are moving and yet
onward the party continues until
the provisions of her

fantasy wear thin. Though this is manifest in
sugar, it still disturbs me when
the Donner Party built to scale with the
Patented Colt Revolvers trimming this cake
melt their weakest into a
desperate sap. Though the world's first sugar
bowl was passed from guest to

guest to show the wealth of Elizabeth's court when
an ounce of sugar traded for
a calf, it's worth more than that. You demur
to mourn lives lost in the frontier raised in scale
and substance to people the
West the Patented Colt Revolvers that
trim a cake were cast to

defend, but I say the bull's-eyes marksmen see mapped
upon the apples poised on the
heads of all things are cut on a lathe whose
smallest revolution of thought is in sync
with that which shapes the metal
of the revolving chamber whose circular
machinations synchronize

with the rings a fly circling the bullet wound
makes in air. Focus my gaze; I
see like a fly whose vision is more like
several interlocking rings left by a tea-
cup on a book but the cake

was six feet high and how could I resist
pistols winding tier up-

on tier up the icing reverberating in
decoration the prudence of
a revolvers' placement in the holsters
of a row of guards under whose raised arms that
beam a private arbor the
bride and bridegroom enter their union. Repetition of pistols

map a rebus of progress marching since the first
firearms to devise a weapon
that can repeat fire without reloading.
Behold the rapid fire pistol inspired
by Colt's meditations on
the wheel of the ship steering him toward
India spinning and

locking in position like the machinations
of fortune pacing through the infinite face of its clock in such baby
steps that I shall reign I reign I reigned adjust
the powers of judgment en-
trusted to calibrate them. Leaning in
to see the gears, like the

wick of one candle used to light the next all along
a dark corridor, leaning in
and replicating, is not unlike the vision
the sugar wife had of her sugar husband
leaning in to see the detail
of a battle painting,
and stirred by the fire there,
enlisting.

Gjertrud Schnackenberg ✳

from "Imaginary Prisons"

A version of "Sleeping Beauty."
In memory of Colin Way Reid

Assigned to live next door, because he's silent,
Though under lock and key, because he's mad,
The ruler's brother sits with elbows propped

And hands holding his face above the trestle,
Regarding through the prison of his fingers
The specter of an empty china platter

As he's regarded it for countless years
Since he was thunderstricken to discover
A trivial flaw disastrous to his theory

In which the world is made of porcelain,
But porcelain that cannot crack or shatter
As demonstrated in his published paper,

"The Paradigm of Glass Unbreakable,"
With which he thought to rectify the anger
Of those like him who'd keenly felt the bitter

Accident of being dropped and broken.
And yet the dunderheads refused to hear!
And given that the blind, refining forces

Which glaze the world in an ideal fire
Appeared to have no meaning to the others,
He ceased evangelizing and retired,

Dropping exhausted to his study chair,
And turned to meditation to restore
His faith and to refresh his memory

By summoning the specter of a platter
To represent our wholly perfect order,
And that's the moment, as I said before,

That this unfortunate was struck by thunder
And terrified to see, and no mistaking,
The surface showed the first hint of a fissure,

A web of cracks across the porcelain
Like black lightning unrolled and fixed forever
Into the lightly shattered glaze was creeping,

A test of faith which lengthened year by year
Before his swearing of a vow to stare
Until the fragile web of laws breaking

The tragic glaze apart come to appear
To be the laws by which it's held together.

Kathy Lou Schultz
on Myung Mi Kim

A FIRST-GENERATION college student, I left a small town in Nebraska in 1985 for Columbia University in New York City. This was only the third year that women were admitted to the college, and the weight of Columbia's patriarchal tradition was evident in the core curriculum, which was bereft of nonmale, nonwhite, and non-Western perspectives. The alienation I experienced quickly led me into feminist activism and scholarship. Yet much of feminist theory excluded me as well; I was from a working-class background. I began to read writings by a number of women of color, including Barbara Smith, Merle Woo, Cherrie Moraga, and Angela Davis, whose feminist analyses addressed issues of racism and class oppression and reflected a more inclusive perspective on the lives of women. Even when their texts did not directly represent women who, like me, were white and working class, I was able to perform a kind of translation process that helped me understand my own complex subject position, and I felt a kinship with their work.

At that time I was unaware of another lineage of feminist writing: contemporary poetry following from a modernist tradition, which Lynn Keller and Cristanne Miller point out in their 1999 essay for *How2*, "Gender and Avant-Garde Editing: Comparing the 1920s with the 1990s," is "concerned with the gendered implications of literary conventions and linguistic structures themselves." I had been writing since I was a child. I had always loved to play with language, but I had had few models for women's writing besides the kind of narrative work that came out of cultural feminist publishing projects in the 1970s and '80s. This work was extremely important to me, but by the time I entered the MFA program at San Francisco State University (SFSU) in 1991, I was ready to absorb new models, including, for example, Susan Howe's innovative use of the page as a field and Lyn Hejinian's autobiographical text, *My Life*, which explores personal subjectivity without relying on linear reconstructions of time.

Myung Mi Kim introduced me to this work in her classes at SFSU, a vibrant but chronically underfunded, overcrowded public institution. Myung and I started at SFSU at the same time, both recent arrivals from the Midwest. From the time I nervously entered her classroom, I was struck by her articulate passion. She talked about writing in a way that my previous teachers never had. In her teaching and writing, Myung encouraged me to rethink my habitual relations to language. "Is it apricot or plum. / Their unripe state likens them," she writes in her third book, *Dura* (1998). To open up the field of perception is to open up the possibility of mistake: apricot or plum? To open up the field of perception is to resee familiar objects anew. She gave assignments that intrigued and delighted me: write a sonnet made of only discarded lines; be open to the possibility of mistake; look at things again. In addition, she taught me to focus on writing as a process and argued, through her teaching and her own work, for "[s]werves, oddities, facts, miscues, remnants—threnody and meditation—the perpetually incomplete task of tracking what enters the field of perception (the writing act)—its variegated and grating musics, cadences, temporalities" (*Commons*, 2002).

Myung also introduced me to new ways of thinking about the role of feminism in my poetics. I was very invested in the relationship between poetry and feminist activism, but I was fighting with brittle representational modes of writing that no longer felt sufficient. After reading my early work, Myung described an art exhibit she had seen in which the outline of a woman's body was filled in with shards of glass. That image has stayed with me, and with it Myung helped me to understand one of the central themes I was working out in my poetry: the fragmentation of female identity.

In addition to the roles of women, including motherhood, some of the other recurring themes in Myung's work that are instructive are commerce and capital and nation-states and the violence used to maintain them. These themes are reflected in her second book, The Bounty (2000), a collection of three long poems, the third of which shares the book's title and is dedicated to her son Malcolm. In "The Bounty," she draws attention to the violence used to maintain the state: "Ordnung ordnance ordonnance in the new / King's name drums / And pig squeals." This work indicates the conditions of living in a nation-state, Under Flag (the title of her first book). "Face for nations albeit feathers father masked ones / To protect our heads from falling projectiles" (The Bounty). Living under flag also often means living in a state of war, where the very language of the colonized, the defeated, is under attack.

Myung explores the condition of language loss in an obsessive return in each of her books to the site of translation, to "[t]he ideas of translation, translatability, transliteration, transcription" (Commons). Also, in Dura phrases such as "an ancestral tablet" and "a short lyric poem / or, the founder of a family" are translated from the Korean alphabet into English. Other "translations" of experience explore the repeated cycles of history: "Torch and fire. Translate: 38th parallel. Translate: / the first shipload of African slaves was landed at Jamestown." She also allows the reader to participate in the act of translating experience:

> _____ arrived in America. Bare to trouble and
> foresworn. Aliens aboard three ships off the coast.
> _____ and _____ clash. Police move in.
> What is nearest is destroyed. (Dura)

Myung's attention to the conditions of history has been an important example for me because her work serves as an antidote to official records. While my own acts of translation do not involve the loss of an original language, I continue to struggle with and be interested in questions of translation, perception, and accessibility related, in part, to my working-class, rural background. The tools Myung gave me allow me to explore these questions on multiple linguistic levels.

In Myung I also saw for the first time what it might mean to live one's life as a poet. I watched Myung juggle teaching, motherhood, marriage, and her own strong creative drives. I watched her carve out a space for her work when writing is not a choice but a necessity. I was also struggling to put poetry at the center of my life: tuition at SFSU was cheap, but living in San Francisco was very expensive, and the creative writing program had no funding for graduate fellowships so I worked full-time (for four of those years at a Bartelby-esque job as a legal proofreader) and had to drop out for a while.

Despite these challenges, as I came of age as a poet in 1990s San Francisco, I had access to a richly creative environment where I was surrounded by talented younger writers including Catalina Cariaga, Renee Gladman, Pamela Lu, Yedda Morrison, D. A. Powell, Jocelyn Saidenberg, giovanni singleton, Rodrigo Toscano, Elizabeth Treadwell, Robin Tremblay-McGaw, and Truong Tran. Among the established writers I came into contact with were Kathy Acker, Michael Amnasan, Dodie Bellamy, Norma Cole, Beverly Dahlen, Kathleen Fraser, Robert Glück, Barbara Guest, Carla Harryman, Lyn Hejinian, Kevin Killian, Laura Moriarty, Michael Palmer, Camille Roy, Aaron Shurin, Mary Margaret Sloan, and Leslie Scalapino. Myung was active in this multigenerational literary community. She and her husband hosted salons in their living room, and from these conversations I recovered not only the courage to give voice to the body, to sex, to the untidy, but also to the will to transgress. I continue to look to her work as I make my way in academia, always aware of the challenges of living as a poet not only on the page but also in the world.

Kathy Lou Schultz ✳

Genealogy IV

By now a song for singing.

The Manthey daughters, twins, married in a double wedding. One was my mother. Their first home a trailer, pipes and utilities dug by my father.

She's beautiful and childlike at eighteen, in one photo seen hugging a large teddy bear.

After the farm and after the farm and after.

I inherit loss as identity.

Body as labor. Body for sale.

In another version I become a great scholar.

Work as bread as.

What aches inside you.

A yawning mouth.

Factory floor 10 degrees hotter than outside, which is 100 degrees.

Soak shirt, chill in the air-conditioned office.

27 years in at the plant, 13 years in at the plant, half her life spent at the plant.

His "experience" consisted of things he had heard on the news, as in the wealthy have no "experience."

What I cannot, finally, defend. Though I know the truth of this.

What your gut finally tells you. Shooting from the hip.

Soft or round. Gamine.

Pig tails. Pony tails. And tall tales.

Biting off more grit than you can chew.

Sky the largest part of everything, I climb the tall tower. The wind: hollowness. The night: a train whistle.

Lives stamped upon lives. Ordered and indexed.

No longer a sure trajectory. We may have arrived at the same destination, but we have taken different journeys. And this is the heart, I mean, art of the matter.

A season to have changed. A crop lost to drought. Destiny foreclosed.

Rounding up the animals for sale. (Keep the kids in the house then.)

Rounding up bids.

The people you see in church. The kids who moved away.

Potluck supper and a bowl for punch. Its pink stickiness goads my thirst.

My tights choking my legs.

Teacher's aide. Restaurant hostess. Deli clerk.

Checkout girl. Fast food worker.

What if any trajectory, from farm to factory?

From hope springs family.

Who shall pay, and who did pay, and who is going to pay?

Though common sense, on closer look, is.

Though my father can fix any machine.

Who shall stand in line, and who apportion?

Who comes really with the bill of goods?

What to have suffered, or is thought of as suffering.

Economies of scale.

That proportion explained it all.

What ordinary actually egregious commonplace outrageous average misunderstood or taken for granted.

Privilege invisible to those who have it.

Corn. Alfalfa. Soybeans and hay.

Oil, gas, electricity, and water.

To slaughter. To market.

I
know
where
meat
comes
from
it
comes
from
the
store

Cream and egg money.

The hook and seed.

Clothes sewn for all.

And Western-style suits.

Book 1: farmer. Book 2: grain elevator employee. Book 3: milking machine salesman.
Book 4: unemployed. Book 5: trip to Las Vegas where you dream of managing a motel. Book 6: grounds keeper.

Book 1: two children, three years apart. Book 1 (revised): a third child, five years later.

Book 1: encourage children to go to college. Book 2: no money to send children to college.

Postscript: never imagine what will happen to children who attend college.

Language wraps round my throat.

I chew each word.

From cradle to grave. Egregious. Misanthropic.

Confused with philanthropic. Or philanderer.

Men strip off coveralls and boots.

On the plains of Dakota or.

As it's nearing dusk.

As I close this page.

Myung Mi Kim ✳

from "The Bounty"

Lilacs to the post foretold

Learning fetch of water

ranges lingering

Funnel thirty

merges temporal wreath

For shelter the pounding sheet rain ponder shir rain roof

Hovers it starts start over field and plain mute forging how compass

Locate a thousand arrows deciphering one degree salted (down)

By granite specked by pink fraction to aim so

Uterus as uphill child's heartbeat repentant am in

Distinct from awash of mother blood rimless to whole

Without specifics, wind broken participle

Pins joints held forth two a nestle axis to tunnel

As axis what revolves three behest insistence

Lilacs to the post foretold

In the first   in three as

Signal and hook   fey   lingual

was all   claim

ocean   seaweed

                              magnet ocean pull cement

                                        the fore the ground wells the water

          smelt smells wells the water

                    water and blood and salt

weight of ten skies falling

                    mother and father to

all done about / lost that / round as bushes

Eleni Sikelianos
on Alice Notley

Mother Mask has twigs in her hair
she is all eye that sometimes closes shut
stars on her eyelids, open are oceans
open are history movies, closed are
blue skies, open are sorrow pain iris clarity events
I forget if closed & open make any difference
—Alice Notley, "Mother Mask," *Homer's Art*

I FIRST MET Alice Notley when I was a student at Naropa, twenty-four years old. The following year I took her workshop, and she read, that summer, from *The Descent of Alette* (1996). In the workshop, she talked about owls and masks and voices, and, as I remember it, I pretty much had no idea what was going on. No fireworks went off. I remember that she read from "Asphodel that Greeny Flower" aloud and began to cry. I was touched and intrigued but didn't know why she was crying. (It took me another year or two to have that response to poetry.[1])

Until then I had been drawn to writers whose technique was transparent enough that I could readily steal things—writers who exhibited either precision and control, like Lorine Niedecker, or a pyrotechnic handling of language, like Louis Zukofsky, or something else, some kind of mysterious carving of language out of the void of history and the blank page, like in Susan Howe's work. As a young poet I was nearly all form and trick and drive; I didn't yet know about content. (I should have noticed the formal innovation of Alice's quotation marks, a new measure for the variable foot; I liked the look of them but wasn't sophisticated enough to know what they meant.)

Bernadette Mayer's and Anne Waldman's work wowed me; Bernadette's bad-girl attitude and Anne's fiery encounters with the world felt immediate.[2] Bernadette's Sonnets had just come out from Lee Ann Brown's newly founded Tender Buttons Press. Those poems knocked my socks off.

I have often said that you have to hit me over the head with a two-by-four for me to realize I'm in love. It's like always wanting to be near someone, making sure you go to the same parties, waiting after class to see them, but not realizing till late in the game that you are falling for that person. My affair with Alice's work was like that. And in a sense my relationship with Alice's work has stayed like that.

I think it was after Naropa, when I was living in San Francisco, that Alice's work crept up on me. I'd gone back to Boulder, heard Alice and her husband, the British poet Douglas Oliver, read; I had bought The Scarlet Cabinet. I wish I could remember the exact scene or moment when the two-by-four hit me over the head. All I remember is that suddenly "Beginning with a Stain" had entered my consciousness and become central.

In this poem, and in others, Alice invented a logic that could leap between things of the world (dream, mind, object, people, emotion) in a way that made intuitive sense to me, that could contradict itself at the level of grammar or punctuation. Some aperture had opened, so that reading her work was like a chiropractic adjustment: the ghost-bones fit. Not everything had to be covered in the poem, and, more important, anything could go in.[3] Bitchiness, dopiness, or (my favorite) sloppiness—all these elements were let onto the page to beautifully disrupt our ideas about what the container of a poem could accommodate.[4] The poem was permeable to everything or anything the poet saw fit to include. My own poems began to slowly open to messy conglomerations and ragged lines.

Just as William James suggested that we should be able to perceive all elements of language, that beyond having a feeling of "blue," we should also be able to apprehend a feeling of "of," I was not being told *what* to feel but was allowed to feel *language*. Gertrude Stein was maneuvering around this in some of her many experiments and was a monumental influence on the fabulous pack of women, born mostly in the '40s, who became important to me and many of my generation.[5] While some mainly picked up on Stein's playful intellect, others, Alice among them, seemed more interested in the lucid and emotional registers Stein captured—how she was able to make language *be* the experience rather than carry it like an exhausted tortoise. Women poets, in an era of poetry that had not yet been extensively marked by the various sounds women might make (as opposed to imitating the poetry sounds men had already made), had access to patterns of anarchic freedom so that their "illogic logic / Made a halo around our syntax and ourselves as we laughed" ("Sonnet," *Selected Poems*).

In Alice's and others' hands, the poem could now register something you might not "understand" but could imagine understanding, not restrictively with the instrument we most commonly associate with knowledge (the brain). The poem could encompass shapes of our most private or original selves, things we understand with perhaps the astral body or brain, like vestigial gill slits that form a ghost syntax hovering around the body.

In San Francisco there was a fantastic series of free workshops at Intersection for the Arts. I took a two- or three-weekend Poets Theatre workshop with Carla Harryman and a weekend workshop with Alice. In Alice's class, we went into "trancelike states" to try to write from an earliest self, a self that was perhaps prelinguistic. (Alice must have been writing the early poems of *Mysteries of Small Houses* then.) We discovered the childlike quality, the freshness that can come about when writing a poem as if you've never written before, when you're working on a poem that discovers itself as it goes. I wanted that freshness in my work, too. In another exercise, we tried to be radios, à la Jack Spicer and early Alice, so that many voices came in and out of the poem.[6]

A transition had begun, if not in how I wrote then in how I thought about writing poetry—a transition I probably wasn't even quite aware of. I think I can say it this way: I had been, to a large extent, in the thrall of silence, of poems as words carefully carved out of space—an enchantment nurtured by my love of Niedecker, Howe, the French (and their obsession with the white page). But, on the other side, or elsewhere, were poems pulled not out of silence but out of noise—often by some generation of the New York School, poets that like Alice, Bernadette, and Anne were reared in the constant and clattering stream of information that is New York City. The noise was not only verbal but also visual, informational, eidetic, hypnogogic, everything. I mean, poems that move toward everything rather than something or one thing.

Blue Guide, the first book in my collection Earliest Worlds (2001) probably displays some awkward marriage between poems more vigilantly hewn out of a hushed space and the occasional influx or burst of clamor. But there are many other things that went into the making of Blue Guide, not least of which is the fact that I had moved back to Paris, and Paris was by then Alice's hometown.

In Paris we began to have frequent dinners in the social circles of expat poets, of which Alice and Doug were a part. We drank wine together in small rooms or in cheap bistros, and often, by the end of the evening, Alice sang shreds of old torch songs, or Doug and my boyfriend Laird agreed to exchange some important and wonderful book. Soon, Alice and I began having lunch every other week or so. We both usually ordered a salade frisée au chèvre chaud and a glass of wine, and we mostly gossiped, but we also talked about poetry or Proust or family.

As in love, I don't always know what I'm learning, most often cannot articulate what it is I'm working out, till much later. There are the things I have learned from a poet's work on the page and the things I have learned from the life of the poet, the choices that poet has made. Alice: a woman who has been willing to live sometimes hand-to-mouth in order to pursue her work; a woman who has removed herself from her cultural and linguistic context and even, to some extent, from her community (although she has found other communities) and family. She has not given in to the American obsession with comfort. And these choices are intrinsic to, reflected in, her work, in a mirror relationship: she writes a book entirely disobedient to contemporary poetic practices, called Disobedience; she makes choices that allow her to write disobediently.

I come from several generations of bohemians, burlesque dancers, jailbirds, and drug addicts, and so for me disobedience is a family trait. It was easy for me to take off with a student loan and money saved from deli jobs to hitchhike through Europe and Africa for eighteen months. It was easy to arrive in Paris with $30 and stay for a year. But in the generation just antecedent to mine, defiant habits took forms of illegality (namely drugs) that made it hard for anyone to get anything done. Perhaps it wasn't so much that Alice reminded me that a person could be disobedient, but that a person could be disobedient *and* productive. Alice's work and life continue to remind me that one can be defiant *in language*, resist received ideas of social and moral and financial and epistemological norms, ideas about the self and the world, and the comfort or place of said self in said world.

I want to say something about the self and the poem, but I am not sure what it is I want to say. It is something about the self in resistance to numbing forces. (Sometimes those forces look like pleasure.) Flaubert spoke of the grinding forces of stupidity like a sea always surrounding us, everrising, ready to drown creativity. But it is also something else. I would like to set down here a history of how we deal with the self in poetry and how our lives lead to the poems we write, but I will settle for a smaller gesture. There is something in Alice's work that keeps me alive to a self that is always coming into and out of being or focus, that creates itself out of its own necessities and interests yet remains, in relation to larger cultural contexts, in this strange common medium that is language.

The several generations before Alice showed us that there are a hundred poses for one poet to strike in a poem. The mask of the "poet's voice" was shattered into a myriad of possible voices. The mask, a recurrent theme in Alice's work, might be perceived as the frozen social "wronglike form" that deprives us of any range of expression, a kind of death mask. Or it might be the betraying political and historical mask ("I wear this mask, but" // "leaks" "skin of the planet" "leaks" "leaks" "white phosphorus"—here, the Vietnam War). It might also be a current state of mind, a place along the path.

But the mask is also everything the poet/speaker can be or say or do, every attitude or feeling or dream she can take on, and it is what helps the poet include "anything" (as a possible set of everything) in the poem. I have long been fascinated and moved by Dante's Aristotelian idea, linked in my mind with Alice's work, that we only know a sliver of ourselves while on earth, whereas in that other world we might know ourselves entirely. Is the mask of the poem a way to gesture our spiritual bodies toward a larger sphere of human and nonhuman knowledge?

The mask is a way to discover the grammar of the poem at hand (changing "masks" from syntactical unit to syntactical unit). And it serves, as in its tribal origins, as a kind of transformational element between states: those "shift[s] of identity to the mythic or other," making a variety of selves, and therefore change, possible. (In Alice's epic poem, *The Descent of Alette* (1996), the heroine, Alette, must take on the features of an owl in order to accomplish her mission of killing a power-hungry tyrant.)

At the same time that they usher in protean possibilities, Alice's masks and poems ask us crucial questions: at how many moments can the poem or the poet or the world or the words be "unmasked"? Can they/we/it ever be unmasked? One of the poet's many jobs is to find nodes between self and language where suddenly language (self?) slips off like a skin, and some other being is present. These gestures are what make the work rise out of itself, into an effervescent dark or light. Whatever slippages occur between self, world, and language, it is in the mess of everything that we find beads of "perfection." The poet is constantly working with words that are "all only one word the perfect / word—" and "Every me I was & wrote / were only & all (gently) / That one perfect word."

NOTES

1. The "Passenger Pigeon" poem in Niedecker's "Lake Superior" brought it on.

2. For whom I was a faculty assistant for Mayer one of those summers.

3. There is herein an implied metonymy, and a connection, in this apposite potential, to the forms the moral, human, and spirit universe takes in Alice's work.

4. See Baraka on this in his essay "How You Sound??"

5. Alice, Anne, Bernadette, Carla Harryman, Lyn Hejinian, Mei-mei Berssenbrugge, Rosmarie Waldrop, Fanny and Susan Howe, to name a few on this long list . . . not all necessarily directly influenced by Stein, but touched in some way by her efforts.

6. I'm thinking here of poems like those in *Songs for the Unborn Second Baby* and *Alice Ordered Me to Be Made* where there is a gathering of surrounding speech.

Eleni Sikelianos ✳

from "The California Poem"

It's o.k. here but we don't have any sourgrass
not so many happy lizards in the sun
seaweed sliding back toward licking the sea
sandflies, sandfleas
jogging men nasty naked along the beach & Joakim's oily eucalyptus
    combusting up toward heaven

I was swimming in the black water underneath my breath & then
dragged by the seaweed vines and belts

the water is yellow with sand and ecology, my friends

are being punished by off-duty fathers in tract houses they are not
    allowed to leave after dark

My family is wily, we live in derelict apartments, are government
subsidized, go
everywhere
at night
on shore

Oil rigs out in the water like lighted bird-palace places

In the dream of dying cephalopods

Cuttlefish feathers & things
invented by sound & light like
the Great Spangled Fritillary monarch, and magnitude
of scales, what lies in inner and outer margins of such
wings "that came with soft
alarm, like hurtless light," and the numberous thunder
of veins

Bluebellies in strange arrangement break their tails
in weedy nooses to grow back new ones
Backs bend in the rows between crop-dusted plants, the little singing
    seeds sting the
fingers & stain them: red, red

Eagle shells crumbling under the eagle's weight croaking at Cachuma Lake

California did not hold its shape
when [the condors] were laid end-to-end
to form a replica of California
with photographs & balsa wood & glue
which was later
beamed to space
(from Big Sur). The message is in regards to
the gardens of the sea: graphed
in the scallop's eyes (bright), amid its tentacular
fringe: writ

in the fossil guts of hermaphroditic oysters hanging
out in kitchen middens, a theatre

acted out on land-
masses between bivalves (motory "self-powered
castanets" fluttering
in zig-
zagging arcs) and hungry
bipeds. This heroic

fantasy is set
in an ominous landscape, a dark world that mirrors our watery arms
and legs but not our muscular
hearts

                                Have I been shaped like
                                  an animal, god, or
                                  have I been good?

Everything I know
occurred in California and everything
I know later, everything I know of California
is shaped like a piece of cardboard
and smells like the black plastic pitch that stretches between Bakersfield
    & apricots

blue & green & the penny arcade, my dream is just like that:
a thousand miles
long & deep into the otter ice water cliffs

almonds Fresno when I was nearly blond & knees straight
as an arrow & my name
was Dylan-in-the-grass-blue-grass, when my home-
stead read: Mary-of-the-villas
of-the-vocables-of-conches Jalama ice plants and Spanish
mosses
        At its Eastern Boundaries of the Ear
        Without answer key or blue fig California

at its goldenest gold, brimfullest bright
of citron, sun, when the blazing pollen falls all, all California blooms
pornographic, hysterical flowers loyal
daughters of the revolution horses whinnying
up State Street stamp the independence of California into the tarmac
    Chumash
dancers with fancy feet but
no state.

In *One-eyed Jacks* Marlon Brando and Karl Malden will escape
on steaming ponies, and the beautiful Mexican girl, and roar
into that sleepy village just north of Salinas with its beautiful low
    Chinese dwarf
cypress in a shady glen & the village is
of Chinese hoteliers, fisher people with grey eyes railroad coolies who
    bent their

backs & did not break in filmy
VistaVision.

Salinas rises from its
valley like a huge dusty mutt mottled
with lettuce and chemicals not of trash in the state's hallways I want to
     make you dream this
just as you
made me dream you in a beginning
of bundles and other beginnings
slash
endings.

"Get up you scum-suckin' pig," growls Brando and plays
a wild card.

Alice Notley ✳

from "Beginning with a Stain"

In the very beginning was it very dark? I think
that it was bluer than it was dark—from an old dream—
I was in space happy flying with another, who was it? a man
That's the first thing I remember from before I was born
I remember that; it is my truest dream

But one time I dreamed I was like a bird, flying
not like a person flying in a dream, & that was a true
dream too, so it is true, a bird flying over gold-spotted
brick-red canyons of the West, in the afternoon—
But I was flying alone so that was much later

So first, or before, when there was no first, never was, I was
flying with someone, then later, was alone. So this is my story:

The creation of the world comes after the real world, but
this is the real world too. In the old real world we were happy
we were together, we didn't have to walk on the ground or
make things; then the separation into canyons & sky came, how, who

made that? I will walk on the earth & call out your name
I will tell it as I do it, & the words will be the same, say, as
mountains: and when I find you, we'll talk about ourselves
incessantly: the words will be as much as all else.

Tracy K. Smith
on Lucie Brock-Broido

BY AUTUMN OF 1992, when I registered for her introductory workshop, "The Practice of Poetry," Lucie Brock-Broido had been Briggs-Copeland Lecturer in Poetry at Harvard long enough to have developed quite a following. From the dining halls and libraries to cafés and literature classes, students espoused views on poetry that included statements like "this poem strikes to the Terrible Crystals" and "there's a very strong sense of the Marvel in this poem." The *Advocate* was publishing poems with a kind of linguistic sheen equivalent to brocade, along with lots and lots of sonnets. I was so new to poetry that it made little real sense to me, but my interest in this particular enclave—this invisible space in which Lucie's name ricocheted like a bird in an atrium—had been piqued. It was her last year at Harvard, and I was eager to be, if not part of her following, then at least aware of from whence it sprung. When I finally met her, the world began to make a different kind of sense.

Notes toward a composite sketch of L—

If certain rooms smell of hyacinth
She has just been
Or will be
There. Like rain,
Arriving first in the mind.

Eyes a particular green you will be
Tempted to believe. (You will.)

Mane a girlish, foalish
Shawl. You'll want
To lace your fingers in, drag
Them slowly through it.
But—Must—Not.

The afternoon of our first class, we met in the creative writing department, then located on the third floor of a wooden house on Prescott Street. I wish I could remember the name or the color of the building or the exact route I took to get there. I realize these details, these moments in time, are farther from me than I'd thought or than I wish. Yet at the same time this memory is a kind of constant I return to as a way of reminding myself that the decision to write is not about precise awareness but rather magic.

We sat around a long mahogany table, legs and bracings sturdy enough for a banquet of Goths, as if it were a given that our poetry would be weighty. Lucie was nearby, but not there. I can say this in retrospect because the room, the whole house, smelled faintly floral. It was as though, if we'd peered outside, we'd have found newly blossomed bulbs pushing up from fresh earth. It was a scent I responded to as though it would soon dissipate—breathing a bit more deeply, consciously, holding the fragrant air in. Only it was autumn. The colored leaves caught the light and cast it in mulberry and gold on its way through the windows. That whole semester, right into the irrefutable onset of winter, through rain and snow and the donning of boots, it was spring.

Memory is tricky. What do I remember about that first day? What is true about what I've said thus far? Lucie arrived. And maybe I was surprised. Or maybe I played it cool, imagining everyone else was already used to the velvet vest, the Renaissance blouse, the hair that flowed over the top and down the back of the chair or hugged her form. Or perhaps she was always there. Perhaps I walked in and took one of the few remaining seats, while everyone spoke in quiet voices, saying the things people say when they are about to begin something together for the first time. It is very likely that I was too shy to offer much and that I sat still, heart agallop, in my seat. It is very likely that I sat one or two seats away from where she sat, on the side closest to the door, and that I drew my legs up beneath me and waited. But for the sake of getting started, let's say the first class began like this:

Lucie took her seat at the head of the table and began to speak, her voice papery, low, her enunciation precise, as if Many of Her Words began with Majuscules. One of the first things she shared was a sheet of paper containing dozens of one-line definitions of a poem. Some were familiar:

> A Poem is an emotional machine made of words.—Philip Larkin
> Poetry is the best words in the best order.—Samuel Taylor Coleridge

Others were completely new to me:

> A poem is always married to someone.—Rene Clair
> All are very naughty, & I am naughtiest of all.—Emily Dickinson

Many were cryptic and from unknown sources:

> A poem is an Egg with Horses in it.
> A poem is smaller than itself.

Several were attributed to her former students, whom she quoted in a way that instantly mythologized them:

> A breeze of dreams, then certain death—Ellis
> A good line is a soul kiss with the universe. Don't ask what a great line is.
> —Stepek

I was sold. I believed in the power of words to enchant—I was, after all, at that very moment, feeling their charm at work on me. And I wanted to do what it took to sound like that, and, more important, to make myself think and feel like that all the time. Like the speaker in Sharon Olds's "First Sex," *I signed on for the duration.*

The duration of that workshop wrought change upon my classmates and me. Even as a twenty-year-old with little awareness of what I wanted to say or had to say, I was determined to push and hone and whittle and trim my own ideas and feelings into lines that could place me in intimate, if fleeting, circumstances with the Universe, whatever and wherever that was.

Eager for material to share, and eager to see Lucie's wiry handwriting in purple ink along the margins of my work (and, if I was lucky, for the Victorian stickers of kittens and cherubim that sometimes accompanied her comments), I stayed in and up during what felt like long nights while my dorm-mates were out gathering lived experience with one another and with boys. I scoured my own life, to the extent that I was aware of what comprised it, for material. I scoured my family and memory and built poems with what I found. I now know that, for the most part, I was too young to really understand what I had to say and too young to understand with any real clarity what many of Lucie's larger insights meant. But I held onto them.

Five years later, after Harvard workshops with Seamus Heaney and Henri Cole, I found myself in Lucie's classroom again, this time in the graduate writing division at Columbia. Much was the same. I recognized her instantly and felt the kind of hopeful assurance a child feels when the familiar adult appears, smiling, at the end of a long and bewildering day. But much had changed. My classmates, fifteen of them, were strangers to one another. Like me, many were strangers to New York. We were to read poems "by way," as Lucie had specified beforehand, "of introduction." There was pressure to measure up, and to prove, as subtly as possible, our seriousness and ability as poets. As I listened to all the unfamiliar voices naming themselves and giving shape to fifteen different private realities, I quaked. I realized that, for all the time and all the poems under my belt, I was still unaware of what exactly I possessed to say. The only surety for me was that this was a vocation I was committed to, for better or worse.

I'd spent the previous year in California with my family, saying good-bye to my mother, who was going through the end stages of terminal illness. I hadn't written much during that year—hadn't *finished* much. But in the long nights when I'd lie awake, imagining the workings of a world so vast it seemed to exist outside of human logic, I knew that poems—the words and sparks of meaning that poems were able to create against one another—were the only things I could rely on or believe in. I'd botched job interviews and sent off countless shoddy resumés. But I'd put my Columbia application together with a devotion that, I'm sure, derived in part from the prospect of picking up where I'd left off in Lucie's workshop not long ago in Cambridge. Sitting there that day, in the classroom where our workshops would be held for the next two years, I felt the movements of the same spirit that had stirred in and around me during my first workshop years ago. And I breathed in the same hyacinth air, feeling certain of something that seemed to exist within and yet outside of words.

Of the familiar material that reached me during that second workshop with Lucie, much of it reached me differently the second time around. I heard different things within some of the same things. Like Lucie's favorite admonitions: *Don't be afraid to tell the truth, even if it's a lie,* and *a poem should be all muscle and sinew; an arm pointing* (and here she'd raise her own lithe limb out to the right or left, triceps taut): *That-a-way.* At times I even understood (although the pang was still present) what she meant when she would say, as she often did when confronted by our sprawling poems, that the *real poem* was four (or three or two) lines long. While my own urge was to find ways of saying more and more, and of pushing against limitations within my own work, she was fond of telling me things like this: *You've mixed all the ingredients together, but now you must roll them out and cut them into pleasing, symmetrical shapes. Like sugar cookies.* She was gentle, yet rigorous. It would be years before I was able to take her up on her advice, but her commitment to equal parts alchemy and craft helped me to make poems, and sense, out of the grief I was still trying to process.

She invited us to parties thrown in her New York apartment, where we danced on Persian rugs, cajoled her cats, and marveled at the gargoyles guarding her shelves lined with slim books of poetry. We bumped into her on Broadway, where she'd greet us quickly, shyly, in grey sweat pants, her long braid bobbing behind as she ran to the gym. We'd speculate about her love life, the rumored Ouija board sessions with students from the years before us, her encounters in the world outside Morningside Heights. We all loved her. And in the way an adolescent loves a beautiful older sibling, our love was part gratitude, part envy. We knew the story of Lucie's luck— that Helen Vendler had been so impressed by her first manuscript she championed it and provided Lucie with a kind of lasting, door-opening, expiration-less benediction. Our devotion was based, perhaps unconsciously, on the belief that our nearness to her would lend itself to likeness—that our luck would one day, by proximity, resemble hers. I wonder if envy isn't always vaguely present in the relationship between student and mentor, perhaps as a persistent urge to catch up, even if the distance that must be covered is vast.

I'm not sure that, at the time, I'd have ever thought to use the word "mentor" to describe Lucie. I'm not sure any of us would have. Surely she was older, better read, and more accomplished than we were; but she felt far too accessible to embody a role so formal. Sometimes that nearness must have been a disadvantage. Because she was youthful—ageless—it was sometimes tempting to forget that she had paid her dues, worked to attain a certain professional standing. I think we felt so close to her from day to day that it was always a surprise when something would remind us that she was a mature poet while we were barely apprentices. The remarkable thing about Lucie was that she never seemed concerned with safety. She never seemed worried about how we would perceive her or whether, as a young woman, she would be able to command the respect of her students. She never tried to posture, protect her reputation, or demand our devotion by keeping us at arm's length. She felt unafraid of the consequences of being herself.

And it worked. We respected her because she was honest, unguarded, even vulnerable. We were grateful for the degree to which she trusted us with her beliefs and her enthusiasm and her self. And I do believe that all of the grandeur of her persona was her real self. How could she have afforded to be so generous within that self were it not real? How could we have trusted her for so long, and learned to trust ourselves by way of her, were she not genuine even down to her Elizabethan flounce? Now I know that all of it was nothing if not mentorship—some of the most important I've received to date—and that Lucie's example of freedom and generosity and joy have served to enrich my own career as a poet and teacher in ways so natural, so seemingly inevitable, I sometimes forget I wasn't born this way.

Our coming of age at Columbia involved the submission of a portfolio of thirty-five pages of our best poems. Lucie's class on "Pageantry, the Art and Architecture of First Books," was designed to make the production of our portfolios meaningful. We read first books by twelve or fourteen poets, analyzed them, took them apart. We unraveled the logic shaping each book's poetic arc and developed (and borrowed) ideas relating to our own work. My own manuscript was called, regrettably, *Driving the Living*, and it included many of the poems worked and reworked over the two years of feedback. Many other poems were new, dashed of in the last months before commencement, as if finishing the program and receiving my MFA on time would somehow render me more ready to embark on life as a poet. Some of my classmates had been working more diligently and with more awareness of why they were writing. Some wisely took an extra semester or year to produce and revise.

Weeks later, I received evaluations of my work. One reader, a respected poet and critic (and, as it happens, a man), demolished my poems, leveling my project as a whole with comments like "these poems fall prey to the snare of infantile narcissism." Lucie's measured praise and thoughtful reflections felt like a firm hand at the center of my back, assuring me of its comforting presence while pushing gently forward. Both readers were right, but while one succeeded in silencing me for months, Lucie managed to dangle the promise of meaning and music just near enough and just far enough away to make me want—no, *need*—to keep striving for it. In the years since, I've returned to the echo of her voice and learned again and again from what I can almost still hear her saying, beckoning.

It's a voice that, thankfully, doesn't go away, and one I've listened to from the various perspectives in which I've found myself since Columbia. Objectively speaking, Lucie knew how to make her students feel important. I've had other teachers, each important in their own ways, who did not know this—teachers whose poetry was generous, innovative, and brave but who did not have (or make) the time to get to know their students as individuals. And how can any of us affect our students if we don't really know them and if we aren't willing to let them know us?

Tracy K. Smith ✳

Theft

In 1963 John Dall, a Ho-Chunk Indian, was taken from his mother's home as part of a federal project to reduce poverty in Native American communities. He moved from foster home to foster home, haunted by recurring dreams and unsure of his own history. Years later, he was located by members of his tribe.

The word Ho-Chunk means "people of the big voice."—*The Chicago Reader*

The world shatters
Through Mother's black hair.
I breathe smoke,
Tincture of sudden berries.
Mother covers my eyes,
But this heat is inside.
It trickles out, a map
Of hot tears across my face.
And rivers, my own rivers,
Pushing out from the desert
Between my legs.

Frantic birds lift off
And their flight takes me.
I float above dark thickets,
Thick air. Above voices
That rush and rise. A mad cloak.
Sirens in my mother's mouth.
Sirens in the far corners
Of the flat black globe.
I wake again and again,
Ears ringing, eyes dry.

★   ★   ★

One night when our bellies groan,
I quiet myself watching bare branches
Scratch against the moon. If night
Has a voice, it is surely this wind
In these trees. Is surely Mother's
Heavy shoes climbing the steps,
Trampling leaves. I am the only one
Who knows what that voice means
To say. It is trying to tell us
To hurry. But it does not say
For what.

                One brother twirls
A pencil over a notebook. Answers
He's erased hover like stalled ghosts.
He shakes his head. All wrong.
Another laughs at the tv. We are many,
Each in his own Now. I have never
Thought to cross from mine to theirs,
But I've held my hand inches
From my brother's back and felt
His heat.

              A knock at the door,
The walls cough. Again.
And mother doesn't ignore it.
I feel what the moon must feel
For the branches night after night.
This can't go on. Come in.
Then I watch our house come undone
And Mother get smaller,
And the road ahead like a serpent
Racing into pitch.

                In the station,
We get blankets and a civics lesson.
We get split up. All night
The drunks and devils
Sing, rattle.

     ★   ★   ★

I live:
        In the house behind the chain link fence
        With smoke stenciling the sky above the roof
        In a room with three boys
        And a window that wheezes winter

I wear my hair shorn

The mother here leans
Against the kitchen counter
Scrubbing forks and bowls
Staring into steam
If you interrupt her
She'll surprise you with an elbow
The back of her hand
Her fist squeaks in yellow gloves

        I live in Chicago
        In America

We have rules:
        Don't flush
        Unless necessary
        And only four squares
        Of tissue a day—
        Two in the morning
        Two at night or
        All at once
        But just four
        And someone
        Is counting

        When you brush
        Turn the water on once
        Then off
        Then on again
        Say Sir and Ma'am

But only when necessary
Otherwise don't talk
And don't stare
What are you stupid
And what kind of Indian
Are you What kind
If you don't know
You must not be

This is my eighth home
I am seven

      ★   ★   ★

When I skip school, I get on the El
And scour the city from inside,
From above. I listen to

The iron percussion, track
Soldered to track. A story
That turns and returns,

Refuses to end. I ride it,
Write it down: I'm my seat
In the first car. A hologram

In the window, in the battered doors.
A stick figure in the chrome poles.
I reach for myself. Grab me by the neck.

What do I hear? Time.
What does it say? I can't tell.
What does it sound like? It sounds

Angry. Why angry? Because we keep it
Waiting. When it's not waiting,
It is always begging us to go.

I get off the train. Walk backwards
Over bridges. Watch perspective
Diminish. Watch my breath,

My ideas hover and drift
In perfect clouds. They'll
Drop eventually, mingle

With a river or lake. Might
Even one day make it back to me.
As rain, maybe, or a tall glass

I drink quickly, blind
With thirst. I shout my name
Into the traffic, and if my voice

Is big enough, someone will hear it.
It will land where it needs to land,
And someone will catch it

And come looking.

Lucie Brock-Broido ✳

Birdie Africa

WOLF

My father calls me Wolf.
He says that I will see things other people will not see
at night. When he holds me, heat comes out
of his big arms & I belong to him.
In the cold of Christmastime he rocks
me in his deep lap in the great shadow of a comforter.
We are wool on wool,
back & forth, singing these songs
whose words I can't even say out loud.
I think they're about God who keeps us in his paws.
My mother watches, standing at my window, arms
folded to her chest. One fingerbone
of moonlight reaches in, tapping on the lock
of her face, restless, not like a mother wolf
but lit like she is going
somewhere else.
But when I wind my arms around
him, put my face into the dimmed scoop
of his neck, he smells like good warm fire
like dark sweet dreams.

THE ROOF

I sleep on the roof now.
She has taken me away from him.
I sleep thinking of his face tucked
next to mine like a big black bear.
There are other children now.
We run like wild
animals. We let our hair go
into puzzles which will never be unraveled.

We let our teeth go fierce.
We leave dirt in our palms
& sleep without nightclothes.
We pee in the yards & eat raw things.
In the dark we watch the traffic lights blinking
from our sleep in the cold night air.
Sometimes I talk to the stars
& the stars keep the traffic
in the sky from bottling up.
Each person gives off a little
torch when they sleep
& mine's the softest one.

BIRDIE

I am Birdie now I don't know why.
I squat at the edge of the top
of our rowhouse & I'm without wings I think.
Philadelphia isn't gentle now. Bad things echo up
& down our neighborhood at night.
I think we wound the people of our street.
I am hurting myself.
I can't tell time you know.

ALL THE AFRICAS

All the Africas live here
like a family of fire.
My mother always wears the bone of moon
across her face. I peer at her
like through a keyhole & I don't know why.
She never touches me.
The grownups eat cooked things
& we go foraging,
carving our designs in trees
& benches in the park & cedar picnic tables
left out in the trash, we never leave our names

& we can't read.
I am the clean seed
of a new race springing
from the dark continent of America.
God keeps me pure & savage here
before Moses
before the gift
before TV and toothbrushes
before the alphabet.

THE LAST AFRICA

The man with the megaphone warns Vincent Leaphart
to get out. He stays on, we stay here with him.
From up top of the bunker, the city
is our karroo dotted with colors of light.
In the dark, we are swept
down to the belly of our house.
They turn water on us
like a devil. We stay on.
We are flooding, there is no light left.
Then the fires & we huddle in the basement
under wet green blankets. Everything smells bad.
My mother stops twisting & I don't know why.
Everybody wailing. I am Birdie & I don't know how.
Then a quiet like I've never heard before.
Ramona Africa pulls me outside to the alley
& I burn there with her, naked on the stones
in the sweet jungle of the city.
When I come home my father will be singing
like an old kind dream. I have seen things
at night that other people have not seen.

Elizabeth Treadwell
on *Paula Gunn Allen*

... they took themselves with themselves on that entire, long, that centuries-
long journey.
—Paula Gunn Allen

ONE AFTERNOON EARLY in the fall of 1987 I sat in a class in which were
enrolled (a) my dearest girlfriend and (b) a guy with whom I had a fairly
sulky connection. English Literary History. This was at Reed College, in
the dank, pretty city of Portland, Oregon. The syllabus was under fire from
a very few trembly quarters and under the protection of naughty others. At
issue was the history, presented by said syllabus, of creative writing in English in which the representative authors included precisely one woman
and one person of color, both embodied by Toni Morrison, whose work
was scheduled for study in the wispy hurry-up time of May. The professor's defense? Not his fault, that's history.

It is very painful to be taught that persons of your type have had no agency in vast expanses of history. It is very boring to hear your boyfriend revel in a version of history that glorifies his type. This kind of lordly sepulcher, estate-sale scholarship did not sit well with me. So although I didn't speak up in that class, I did leave that school.[1]

I had arrived at Reed on the whackadelic charms of the high school dream of the small liberal arts college, rampant amongst folk of a certain ilk in my hometown of Berkeley, California. Once there I received care packages of candy and small bills from my Grammy in Tucson and lots of emotional and financial support from my Mom. Although I mightn't have admitted it then, the school was beyond our means both financially and emotionally. Nor did I then have much notion of how my experience resonated in and grew from their dreams and hard-won ships and beauties. In any case, my high school had been big, diverse, and chaotic. As it turned out, I needed more out of a college than leaves and bricks. The University of California at Berkeley would fill the bill, even if it was not nearly as diverse as Berkeley High.

So I was back in my hometown, eventually, in the fall of 1989, a junior at Cal with a $300-a-month hardwood one bedroom on Oxford, appointed with built-ins and liberties. Out I would go in my thrifty dresses and frail jeans on my blue bike, about town.

It was life changing to cross paths with Paula Gunn Allen at Berkeley, and extremely fortunate, as we were both there so briefly. It's a bit daunting to express the effect she had on me: she made me feel intellectually at ease, comfortable, right with the world; she made me feel that intellectual venturing can be purposeful, even inspired, not always cracked, fake, and oppressive. In other words, here was teaching that made sense on this continent, in my context. Gunn Allen is extremely present as a teacher, poet, and scholar: she brings everything to bear. She lets everything be. She made me feel there's a sacred continuum between the talk of grandmothers, the play of children, and the concerns of the academy. Or, she showed me there could be. And this is the only way any transmission of knowledge or culture makes good sense to me.

When I mention grandmothers, I'm talking about my own, her own, your own. And I'm talking about scholars like Dale Spender and Janet Todd, whose research disinterred works of English literary history by women and led me so happily later on to, say, a newly minted paperback copy of Eliza Haywood's fabulous 1751 novel *The History of Miss Betsy Thoughtless*. Gunn

Allen's work is, among other things, part of a new wave of feminist scholarship that hit not a minute too soon as far as I was concerned.

Once while at Cal I complained (to my sister Carol probably) of a writing workshop, "they race-class-and-gendered my story!" By which I meant that the students who spoke reduced my writing to less than the sum of the categories into which they had placed me on sight. And indeed there was a lot of simplistic analysis going on. But such half-thought-through or even spiteful gestures were simply the laziest, cheapest, dumbest outcropping of a profound and necessary change that was occurring—a long and tidal change, expressed partly as the very existence of the ethnic studies programs at Cal that allowed me to focus on Native American history and literature in the Native American studies department rather than on mainstream and otherwise canonical literature in the English department. Gunn Allen's work as a scholar and teacher has been profoundly valuable to me. For it validates, complicates, and extends ways of thought and story and living and dreaming that make my brain and heart and senses feel recognized and, by such recognition, propelled.

It was very important to me to understand the line of progression I knew the (current) tail end of as my Mom and Grammy. My maternal relatives are most recently from Oklahoma, "Indian Territory," the red earth, the wild west. It is amazing, really, that after centuries of no such luck, I found my way (partially) via this big school.

I had a friend, Karen, in the Native American studies program. We would cut class on $2 Tuesdays and go see movie matinees (thus exposing ourselves to, for example, the pop imperialism of the absurd early Tom Hanks/Meg Ryan vehicle *Joe vs. The Volcano*). Neither Karen nor I were recognized in the department as being Native and this was part of our bond. We learned about the "relocation" program of the federal government in the 1950s and '60s whereby folks were enticed/compelled to leave the reservations in search of a better destiny on, say, the blank, weary streets of Los Angeles and, once there, sweet talked/coerced into giving their babies up for adoption. Later, Karen did the research (she knew she was adopted) and found out that she was one of those kids. My story is both less and more clearly demarcated: very briefly, my ancestors are Cherokee, English, Irish, and unknown. As another professor at Berkeley, Sarah Parker, once said to me, we Cherokees always get teased. Indeed there is a sort of cocktail party joke about everyone's Cherokee grandmother. But the Cherokee has been a large and varied nation for a long time, so it makes sense that its diaspora is also large and varied. There is the joke and then there is my Grammy, real live flesh and blood, a mixed-race person born in Shawnee, Oklahoma, in 1922, who nurtured me from my birth to her death, a person with a complicated life and dear self, a person I am still comforted by and learning from. Dare I say also that when my Mom attended graduation I think I got a bit more credibility. (She's darker than I am.) We are all trapped in history and by historical devices; besides, my classmates and I were all at a very prickly age.

Now that I am a mother, I am less willing than ever to have the Cherokee stamped out of me by anyone, on any side. And lucky to be living at a time in history when I can say so.

The fact that Paula Gunn Allen felt so familiar to me was part and parcel of the intellectual excitement I found under her tutelage. From the start, my sister Carol and I said to each other that she reminded us of Grammy—in her snappy attentiveness, for one thing, and the patterns of her voice. Of course she's much closer in age to our Mom and very much like Mom in her story, which might be writ as one of coming from an "unlikely" spot to go on to get advanced degrees besides also being a working mother.

Gunn Allen was born in Albuquerque, New Mexico, in 1939; raised in Cubero, New Mexico, a Spanish land-grant village adjacent to Laguna Pueblo; and is of Laguna-Sioux-Lebanese-Scottish-American descent. She received her doctorate in American studies from the University of New Mexico and retired as a professor of English at UCLA. She has been highly valued, I am quite sure, by many students. In addition to teaching, she has written and edited many important books, including *Pocahontas: Medicine Woman, Spy, Entrepreneur, Diplomat* (2003), which the *New York Sun* calls "nothing less than a watershed event in the historiography of the Americas, not to mention one of the wittiest and wisest biographies I have ever read."[2] Gunn Allen is also a mother and grandmother, and I had coffee with her a few years ago on the alarmingly suburbanized Fourth Street in Berkeley, showing off photos of my niece, hearing of her latest projects, and soaking up her singular advice. I invited her to read at Small Press Traffic, which she did some months later, including a transliteration of Rumi and speaking also of Native reactions to 9/11.

In the spring of 1990, I took her seminar on Native American women's literature and read, among others, her book *Spider Woman's Granddaughters:*

Traditional Tales and Contemporary Writing by Native American Women (winner of an American Book Award that year). We studied works in which English literary history and the histories of the indigenous literatures of this continent began to become part of each other. We learned of writers such as Zitkala-Ša, a.k.a. Gertrude Bonnin, a mixed-race Sioux who began editing *American Indian Magazine* in 1916, and Mourning Dove, a.k.a. Christine Quintasket Humishuma, an Okanogan and author of the 1927 novel *Cogewea, the Half-Blood*, which Gunn Allen cites as a turning point in this new mixed literature. After *Cogewea*, writes Gunn Allen in *The Sacred Hoop: Recovering the Feminine in American Indian Traditions* (1986), "acquiescence to Western publishing tastes is offset by a counterdevice [wherein] the protagonists are also participants in a ritual tradition, symbolizing the essential unity of a human being's psyche in spite of conflict."

Carol and I both took Gunn Allen's creative writing workshop through the Native American studies department. Class was held at my nearby apartment, since neither students nor teacher were too keen on our close, shinydusty assigned room in Dwinelle Hall. So once a week we met in my oddly chair-impaired digs. She assigned collaborations and random operations to push us beyond self-imposed limits. I was so encouraged by the short line "it works" in her neat penciled hand on one of my poems. This is a sentence I doodled in *The Sacred Hoop*: "Traditional tribal narratives possess a circular structure, incorporating event within event, piling meaning upon meaning, until the accretion finally results in a story."

Many of Gunn Allen's bon mots have found special spots in my brain. For example, "gossip is literature." (The continuum again.) She noted and demonstrated the idea that the spirit is, of course, strong enough to come through even in the ugliest situations. (I do not mean to make this sound simple or easy. I think it has taken me years to take in the despair present in her novel *The Woman Who Owned the Shadows*.) She once mentioned that lost feathers, wherever they're found, are like bird thoughts, little notes from the birds. And, there they are—camping, hiking, citytrudging—on the dirtyclean sidewalks near my current job in San Francisco, on the blank, weary streets of L.A. Such living metaphors or poetic mechanics of understanding this metaphysical reality come to those who are open to them—writing and reading are only two methods of connecting with the spirit world of this continent. It seems to me that much contemporary Native writing and art affirms the hope and truth that spirit and traditions continue, morph, and thrive.

The final meeting of the creative writing class was to be held on campus. Earlier that day, at Moe's Bookstore on Telegraph, I bought Paula my two favorite Fay Weldon books, *Puffball* and *Praxis*, feeling the sturdy, ugly, funny takes on spirituality and feminism in these new English novels would speak to her, too.

After class, she asked Carol and me to stay and then told us to take ourselves seriously, to really commit ourselves to being writers. This was very important and encouraging, and we have.

NOTES

1. To be fair to Reed, it was there, in Christopher Zinn's Studies in American Modernism class, that I was first introduced to my dear Gertrude Stein.

2. Now, in December 2006 as I edit this essay for publication, I am in the midst of using *Pocahontas* as a primary source in composing what I imagine will be a book-length poem titled *Virginia or the Mud-flap Girl*.

Elizabeth Treadwell ✳

distomap for the coded mountains, pale frontier, or the devotions

for my sisters, Margaret & Carol

This faith was expressed using symbols of shaped metal, embroidered cloth,
carved wood, and painted canvas.
—curator, San Xavier Mission, Tucson, Arizona, U.S.A.

in a well-sought dream remember think of something plain like
Grammy's tears; think of something plain like the color and curvature of
gingerale nightgown & bend & kink of patio, how the 3rd vowel of her
name was scratched in.

think of some plain dream of something like how the buildings of a
particular high school became part of your body—its grubby lockers,
the glass of its metal panes, the terrors of gum on things, or, if in
Arizona, its trellised breezeways &

saint-abrasive walls

that one boy's back of head withdrawal crinkly toward your new sugar
paws, the inept hairstyle of a still-favorite teacher (chem lab particular:
insulting miracles, too; with atoms slamming you into that seat all
worn out—

why am I a girl

(I'veneverbeenthisfuckedup). in a well sought dream remember pop
song proclamations, Nicole's big shoes and how she tipped them,
flirty, Clementine, third grade flat rug, your leotard itch—committing
with mastodon eyes the masturbations of Marilyn Monroe—or, mass-
produce doodles of perfect ballerinas

the decoration of the senses
the pornographic mailbox
widow to the investigation

go home & eat bowls of cereal. the kitchen circa 1903 w/new cabinets

committing with resolute arms
the acts of Cleopatra

lies & other orthographies: my *.

The water's edge so overgrown with grapes that the surging waves flowed over them—
—Captain Amadas

The generations changed too quickly & the children began to turn out all weird & bitter.

well sought remember were days and nights of highway the trucker STOP
the LOGOS merging with your SIGHT & fear & thrill the Marlboro
Menthols with green packaging the digital tune the particular cap the
safety the way the truckers stopped and slept the road became quite thin
and empty the final Tulsa sunrise sleep in a hospital lot and next, the
youngest her warmest warmest coats how she looked up

then also a blue mountain the way its sweatshirt ponytails paraded about
the smooth bent of Honda the Honda was our age nearly the sweatshirt
was the color of skin or sky or blue mountain so named the photo was full
of light our sunglasses formed the darkest spots there were birds there and
certain trees, Mom *text itself beats winged* you tried out—"boiled peanuts &
the southern-accented Cherokee waitress"—learning to see past the Bible
and Vegas and how it was ALL OK talking past canyons and rivers and
shops in the middle of blind flat states called Uncle Junk and how you
didn't stop there but stopped there and there was a well-earned you felt dip
in a mastodon chlorine—that means you laid down some cash for the
Holiday Inn in Rapid City—and in OK City you shared a parking lot teem-
ing with participants in the Red Earth Festival it was July and the guy at
the counter gave you a discount thus porch strung about doors stung with
conversation you merely listening and near Graceland a nice old German-
descended lady said, here take some cookies, GIRLS
cable and frybread and what Grammy remembered and was willing to *give
up* or with which to *gamble*

> * *Pocahontas*, your false house & impossible letter,
> crown, marriage, shields, swearing, bending, robe,
> my play on play on play, Rebecca, ornamental
> *bearing*—

Paula Gunn Allen ✳

Pocahontas to Her English Husband, John Rolfe

In a way, then, Pocahontas was a kind of traitor to her people. . . . Perhaps
I am being a little too hard on her. The crucial point, it seems to me, is to
remember that Pocahontas was a hostage. Would she have converted freely
to Christianity if she had not been in captivity? There is no easy answer to this
question other than to note that once she was free to do what she wanted,
she avoided her own people like the plague. . . .

Pocahontas was a white dream—a dream of cultural superiority.
—Charles Larson, *American Indian Fiction*

Had I not cradled you in my arms,
oh beloved perfidious one,
you would have died.
And how many times did I pluck you
from certain death in the wilderness—
my world through which you stumbled
as though blind?
Had I not set you tasks,
your masters far across the sea
would have abandoned you—
did abandon you, as many times
they left you
to reap the harvest of their lies.
Still you survived, oh my fair husband,
and brought them gold
wrung from a harvest I taught you
to plant. Tobacco.
It is not without irony that by this crop
your descendants die, for other
powers than you know
take part in this as in all things.
And indeed I did rescue you—
not once but a thousand thousand times

and in my arms you slept, a foolish child,
and under my protecting gaze you played,
chattering nonsense about a God
you had not wit to name. I'm sure
you wondered at my silence, saying I was
a simple wanton, a savage maid,
dusky daughter of heathen sires
who cartwheeled naked through the muddy towns
learning the ways of grace only
by your firm guidance, through
your husbandly rule:
no doubt, no doubt.
I spoke little, you said.
And you listened less,
but played with your gaudy dreams
and sent ponderous missives to the throne
striving thereby to curry favor
with your king.
I saw you well. I
understood your ploys and still
protected you, going so far as to die
in your keeping—a wasting,
putrefying Christian death—and you,
deceiver, whiteman, father of my son,
survived, reaping wealth greater
than any you had ever dreamed
from what I taught you and
from the wasting of my bones.

Crystal Williams
on Lucille Clifton

I HAD HEARD tell that, like her poems, Lucille Clifton is warm, generous, deceptively easygoing. But in all the years I'd been around poetry and its myriad groupings of folk, I hadn't met her, so I was forced to rely on rumors, innuendo, and the knowing nods of the lucky ones. Meanwhile, understand: I'm not often rendered goofy when faced with well-known or respected artists. Danny Glover, bah. Oprah, bah. Impressive but just folk. But Lucille, well, Lucille Clifton is Lucille Clifton: the ultimate enigma, a truly great artist. Certainly she is a woman with a life full of triumphs and tragedies. She is a poet who has, for upwards of thirty years, beat her own drum and written powerful, important poems. So it was not surprising that, when I finally met her at a writer's conference, the most I could do was blather, stick my face too close to hers as if performing some sort of inspection, thank her for her work, offer her my chair, and ask if she needed water. I wonder how many fools she had to suffer that day and hope she doesn't remember this one.

The thing is: Lucille Clifton's is the rare body of work to which I return over and over again. The poems of which I never tire, the ones that provide a roadmap: *This is how to be a poet, Child*, they seem to say. *This is what it should be.*

When I was young, in high school, and just beginning to poke my snot-nose into poetry, I fancied Nikki Giovanni, Sonia Sanchez, and Langston Hughes for their directness, their political content, for giving a brown girl like me a voice. Later, having given up on what was to be my theater career and moving instead into writing, I was intrigued by the storytellers, poets like Walt Whitman and Robert Frost. Also I was in awe of Ntozake Shange, who, it seemed, had done with "For Colored Girls Who Have Considered Suicide / When the Rainbow Is Enuf" something just short of miraculous. (Even now it is hard for me to conceptualize the mechanics of such a work, how such disparate voices and movements, the interior workings of a piece, meld together to form a choreopoem. I mean: what is a *choreopoem*?! How does a body come up with the idea to write one?) Anyway, my poetic meanderings, the excursions taken from the moment I wrote that first poem until now, were all leading me to Lucille, the poet who gives us brown girls fierce, undaunting voices. She is an astute social commentator; tells enormous stories in small, confined spaces; and is inspired in such a way that she seems like an oracle, a soothsayer, or, yes, a for real and sure enough poet.

I started writing when I was fourteen. Mrs. Arthuree Leach, my high school English teacher, had demanded that we each write a poem. "The exotic beauty my darkness beholds" was my unfortunate first line. Nevertheless, she thought something of the poem, read it aloud, and squawked about talent. That's really all it took. From then on I was writing horrible little poems on everything I could, hoarding them through high school and my early college years in drawers and such. I actually had the nerve to compile a sheaf of them and send the pitiful things to the Library of Congress in case someone might want to "steal" them from me.

At that time I was still working on becoming a great actress. This was in Washington, D.C. I was twenty years old and broke, and so when a friend started holding talent shows that boasted a hundred dollar first prize, I began writing dramatic monologues in order to compete. Later, after moving to New York—watch out, Dorothy Dandridge—I found my way to the Nuyorican Poets Cafe, that now infamous cauldron of Lower East Side angst from which many a talented artist has since emerged. Suffice it to say I ain't no Dorothy and didn't fancy myself a "great character actress," which is what I was told by a well-known acting coach who had agreed to take me on as a student. I was young, stupid; "great character actress" sounded lame. I soon found that with a little tweaking, the dramatic monologues easily became spoken word poetry. Spoken word became my life.

The great thing about spoken word is that it demands that you (a) be able to tell a compelling story, (b) engage your audience emotionally (and you will know because they *are* in your face and *will* turn their heads and continue a conversation if what you've got to say isn't important), (c) be a fairly astute social commentator or have a view so outrageous that it merits skeptical consideration, and (d) be funny, or at least understand the function of humor. (I've since come to know that these factors are equally important for page poets.) In the early '90s, the Nuyorican was home to an extraordinary array of fine writers and artists—Carl Hancock Rux, Dael Orlandersmith, Paul Beatty, Ava Chin, MuMs, Tracie Morris, Willie Perdomo, Sarah Jones, Hal Sirowitz, Regie Cabico, Saul Williams, among others—who have since gone on to publish, produce, perform, and win myriad awards.

These were the proverbial good times. But after three years of hanging out and cutting my poetic teeth at the Nuyorican, I found myself writing shorter, quieter poems and becoming less interested in performing them on stage. I was finishing my undergraduate degree in creative writing and studying with poets Ruth Danon and Karen Volkman, whose primary concern was the written word. My work shifted accordingly. I started focusing on line breaks, how metaphors and images were working within the poem. I was becoming more sophisticated (I hope), which was both a function of moving beyond my comfort zone and getting older and more interested in the craft of my chosen genre.

Soon enough I figured out that working a day job and prowling poetry at night could and probably, for my sanity, should be integrated. So I set about getting an MFA at Cornell and began pursuing a substantially different career path: professordom. That's when I really discovered Lucille. And thank God.

You see, soon after that MFA honeymoon period in which we were each desperately in love with the work of our peers, I found myself being accused of many things by some, not all, of those same peers. "Coding" was perhaps the most devious accusation because the word was in fact itself a code used to obscure what was really being said: I was thought to be writing "black" poems—poems written by a black person for consumption by other black folks and only black folks. Further, my understanding of and dedication to writing poems most everyone could get a hold of directly conflicted, at least in the eyes of some of my peers, with what "real poetry" is and should be. They thought that writing cryptic, indefinite poems, poems mired in obscurity, poems that would flummox or, if you rather, "challenge" their readers signaled success. I believed that the challenge should be in what I say, not in how I say it. It was James Baldwin who said something like "if you've got something important to say, you find a way to say it to as many people as possible." Had I known it then, I would have been screaming it in the corridors of Ezra Cornell's Goldwin Smith Hall.

Instead, my use of colloquial language and slang was labeled "code," while their use of Greek mythological references was accepted as capital Normal. And yet, in my head, if poetry is largely the contextual study of the human through concise use of language, then our language, the symbolism we use to express ourselves, is in itself most important. How, then, can slang be considered a "code" by fellow Americans who pull from largely the same cultural iconography? Isn't Detroit in America? Who doesn't know what "ain't" means? It's a simple conjunction. Why is commenting on how groups of people make language come alive, make language jump and hop, make people laugh, cry—how is that not the norm? How is Zeus the norm? In Detroit, Zeus is the name of many a dog, most of them pit bulls. Everyone understands "ain't," as in "ain't no Zeus 'round these parts, Man." Code.

There I was, the girl who'd cut her teeth on Giovanni and Hughes, being told that my kind of work wasn't their kind of work, that what I was writing wasn't as meritorious and was not, therefore, to be taken as seriously. Although I am quite sure my peers at Cornell would vigorously deny such accusations and claim that I am being too sensitive, the fact, however, is that they did not value the work of black writers in the same way that they valued the work of white writers. Quantify valuable to a writer: whom do you read and return to?

They didn't read the work of young black poets (or even non–prize-winning established black poets) as they read the work of young and/or established white poets. They were uninterested unless someone in authority had said "this is a poet worth your attention" (read: this is a winner of a national or international prize). This point can only really be talked about comparatively: my poetry peers who are black are among the most well-read people I know. They read across race, class, and gender all the time. They want to know who's doing what, when, where, why, how. You might say they're nosy. My peers who are white, on the other hand, well, they largely read other white poets. This is nothing less than cultural elitism and is, I think, directly related to their status as members of the dominant culture. Dominant cultures tend to be less interested in what other folks are doing—they don't have to know who's doing what, when, where. And, I certainly don't mean to insinuate that all white poets diminish the value and importance of work produced by ethnic minorities. That's clearly not the case. Still, my graduate school experience, I suspect, is not singular. And how sad, really, because there I was, a lover of poetry, being accused, albeit often silently, of being a danger to "real poetry" by the simple fact that I was a brown girl writing poems in a brown girl voice, asserting that I have not only a place in the pantheon of American literature but also a right to be there and a duty to be there in whatever manner I saw fit. And, in the beginning of that fight against that particular set of wacky beliefs, I found Lucille.

I am sure there are people who can much more eloquently speak to the breadth and scope of Clifton's work, to the general tenor and importance of it in the scheme of American letters. I will leave that to them. What I can say is that, when I seriously began to study her work, I was astonished and deeply saddened that she seems, still, to be widely considered a secondary player. She is, to my knowledge, the only writer to have had two books (Next and Good Woman) considered for a Pulitzer Prize in the same year—and rightly so. Let me be clear, too: secondary ain't obscure. She is not that. But to my mind, Clifton is a major American writer and should be known like Hughes and Morrison: across cultures, geography, taught in all schools, to all ages.

And she, by the way, is one of a very few writers who could be taught in all schools, to all ages. That in itself is phenomenal.

Clifton's ability to examine and write about faith as more than a series of external events replete with religious iconography and traditions into which the mind/body are inserted (i.e., going to church, being a choir boy, going to temple, fasting), her belief that faith is a fundamental element of humanity and is a vehicle *through* which the mind and body more fully and gracefully emerge, is one example of her brilliance. To create a body of work that among other things argues that our perceptions of and experiences with each other are all to do with our belief is atypical and is an incredibly powerful lens that Clifton loans us each time we read her work. This strain runs so long and deep through her corpus that one cannot fully consider her poetry without addressing faith. In fact, it is precisely this embedded world-view that lends to Clifton's work an ever-deepening sense of generosity, exquisite understanding, wisdom. To be reminded that we are beings of faith, not of faith's trappings, is a powerful thing. That her poems routinely address difficult issues—abuse, racism, poverty, spirituality—is further proof of her greatness. Furthermore, I think everyone who reads her work agrees that it is deceptively well crafted. In fact, when I teach Clifton poems, and I always do, some student inevitably asserts "well, this poet didn't revise" or some such nonsense. I love these students; am waiting, really, for their assertions, because therein lies the lesson: Lucille Clifton's poems are so exquisitely crafted that their mechanics are invisible.

I wonder if it is this very fact that has thus far kept her out of the canonical circle. Clifton poems may be too well crafted, too "simple." She does not, as has become terrifically popular to do these days, use abstraction to code her poems as being "complex." But then, Langston Hughes's career was similar in that his work was also defined as easy, and only with time and context have people come to see the deep, deep complexity and importance of his body of work.

Clifton's praise songs/poems are organically generous. We are complicated animals, she seems to say, but ultimately, given the proper nourishment and attention, we will thrive, work beyond our current constraints, get better, be bigger spirits than we once thought possible. She often says this with humor and deference to the ancestors who are always calling out from her poems. When I read her work I believe, no matter how difficult the subject matter, that Clifton herself has hope and faith, that she believes generosity is an attainable attribute. Of course, I am prone to believing this anyway. Nevertheless, Lucille Clifton's work changed my life as a poet because her constant assertions, as I interpret them, gave me voice and space to make my own assertions.

Really, this is all my way of saying that for me Lucille Clifton's work has become a model of what kind of work there is to produce: work that is at once thematically complex and stylistically accessible, poetry that allows me to move in and out of the duality that is the language/space I inhabit. Clifton asserts in Bill Moyers's *The Language is Life* that "poetry began when somebody walked off a savanna or out of a cave and looked up at the sky with wonder and said, 'Ah-h-h!'" That "Ah-h-h" is for everyone—equally, undeniably.

Crystal Williams ✳

Girls in Tornado

It smelled bad, she tells the interviewer, like everything in the world
all at once. The tornado pulled up the earth & all its secrets.
It is not the wind that kills you

but everything picked up along the way. The wind's machine-gun
propels rocks & wood, chunks of houses, bodies,
travesties. There is no hiding from them.

She thinks the fierce noise was angels calling for help
to keep the church walls up around those hunched people.
She believes it was angels she heard, wailing, screaming for backup,

fighting it out with the demons who were pushing the walls inward
from the other side. That those folk are alive is proof:
good prevails, she claims.

I want to tell her it is never
this simple & wonder what will become of her belief.
Will it, like the tornado, pick up debris along the way

or will it remain simple? Will the walls,
the struggle between sides, hold? Or will she get crushed
amid other suffers? I would like to know

what became of that young girl, hope she will never know:
Just as midst a tornado you should be fearful when there is no wind,
no movement, no startling, so too should you fear your friend on edge,

your friend whose eyes no longer assert the angels or their brother demons.
Your friend who is silent, tearless, simple & decided, your friend who is ready
to push down into the earth & pull up everything, everything all at once.

after Reetika

God Is Good

on my thirty-first birthday

It's dark today, the sky has morning mouth,
trees hang their flabby heads & I am not sure
if they are looking into the sour eyes of last year
or the lanky eyes of this one.

Someone is always saying: this year is a good year,
this twenty-fifth year, this thirty-first year.
Someone is always pointing, however coyly, to God.
More of this, more of that, they chirp, it's all good:
Understanding will blossom like a girl's breasts—slowly
until they are, it is, a fact.

Today my accomplishments crouch in the corner,
not jabbering happily or raising their hands,
but with their grubby heads down murmuring something dull.

I have never heard the clock's boom or listened to the ground's gossip,
to the trees' riddles. I've not wanted to be a woman running naked
through the woods. & yet this morning I glanced again, guilty,
at the dusty candle, the pillows, the lighter,
the slow growing moan in my chest.

Today is dark & I am on the ground, the trees do sigh,
the clock does beat. Maybe this is the good life, this sudden uncertainty.
Maybe this is the woman all women once were. Maybe this is the way:
the body as quiver: a single hair on an arm in the middle of a scary movie;
awareness: the story in flickers: wooden floors & dust motes,
a lopsided tricycle, a grammar book propped open on the table—
pages twinkling in the breeze, a giggle through the window,
a hand about the waist, a pillow fight when even the trees snore.

The year has already slimmed its eyes. & I am left to insert myself,
to press myself, again, between the god & the good.

Parable on Kings & Queens

After Jack

Up & down MLK Blvd.
the story jabbers about,
pops upside Deshawn's head.
Deshawn who is cutting school
& her eyes, waps along the sidewalks
where Marcus is getting his Mack on,
where Tika is dragging her son
who wants a lollipop,
wants a lollipop,
wants, wants a lollipop.

According to some,
before the white folks came & got us,
it was all good.
Africa was a land of plenitude & glory
where no one went poor or hungry,
no one slapped his wife as if she were a fly,
no wife smacked her child.
The days shimmered long
& only just hot enough to be comfortable,
the nights were full of lovemaking
wherein
hands were held, souls were made one,
& regal children got produced.
In Africa we were better.
We were not ourselves.
Not one of us cut our eyes or sucked our teeth
or was trifling or stinky or dumb.
Not one of us was a fool
just sorta walkin' around.

Lucille Clifton ✳

my dream about God

He is wearing my grandfather's hat.
He is taller than my last uncle.
when He sits to listen
He leans forward tilting the chair

where His chin cups in my father's hand.
it is swollen and hard from creation.
His fingers drum on His knee
dads stern tattoo.

and who do i dream i am
accepting His attentions?

i am the good daughter who stays at home
singing and sewing.
when i whisper He strains to hear me and
He does whatever i say.

Rebecca Wolff
on Molly Peacock

CONSIDERING THAT I had always declared myself, and believed myself, free from poetic influence, having sprung from the forehead of Zeus, poem in hand, at age thirteen, imagine my surprise—of the worldview-changing kind—when, going back to the stacks for the poems of my high school poetry teacher Molly Peacock, I discovered with a thud of recognition that I had instead sprung from the forehead of this kind, unpatronizing, baklava-munching, New Yorker cartoon of a middle-aged, Upper-West-Side-dwelling poet instead. This entrée itself has the ring of a Molly-ism: there's something painfully proximate in it; something gruesomely fleshly; its specificity is intended to leave the reader no choice but to know exactly what I'm talking about. The intimacy of autobiographical detail, the direct address from speaker to reader, the vernacular of the lucid disclosure: all Molly.

I have no idea how old Molly was, actually, when she first became my dedicated poetry teacher. I was at that age when adults seem just "old"—out of my league, as it were. I remember thinking that she was a particularly forthright version of the usual model. I know that I was in ninth grade, and therefore thirteen years old, and that I had made the lucky leap into her senior poetry elective by virtue of a poem I had shown to Mr. Singer, my regular ninth-grade English teacher. He showed the poem to Molly, and she suggested that I might enjoy her upper-level class, in which the students would be reading poems by famous, dead-type poets and writing their own as per her assignments. As I recall it now, many of her assignments involved the use of formal devices such as the sestina, the villanelle, the sonnet, and I think even the prose poem. I believe that she added that last one in a show of flexibility when it became apparent that several of the students simply could not muster the impulse or strength required to break a line. With my adult knowledge of her own work, I know that she taught forms not only as a way to get a bunch of teenagers to have fun with words but also because she simply loves forms and finds them to be inestimably valuable to her process of expressing language and its concomitant emotion.

After the ninth grade, I switched to a public school down the street but continued to work with Molly privately, every week. We met after school at a coffee shop on the corner, where she would return to me my poems from the week before and discuss with me every green-felt-tipped-pen comment, many of which brandished exclamation points and said things like: "Marvelous! Your best yet." It didn't ever occur to me until much later that my parents were paying Molly to meet with me; it felt to me at the time as though we were friends, if not colleagues. The poems I wrote in the three years I worked with Molly were, in some ways, typical of any teenage girl's poems: they were often concerned, either overtly or subtextually, with feelings of deep self-consciousness and alienation. They were often concerned with sex and boys. The few whose subjects stepped a bit away from my own little life were met with encouragement from Molly: I remember one about a homeless, deranged man called "flat outrage doorway"— "great title," she enthused in her green marker. But for the most part these were poems based on early childhood memories, poems about love affairs real and imagined, about friendships and their injustices, about wishing to be prettier, about an unsubtle dream I had in which a man asked me to take care of a doll-sized woman in a red cardigan. He said that she had been raped and that if I wanted to I could rape her again. Then the doll-sized woman flew out the window.

If there is anything remarkable in these poems it is the consistency with which I employed the form known as "free verse"; I never fell in love with Molly's devices. I remember one embarrassing villanelle I wrote for that ninth-grade class about, seriously, how much I loved to watch black girls dance. The repeating line was, I believe, "I love to watch black girls dance." I don't know if I was talking about *Soul Train* or some closer encounter, but I do recall the sentiment, or fugue state, behind the composition of that embarrassing line: it is the very same lifesaving trance that still descends and allows me to briefly suspend my native world-weariness when writing a line for a poem, and to therefore write whatever in the world comes to mind and only later to consider the consequences. God bless Molly for not mentioning all the things that were potentially problematic about that poem in class—I believe she only commented on the end rhymes and talked about how difficult it is to find a line that you can repeat in a "natural" sounding way.

Molly encouraged me in the naturalism I tended toward and never placed undue emphasis on form. She did, however, gently allow me to recognize that a poem is a made thing, when it would have been all too easy to allow me to wallow in the very real illusion of the inspired, irrevocable utterance; the allure of the truly true. I do remember her admonishing me, leaning over my poem as it lay on the table at our regular booth in the back of Joe Junior's on the corner of Third Avenue and Sixteenth Street, to pay more attention to the length of my lines. I tended, in the tenth and eleventh grades, toward very short lines. Three words or so per, max. I remember asking her why it was important, attention to line length, and her response being categorical: it is always important to pay attention.

It is perhaps also remarkable how sure-footedly I found my way into the heart of confessional subject matter at such a tender age. I remember a poem I wrote about how I hated to get my period when I hadn't had sex recently (with the man I purportedly loved) because it felt pointless without the possibility of conception. Never mind the assumed precociousness of sexual awareness: What was I reading? This was 1980; Sharon Olds was just a twinkle in Knopf's eye. I had read, I think, some Anne Sexton, but not enough to really give that sort of permission. I think, dear reader, that it was Molly I was reading.

Molly Peacock's poetry (five books including a volume of new and selected poems) has been recognized by critics and fans alike for what it appears to be: formalism, confessionalism, New Formalism. New Formalism, I loosely understand, designates the work of a group of youngish poets, arising in the 1980s and '90s, who use formal devices such as those named above. Apparently there has been a further development in the particularly fervid corner of criticism that regards the use of form in contemporary poetry: New Formalism, along with its cousin New Narrative, is now a subgenre of Expansive Poetry, a term coined by one Wade Newman in 1989. Like "Language Poetry," the term "Expansive Poetry" has apparently been disclaimed by many of the poets whose names are most often linked with it, including Lucie Brock-Broido, Rita Dove, Rachel Hadas, Ed Hirsch, Andrew Hudgins, Brad Leithauser, Phillis Levin, William Logan, Thomas Lux, Mary Jo Salter, Gjertrud Schnackenberg, David Wojahn, and poet/critic/businessman/Director-of-the-National-Endowment-for-the-Arts Dana Gioia, although this last figure is quite enthusiastic about the world-changing possibilities implied thereby. In the words of Dick Allen:

> Expansive Poetry's emphasis on significant content, strong narrative and dramatic elements, and a renewal of variations of traditional forms, say its poets, once again expands poetry's reaching out to a wider, more general reading audience. Like Language Poetry (which Expansive Poets generally regard as trivial Dadaism), Expansive Poetry is a reaction against the domination of free verse lyric confessional poetry's excesses of nominalism and narcissism. But unlike Language Poetry, Expansive Poetry's emphasis is on meaning carried by variations on traditional technique, rather than on the use of technique as a way to meaning. While not slighting form, Expansivists treat form as it had been commonly treated until the last half of our century: not as organic, but as a vehicle whose shape follows from its subject rather than occurs simultaneously with it. (see http:// www.n2hos.com/acm/culttwo.html for his complete thoughts on the subject)

Setting aside questions of form and content for a moment, I would argue that Molly Peacock's use of the "I" is about as clear, un-ironic, and organic—that is, arising without convolution out of her actual sense of self—as an I can be. The poems are, therefore, Confessional with a capital C: she writes about her sex life, she writes about her childhood, she writes about the world as seen through her own eyes. In her well-known and much-anthologized poem "The Lull," in which the speaker approaches a dead possum on the railroad tracks, she says: "That's my bargain, the Pax / Peacock, with the world. Look hard, life's soft. Life's cache / is flesh, flesh, and flesh." This question of the persona/speaker/poet is especially vexing to me because for about five years, in college and early graduate school, the tenet I held dearest was that NO poem—no speaker in any poem—was actually representative of the life of that poem's poet. I had arrived rather painfully at a set of beliefs regarding the magical, sometimes diabolical powers of artifice to transform, to remove, to render beautifully inert and indecipherable whatever voice, whatever content, whatever product of the writing moment. We shall not here look into the particular reasons that I might have found it useful to be rendered simultaneously indecipherable and diabolical, but instead look backward again, to my first lessons with Molly in naturalism.

But first let's entertain Mr. Allen's statement by positing the contrary albeit supportive notion that formal devices such as the sonnets and sestinas and villanelles, even the simple *abab* rhymes that Molly Peacock has made her trademark, all do serve to render what is, content-wise, pure confession, into something not necessarily better or bigger but at least other. For the sake of the visionary optimism I prefer to cynicism, it is important to me to believe that Molly's forms are as organic to the content, to the poem, as anyone else's—as any Language Poet's. Why would anyone write a poem, a poem as such, if it were not because she had to? If organic formal device meets the organic Confessional "I," and each is to each as each is to its own, then this is how it is and how it must be.

A poem is, for me, the proof, a priori, of the existence of a shared reality. It is in the writing of a poem that I make myself, like the hot-dog vendor's best customer, One with Everything—or at least with everything in the poem. That everything in the poem is language is, if not immaterial, at least reconcilable: I find the words; the words find me; everybody's happy.

My own poem on finding a possum dead on the tracks was written during my first graduate workshop at the University of Iowa, Heather McHugh presiding. I wrote poems rather feverishly in the four or so years between my last meeting with Molly and my first semester at Iowa. Those poems, some three hundred of them, were read by teachers at Bennington College and at the University of Massachusetts at Amherst. It was only sometime during my second year at UMass that I finally conquered my horrifying tendency to cry when a suggestion for a change to one of my poems was made in workshop. It seems the lesson about artifice had not fully been absorbed: how could it, when the need to write a poem felt as inarguable as the need to swallow? Swallowing being one of those things that can really start to seem impossible if you think too hard about it.

I remember meeting with Molly at least twice after high school; once at a diner uptown, near her apartment, and once at a perfectly Molly-esque tea shop in the West Village. This latter time I remember I had sent her, beforehand, a big batch of my new work, poems written during my second year at Iowa. During this year I had had a breakthrough of sorts, and the poems had moved much farther away than I ever dreamed they would from the poems I started out with, fully formed at thirteen. Most significantly, the compositional process had shifted away (never yet to shift back) from the kind of one-off, bolt-of-lightning, sit-down-and-write-an-entire-poem experience of my youth and into a more streaming, long-running, collagelike event, one sometimes taking place over many hours or weeks or even months. I remember the first time this happened: I was sitting in my apartment watching The Ghost and Mrs. Muir, starring Gene Tierney and Rex Harrison. I wrote a poem during the entire movie, moving freely into and out of the narrative of the film and into and out of the nonnarrative of my poem. I remember at first being uncertain that it could rightfully be called a poem, for its striated texture, but then later being impressed by its flexibility and strength.

What might have caused me most trepidation, showing the poems to Molly, was that the poems had lost their speaker, the speaker that she had known—the speaker that would be easily recognized as me, Rebecca, her former student. Bluntly put, I was no longer writing personal narratives, no longer telling stories of my little life in the manner in which I knew they would be appreciated; I had finally been swallowed by my own tail and the utterances that resulted were pleasing to my ear as well as to a new audience I had recently subsumed into my "process": Iowa. At Iowa it had become clear to me that what Molly did, what I had done in the past, rendering experience in a solid form, in language true but untested, valid but unvexed, was not the thing. And I was interested in learning the thing. I am trying to avoid saying that my poems have been enslaved by fashion;

it's not quite so. Rather, I have had the good fortune to fall into congenial surroundings at appropriate moments: when I was looking to tell stories, I had a listener; when I no longer felt compelled by my own story but instead by the language it was made of, I found my way into that material.

Several years ago Molly was the subject of a documentary film about women who choose not to have children. In 1998, Molly published a book about this decision of hers, a memoir called *Paradise, Piece by Piece*, and the filmmaker had asked her to be in the film as an example of a woman who had fulfilled her self as a nurturer by being a mentor. As a former student of Molly, I was invited to be interviewed for the film.

It was strange to have that relationship presumed for us; had she really been a mothering kind of influence on me? My own mother was very much present during those years, if not even a little bit less maternal than your average grade-school teacher. With the benefit of a rather squinty-eyed hindsight I can say that I thought of Molly more as an older friend, the kind you want to teach you how to put on makeup; sort of like a sister, maybe a close cousin. Our relationship took place before Molly gained the notoriety she has today, as Formalist, as memoirist; she was, at the time, a poet with her first book out, teaching grade school for a living—more a lesson in humility than a primer in public living. Whatever energy I have shored up and disbursed, shored up and disbursed in my role as editor of *Fence* seems to come more from a slight and benign psychosis than from any lessons learned at Molly's knee. So as I sat under the hot lights, with lots of makeup on, being interviewed about the role Molly had played in my life, I found myself stuttering something unexpectedly heartfelt about how Molly had given me the initial permission to write and how I probably wouldn't have been capable of rejecting her first teachings if she hadn't been as accepting of my first learnings.

Molly was my first audience! And now twenty-plus years later I am unembarrassed to use an exclamation point—and all the personal enthusiasm it implies.

Rebecca Wolff ✳

The King

Alone at last with my feelings,
the King an unlikely sentry

the king a peculiar
the king a makeshift

Thinking is dry, and frivolous

I often have a hidden agenda
               (a secret)

    KING II
And why the King should choose
to starve his son to death,
in isolation
and torture him with
water running pitiless on his nakedness,

I'll never know.

I woke up, changed.
You've got to spend money
to make money.

    KING III
In the kingdom
you will live together forever
because she is a fag
hag and you are a fag
hag hag. Family

foundation.

KING IV

I wanted to make my son
look like a king

but I could not bring myself
to bind his forehead
to flatten the back of his head
on a flattening board

Generally I am opposed to mutilation

Even manipulation

You Say There Are No Standards But There Are

behaviours

sticks, rods
entreaties what cause shame

Varieties of morning.
I trade in that

Dawn—a more retractive
a "less and less"
—am revising.

Most of all to be at my leisure
is most important to me

As a witch I have to be conscientious
the energy I expend

contradiction next to me
a mutual breast

contradiction accepts me
a necessary levy
eroded standards

next to me a mutual breast
Font Royale
we mindlessly rifle
your pages
while we nurse

Breeder Sonnet

corpulent
filament

rotting clams and oysters

I hate to wait
a liar and a thief
the underclass motif
posture of mean streets

a medium calm sweeps over the water
destroying the calm that was here before
a harbor—a tranquil, a desert of ocean
existed where nothing was here

it's kind of hard to say it with a
straight face: anxiety disorder

spiders and snakes

missed you.

Boo hoo.
A special kind of "unhappy":

juvenate
and
rejuve
-nate

soot and suet together
a nice paste
for innovation

wake up wake up wake up

he said and slapped me

I deserved it/I was sleeping

in this defensive posture

Are you meant to be born
Were you meant?

a
b
a
b

c
d
c
d

e
f
e
f

g
g

Molly Peacock ✳

The Lull

The possum lay on the tracks fully dead.
I'm the kind of person who stops to look.
It was big and white with flies on its head,
a thick healthy hairless tail, and strong, hooked
nails on its racoon-like feet. It was a full-
grown possum. It was sturdy and adult.
Only its head was smashed. In the lull
that it took to look, you took the time to insult
the corpse, the flies, the world, the fact that we were
traipsing in our dress shoes down the railroad tracks.
"That's disgusting." You said that. Dreams, brains, fur
and guts: what we are. That's my bargain, the Pax
Peacock, with the world. Look hard, life's soft. Life's cache
is flesh, flesh, and flesh.

CONTRIBUTORS

PAULA GUNN ALLEN was born in 1939, in Cubero, New Mexico, a member of the Laguna Pueblo tribe. She received her BA and MFA from the University of Oregon and a PhD from the University of New Mexico. Her books include *Life Is a Fatal Disease: Collected Poems, 1962–1995* (1997); *Skins and Bones* (1988); *Shadow Country* (1982); and *The Blind Lion* (1974). She is the editor of a number of books on Native American art, literature, and poetry, including *Spider Woman's Granddaughters: Traditional Tales and Contemporary Writing by Native American Women* (1989) as well as novels and nonfiction volumes on Native American traditions and womanhood. She has taught at San Francisco State University, the University of California–Berkeley, and the University of California–Los Angeles. Her awards include a National Endowment for the Arts fellowship, an American Book Award from the Before Columbus Foundation, and the Native American Prize for Literature.

LUCIE BROCK-BROIDO was born in 1956 in Pittsburgh and raised there. She received her BA and MA from Johns Hopkins University and her MFA from Columbia University. Her books of poetry include *Trouble in Mind* (2004), *The Master Letters* (1995), and *A Hunger* (1988). Her awards and honors include the Wittner Bynner prize in poetry from the Academy of American Arts and Letters, two National Endowment for the Arts fellowships, and a Guggenheim fellowship. Brock-Broido has taught at Bennington College, at Princeton University, and at Harvard University as the director of the creative writing program and as a Briggs-Copeland Lecturer. She is director of poetry in the writing division in the School of the Arts at Columbia University and divides her time between New York City and Cambridge, Massachusetts.

LUCILLE CLIFTON was born in Depew, New York, in 1936. She attended Howard University and Fredonia State Teachers College. Her books of poetry include *Blessing the Boats: New and Selected Poems 1988–2000* (2000), winner of the National Book Award; *The Terrible Stories* (1995), nominated for the National Book Award; *Good Woman: Poems and a Memoir 1969–1980* (1987), nominated for the Pulitzer Prize; *Two-Headed Woman* (1980), also a Pulitzer Prize nominee and winner of the University of Massachusetts Press Juniper Prize; and *Good Times* (1969). She has also written *Generations: A Memoir* (1976) and more than sixteen books for children. Her honors include an Emmy Award, a Lannan Literary Award, two fellowships from the National Endowment for the Arts, and the YM-YWHA Poetry Center Discovery Award. In 1999 she was elected a chancellor of the Academy of American Poets. She has served as poet laureate for the State of Maryland and is currently Distinguished Professor of Humanities at St. Mary's College of Maryland.

TOI DERRICOTTE was born in Detroit in 1941. She holds a BA from Wayne State University and an MA from New York University. Her books of poetry include *Tender* (1997), *Captivity* (1989), *Natural Birth* (1983), and *The Empress of the Death House* (1978), as well as the memoir *The Black Notebooks* (1997). Her honors include fellowships from the National Endowment for the Arts, the New Jersey State Council on the Arts, and the MacDowell Colony, a Pushcart Prize, a Poetry Committee Book Award from the Folger Shakespeare Library, the Distinguished Pioneering of the Arts Award from United Black Artists, Inc., and the Lucille Medmick Memorial Award from the Poetry Society of America. She has been a visiting poet at many colleges and universities and is an associate professor at the University of Pittsburgh, where she lives.

RITA DOVE was born in Akron, Ohio, in 1952. She received a BA from Miami University and an MFA from the University of Iowa Writers' Workshop. Her books of poetry include *American Smooth* (2004); *On the Bus with Rosa Parks* (1999), named a *New York Times* Notable Book of the Year and a finalist for the National Book Critics Circle Award; *Selected Poems* (1993); and *Thomas and Beulah* (1986), winner of the Pulitzer Prize. She also has published short stories, a novel, and a verse drama and has edited *The Best American Poetry* 2000. Dove's honors include the Heinz Award, a National Humanities Medal, an NAACP Great American Artist award, the Common Wealth Award, and fellowships from the National Endowment for the Arts, the Fulbright Foundation, the Guggenheim Foundation, and the National Endowment for the Humanities. Dove served as U.S. poet laureate from 1993 to 1995. From 1994 to 2000, she was a senator of Phi Beta Kappa; in 2006 she was elected a chancellor of the Academy of American Poets. Dove is Commonwealth Professor of English at the University of Virginia. She lives in Charlottesville, Virginia.

DENISE DUHAMEL was born in Woonsocket, Rhode Island, in 1961. She received a BFA from Emerson College and an MFA from Sarah Lawrence College. She is the author of numerous books and chapbooks of poetry including *Two and Two* (2005); *Queen for a Day: Selected and New Poems* (2001); *The Star-Spangled Banner* (1999), winner of the Crab Orchard Poetry Prize; and *Kinky* (1997). Duhamel has also collaborated with Maureen Seaton on three volumes: *Little Novels, Oyl,* and *Exquisite Politics*. She is co-editor, with Nick Carbó, of the anthology *Sweet Jesus: Poems about the Ultimate Icon* and a coeditor of the collaboration anthology *Saints of Hysteria* with David Trinidad and Maureen Seaton. A winner of a National Endowment for the Arts fellowship, she has been anthologized widely, including four volumes of *The Best American Poetry*. Duhamel teaches creative writing and literature at Florida International University and lives in Hollywood, Florida, with her husband, the poet Nick Carbó.

JENNY FACTOR was born in 1969 in New Haven, Connecticut, and is the author of *Unraveling at the Name* (2002), winner of the Hayden Carruth Award. She graduated from Harvard and Radcliffe Colleges and received an MFA from Bennington College in 2000. She formerly worked as an editor at EarthLink and currently serves as Core Faculty in poetry for the Antioch College MFA program and lives in San Marino, California, with her son, Lev, and her partner, Marilyn Hoyt.

BETH ANN FENNELLY was born in 1971 in Rahway, New Jersey. She is the author of *Open House* (2002), winner of the 2001 *Kenyon Review* Prize for a First Book and the GLCA New Writers Award; *Tender Hooks* (2004); and the nonfiction book *Great with Child: Letters to a Young Mother* (2006). She is the recipient of a 2003 National Endowment for the Arts fellowship and the Diane Middlebrook Poetry Fellowship at the Wisconsin Institute for Creative Writing, and has been included in *The Best American Poetry* series three times. She received an MFA from the University of Arkansas and is currently an assistant professor of English at the University of Mississippi and lives in Oxford, Mississippi.

MIRANDA FIELD was born in 1962 in London, England, and received an MFA from Vermont College. Her first collection of poems, *Swallow*, won a 2002 Katharine Bakeless Nason Literary Publication Prize. She has also received a Discovery/*The Nation* Award and a Pushcart Prize. She currently teaches at the New School in New York City, where she lives with the poet Tom Thompson and their two sons.

KATIE FORD was born in Denver, Colorado, in 1975 and holds a Masters of Divinity from Harvard University and an MFA from the University of Iowa Writers' Workshop. She is the author of *Deposition* (2002) and *Colosseum* (2008). She has received an Academy of American Poets prize and is a contributor to the anthology *Legitimate Dangers: American Poets of the New Century* (2006). She is poetry editor of the *New Orleans Review* and has taught at Loyola University, Reed College, and Franklin and Marshall College. She lives in Philadelphia with her husband, the novelist Josh Emmons.

DAPHNE GOTTLIEB was born in Philadelphia in 1968. She is the author of *Pelt* (1999); *Why Things Burn* (2001), which won the Firecracker Alternative Book Award for Spoken Word; *Final Girl* (2003); and the forthcoming *Kissing Dead Girls* (2007). She is also the editor of *Homewrecker: An Adultery Reader* (2005) and author, with illustrator Diane DiMassa, of the graphic novel *Jokes and the Unconscious* (2006). She received an MFA from Mills College and is currently on faculty at the New College of California. She lives in San Francisco.

JORIE GRAHAM was born in New York City in 1950 and spent her youth in Italy. She attended New York University as an undergraduate and received an MFA from the University of Iowa Writers' Workshop. She is the author of numerous collections of poetry, including *Overlord* (2005); *Swarm* (2000); *The Errancy* (1997); *The Dream of the Unified Field: Selected Poems*

1974–1994, which won the 1996 Pulitzer Prize for Poetry; *The End of Beauty* (1987); and *Hybrids of Plants and of Ghosts* (1980). She has also edited two anthologies, *Earth Took of Earth: 100 Great Poems of the English Language* (1996) and *The Best American Poetry 1990*. Her honors include a John D. and Catherine T. MacArthur fellowship and the Morton Dauwen Zabel Award from the American Academy and Institute of Arts and Letters. She has taught at the University of Iowa Writers' Workshop and is currently the Boylston Professor of Rhetoric and Oratory at Harvard University. She served as a chancellor of the Academy of American Poets from 1997 to 2003.

ARIELLE GREENBERG was born in 1972 in Columbus, Ohio, and raised in upstate New York. She received her BA from the State University of New York at Purchase and her MFA from Syracuse University. She is the author of *My Kafka Century* (2005) and *Given* (2002) and the editor of a composition course reader, *Youth Subcultures: Exploring Underground America* (2006). She has received an Academy of American Poets prize, a Saltonstall grant, and a MacDowell Colony fellowship and has been included in two editions of *The Best American Poetry*. She is the poetry editor of *Black Clock* and an assistant professor in the poetry program at Columbia College Chicago, where she is a founding coeditor of the journal *Court Green*. She lives with Rob Morris and their daughter Willa in Evanston, Illinois.

MARILYN HACKER was born in New York City in 1942. She received a BA from New York University. She is the author of several books of poetry, including *Desesperanto: Poems 1999–2002* (2003); *First Cities: Collected Early Poems 1960–1979* (2003); *Winter Numbers* (1994), which won the Lenore Marshall Poetry Prize and a Lambda Literary Award; *Selected Poems, 1965–1990* (1994), which received the Poets' Prize; *Love, Death, and the Changing of the Seasons* (1986); *Going Back to the River* (1990), for which she received a Lambda Literary Award; and *Presentation Piece* (1974), which was the Lamont Poetry Selection of the Academy of American Poets and a National Book Award winner. She also translated Venus Khoury-Ghata's poetry, published in *She Says* (2003) and *Here There Was Once a Country* (2001). Hacker was editor of the *Kenyon Review* from 1990 to 1994 and has received honors including the John Masefield Memorial Award of the Poetry Society of America and fellowships from the Guggenheim Foundation and the Ingram Merrill Foundation. She lives in New York City and Paris.

JOY HARJO was born in Tulsa, Oklahoma, in 1951. She received a BA from the University of New Mexico and an MFA from the University of Iowa

Writers' Workshop. Her books of poetry include *How We Became Human: New and Selected Poems* (2002); *A Map to the Next World: Poems* (2000); *The Woman Who Fell from the Sky* (1994), which received the Oklahoma Book Arts Award; *In Mad Love and War* (1990), which received an American Book Award and the Delmore Schwartz Memorial Award; *Secrets from the Center of the World* (1989); *She Had Some Horses* (1983); and *What Moon Drove Me to This?* (1979). She also performs her poetry and plays saxophone with her band, Poetic Justice. Her honors include the American Indian Distinguished Achievement in the Arts Award, the Josephine Miles Poetry Award, the William Carlos Williams Award, and fellowships from the Arizona Commission on the Arts, the Wittner Bynner Foundation, and the National Endowment for the Arts. She lives in Hawaii.

MATTHEA HARVEY was born in Bad Homburg, Germany, in 1973. She is the author of *Pity the Bathtub Its Forced Embrace of the Human Form*, winner of the New York/New England Prize from Alice James Books in 2000; *Sad Little Breathing Machine* (2004); and *Modern Life* (2007). She received her MFA from the University of Iowa Writers' Workshop in 1998. She is a contributing editor for *jubilat* and *BOMB* magazines and is an assistant professor at Sarah Lawrence College. She lives in Brooklyn, New York.

LYN HEJINIAN was born in the San Francisco Bay area in 1941. She received a BA from Harvard University. Poet, essayist, and translator, she is also the author or coauthor of fourteen books of poetry, including *The Beginner* (2000), *Happily* (2000), *Sight* (with Leslie Scalapino, 1999), *The Cold of Poetry* (1994), *The Cell* (1992), *My Life* (1980), *Writing Is an Aid to Memory* (1978), and *A Thought Is the Bride of What Thinking* (1976). From 1976 to 1984, Hejinian was editor of Tuumba Press, and since 1981 she has been coeditor of *Poetics Journal*. She is also the codirector of Atelos, a literary project commissioning and publishing cross-genre work by poets. Her honors include a writing fellowship from the California Arts Council, a grant from the Fund for Poetry, and a translation fellowship from the National Endowment for the Arts. She recently received the sixty-sixth fellowship from the Academy of American Poets for distinguished poetic achievement at midcareer. She lives in Berkeley, California.

FANNY HOWE was born in Buffalo, New York, in 1940 and attended Stanford University. She is the author of more than twenty-five books, including the novels *Nod* (1998) and *Famous Questions* (1989) and fiction for young adults, including *The Race of the Radical* (1985). Her books of poetry include *Indivisible* (2000), *One Crossed Out* (1997), and *Robeson Street* (1985); her *Selected Poems* (2000) won the Lenore Marshall Poetry Prize. Other honors received include MacDowell Colony fellowships, a California Arts Council award for poetry, a National Poetry Foundation Award, National Endowment for the Arts grants, and the *Village Voice* Award for Fiction. She has taught at many institutions, including the University of California–San Diego, Bard College, and Mills College. She lives in La Jolla, California.

SUSAN HOWE was born in 1937 in Boston and attended the Boston Museum School of Fine Arts. Her books of poems include *The Midnight* (2003), *Pierce-Arrow* (1999), *Frame Structures: Early Poems 1974–1979* (1996), *The Nonconformist's Memorial* (1993), *The Europe of Trusts: Selected Poems* (1990), and *Singularities* (1990). Her books of criticism are *The Birth-Mark: Unsettling the Wilderness in American Literary History* (1993), a *Times Literary Supplement* International Book of the Year, and *My Emily Dickinson* (1985). Her work also has appeared in *Anthology of American Poetry* (1999), *The Norton Anthology of Contemporary American Poetry* (2003), and *Poems for the Millennium, Volume 2* (1998). She has received two American Book Awards from the Before Columbus Foundation and was elected to the American Academy of Arts and Sciences in 1999. She has been awarded a Guggenheim fellowship and was a distinguished fellow at the Stanford Institute of the Humanities. She was the Samuel P. Capen Chair of Poetry and the Humanities at the State University of New York at Buffalo and was elected a chancellor of the Academy of American Poets in 2000. She lives in Guilford, Connecticut.

KIRSTEN KASCHOCK was born in 1972 in Ithaca, New York. She is the author of *Unfathoms* (2004), a finalist for the Norma Farber First Book Award. She received an MFA from Syracuse University and a PhD from the University of Georgia; she also holds an MFA in choreography from the University of Iowa and has received a grant from the Pennsylvania Council in the Arts for dance. She lives in Philadelphia.

JOY KATZ was born in Newark, New Jersey, in 1963. She is the author of *Fabulae* (2002) and *The Garden Room* (2006). She also is coeditor of the anthology *Dark Horses: Poets on Overlooked Poems* (2007). She held a Stegner Fellowship at Stanford and serves as a senior editor at *Pleiades* magazine. She received her MFA from Washington University in St. Louis and works as a book designer and as a creative writing instructor at The New School. She served as writer-in-residence at the University of Missouri–St. Louis in 2007. She lives in Brooklyn.

MYUNG MI KIM was born in 1957 in Seoul, Korea. She received her BA from Oberlin College, her MA from Johns Hopkins University, and her MFA from the University of Iowa Writers' Workshop. She is the author of several books, including *Commons* (2002), *Dura* (1998), *The Bounty* (1996), and *Under Flag* (1991). Her work has been included in the anthologies *Forbidden Stitch: An Asian American Women's Anthology* and the *Anthology of Asian American Writing*. She is the recipient of Gertrude Stein awards for innovative North American poetry and a Fund for Poetry award, among others. She teaches at San Francisco State University.

KATY LEDERER was born in 1972 in Concord, New Hampshire. She is the author of *Winter Sex* (2002) and three chapbooks and is the recipient of a New York Foundation for the Arts grant. She currently serves as a poetry editor of *Fence* magazine. From 1996 until 2005, she edited *Explosive Magazine* and continues to edit the chapbook imprint *Spectacular Books*. Lederer is also the author of *Poker Face: A Girlhood Among Gamblers*, an *Esquire* choice for best books of 2003, a *Publishers Weekly* choice for best nonfiction books of 2003, and a Barnes and Noble Discover Great New Writers pick. Lederer holds a BA from the University of California–Berkeley and an MFA in poetry from the University of Iowa Writers' Workshop, where she was an Iowa Arts Fellow. She lives in Manhattan, where she works for a quantitative hedge fund.

VALERIE MARTÍNEZ was born in 1961 in Santa Fe, New Mexico. She is the author of *Absence, Luminescent* (1998), winner of the Larry Levis Prize and a Greenwall Fund grant from the Academy of American Poets; *World to World* (2004); and *A Flock of Scarlet Doves: Selected Translations of Delmira Agustini* (2005). She also served as assistant editor of *Reinventing the Enemy's Language: Contemporary Writing by Native Women of North America* (with Joy Harjo and Gloria Bird) (1997). She received an MFA from the University of Arizona and is currently assistant professor of English and creative writing and Director of Interdisciplinary Studies at the College of Santa Fe.

ERIKA MEITNER was born in 1975 in Queens, New York. She holds a BA from Dartmouth College and an MFA from the University of Virginia, where she was a Henry Hoyns Fellow. She received a Diane Middlebrook Poetry Fellowship at the Wisconsin Institute for Creative Writing and is pursuing a PhD in religious studies at the University of Virginia. Her first book, *Inventory at the All-Night Drugstore* (2003), won the Anhinga Prize for Poetry. In addition to teaching creative writing at the University of Virginia, the University of Wisconsin–Madison, and the University of California–Santa Cruz, Meitner has worked as a dating columnist, an office temp, a Hebrew school instructor, a computer programmer, a lifeguard, a documentary film production assistant, and a middle-school teacher in the New York City public school system, where she is the Morgenstern Fellow in Jewish Studies. She is currently an assistant professor of English at Virginia Tech and lives in Virginia with her husband and son.

JENNIFER MOXLEY was born in 1964 in San Diego, California. She is the author of *The Line* (2007), *Often Capital* (2005), *The Sense Record* (2002), and *Imagination Verses* (1996). She is poetry editor of *The Baffler* and contributing editor of *The Poker*. She received her MFA from Brown in 1994. She is an assistant professor at the University of Maine and lives in Orono.

AIMEE NEZHUKUMATATHIL was born in 1974 in Chicago to an Indian father and Filipina mother. She received her MFA in poetry and creative nonfiction from Ohio State University and was the Diane Middlebrook Poetry Fellow at the Wisconsin Institute for Creative Writing. She is the author of *Miracle Fruit* (2003), winner of the Tupelo Press Prize and the ForeWord Magazine Book of the Year Award for poetry, and *At the Drive-In Volcano* (2007). She lives in western New York with her husband, son, and their geriatric dachshund, Villanelle. She is an associate professor of English at SUNY Fredonia.

ALICE NOTLEY was born in 1945 in Bisbee, Arizona, and grew up in Needles, California. She received a BA from Barnard College and an MFA from the University of Iowa Writers' Workshop. She married the poet Ted Berrigan in 1972. Notley's numerous collections of verse include *Disobedience* (2001); *Mysteries of Small Houses* (1998), winner of the *Los Angeles Times* Book Award for Poetry; *The Descent of Alette* (1996); *Selected Poems of Alice Notley* (1993); *At Night the States* (1988); *Parts of a Wedding* (1986); *Margaret and Dusty* (1985); *Sorrento* (1984); *How Spring Comes* (1981), which received a 1982 San Francisco Poetry Center Book Award; *Waltzing Matilda* (1981); *Songs for the Unborn Second Baby* (1979); *Alice Ordered Me To Be Made* (1976); and *165 Meeting House Lane* (1971). She has also published *Coming After: Essays on Poetry* (2005) and is editor, with her sons Anselm Berrigan and Edmund Berrigan, of *The Collected Poems of Ted Berrigan* (2005). Her awards include a National Endowment for the Arts grant, a Poetry Center award, and a Fund for Poetry grant. She lives in Paris and edits the magazine *Gare du Nord*.

NAOMI SHIHAB NYE was born in 1952 in St. Louis to a Palestinian father and an American mother. During her high school years she studied in the Old City in Jerusalem and San Antonio, Texas. She received a BA in English and world religions from Trinity University. Nye is the author of numerous books, including *You and Yours* (2005), which received the Isabella Gardner Poetry Award; 19 *Varieties of Gazelle: Poems of the Middle East* (2002); *Fuel* (1998); *Red Suitcase* (1994); and *Hugging the Jukebox* (1982). She has written many volumes for children and has edited seven anthologies of poetry for young readers. Nye was a finalist for the National Book Award and received the Jane Addams Children's Book Award twice. She has also received four Pushcart Prizes, a Lannan fellowship, a Guggenheim fellowship, a Wittner Bynner fellowship, and the Academy of American Poets' Lavan Award, selected by W. S. Merwin. She travels widely, promoting international goodwill through the arts, and lives in San Antonio with the photographer Michael Nye and their son.

MENDI LEWIS OBADIKE was born in Palo Alto, California, in 1973 and grew up in Nashville, Tennessee. Her works include *Armor and Flesh*, which won the 2004 Naomi Long Madgett poetry prize from Lotus Press, and *The Sour Thunder* (2004), an Internet opera composed with her husband and collaborator, Keith Obadike. They recently developed *Four Electric Ghosts* (songs and stories based on Amos Tutuola's novel *My Life in the Bush of Ghosts* and the video game Pac Man) and received the Rockefeller Media Arts fellowship; they have also received commissions from the Whitney Museum, Yale University, the New York African Film Festival, and Electronic Arts Intermix. She earned a BA in English from Spelman College (1995) and a PhD in literature from Duke University (2005). She lives in the New York area and from 2006–2009 she will be a Cotsen Fellow in the Society of Fellows at Princeton University, where she is working on a book on sound and stereotype.

SHARON OLDS was born in San Francisco in 1942. She studied at Stanford University and received a master's degree from Columbia University. Her honors include a National Endowment for the Arts grant, a Guggenheim Foundation fellowship, the San Francisco Poetry Center Award for her first collection, *Satan Says* (1980), and the Lamont Poetry Selection and the National Book Critics Circle Award for *The Dead & the Living* (1983). Her other books of poetry are *Strike Sparks: Selected Poems* (2004); *Blood, Tin, Straw* (1999); *The Gold Cell* (1997); *The Wellspring* (1995); and *The*

Father (1992). Named New York State Poet in 1998, Olds teaches poetry workshops at New York University's Graduate Creative Writing Program, along with a workshop at Goldwater Hospital on Roosevelt Island in New York. She lives in New York City.

DANIELLE PAFUNDA was born in 1977 in Albany, New York. She is author of *Pretty Young Thing* (Soft Skull Press, 2005) and coeditor of the online literary journal *La Petite Zine*. She studied creative writing and Russian literature at Bard College and then received her MFA in poetry from New School University, during which time she was publicist for the KGB Bar poetry reading series. She is currently pursuing her PhD in creative writing at the University of Georgia, where she teaches creative writing and composition and curates the Vox Reading Series. She is spending 2007 in Valdivia, Chile, with her partner Adam and daughter Hazel.

MOLLY PEACOCK was born in 1947 in Buffalo. She attended the State University of New York at Binghamton and Johns Hopkins University, where she received an MA in 1977. Her collections of poetry include *Cornucopia* (2002), *Original Love* (1995), *Take Heart* (1989), *Raw Heaven* (1984), and *And Live Apart* (1980). She is also an author of prose, including *How to Read a Poem, and Start a Poetry Circle* (1999) and her literary memoir *Paradise, Piece by Piece* (1998). She is the editor of the anthology *The Private I: Privacy in a Public World* (2001) and coeditor of *Poetry in Motion: 100 Poems from the Subways and Buses* (1996). A president emerita of the Poetry Society of America, she was one of the originators of Poetry in Motion. Peacock has been a writer-in-residence and teacher at numerous universities and is currently a member of the graduate faculty of Spalding University's Brief Residency MFA Program and a lecturer at the Unterberg Poetry Center of the Ninety-second Street Y. She has received awards from the Danforth Foundation, the Ingram Merrill Foundation, the New York Foundation for the Arts, the National Endowment for the Arts, and the Woodrow Wilson Foundation. Peacock has performed her one-woman show in poems, *The Shimmering Verge*, off Broadway and throughout North America. She lives in Toronto.

KRISTIN PREVALLET was born in Denver, Colorado, in 1966. She is the author of *Shadow Evidence Intelligence* (2006) and *Scratch Sides: Poetry, Documentation and Image-text Projects* (2003). She won a PEN translation fund grant in 2004 for her translations of the Congolese writer Sony Labou Tansi. She is the editor of materialword.com (a journal of word/image studies) and coeditor of DoubleChange.com (a journal of French/English poetic exchange). She received a MA in poetics and media studies from the University of Buffalo. She is currently on the writing faculty of Naropa University's online MFA program and a professor at St. John's College. She lives in Brooklyn with her daughter, Sophie.

ANNA RABINOWITZ was born and raised in Brooklyn, New York. She received her MFA from Columbia University. Her most recent volume of poetry is *The Wanton Sublime: A Florilegium of Whethers and Wonders* (2006). Her book-length acrostic poem, *Darkling: A Poem*, has been adapted into an experimental multimedia music theater work by American Opera Projects. Rabinowitz's other books include *At the Site of Inside Out* (1997), which won the Juniper Prize. She has received a National Endowment for the Arts fellowship, and her work has been anthologized in *The Best American Poetry 1989*, *The KGB Bar Reader*, *The Poets' Grimm*, and *Poetry after 9/11*. Rabinowitz edits and publishes the literary journal *American Letters & Commentary* and is a vice president of the Poetry Society of America.

CIN SALACH was born in 1962 in Chicago and is the author of *Looking for a Soft Place to Land* (1996). She performs and records with her band Ten Tongues and is the founder and ongoing director of *words@play*, an after-school poetry program in collaboration with the Chicago Park District and the Children's Humanities Festival. She also works as a copywriter and teacher of performance poetry workshops and has studied glassblowing and seido karate. She is about to adopt her first child with her partner, Chris. They live in the Andersonville neighborhood in Chicago.

ROBYN SCHIFF was born in New Jersey in 1973. She is the author of *Worth* (2002), which received the Academy of American Poet's Greenwall Fund award; her second book, titled *51*, is forthcoming in 2008. She received her MFA from the University of Iowa Writers' Workshop and an MA in medieval studies from the University of Bristol. She is currently a visiting assistant professor of English at Northwestern University and is editor at large for *The Canary*. She is married to the poet Nick Twemlow. They live in Chicago.

GJERTRUD SCHNACKENBERG was born in 1953 in Tacoma, Washington. She received her BA from Mount Holyoke College and was a Bunting Institute fellow at Radcliffe. Her books include *Supernatural Love: Poems, 1978–1992* (2000), *The Throne of Labdacus* (2000), *A Gilded Lapse of Time* (1992), *Portraits and Elegies* (1986), and *The Lamplit Answer* (1985). Her awards include the Amy Lowell prize, the Rome Prize in literature from the American Academy of Arts and Letters, a Lavan Award, a National Endowment for the Arts fellowship, and a Guggenheim fellowship. She lives in Boston.

KATHY LOU SCHULTZ was born in Burke, South Dakota, in 1966. Her most recent book of poetry and experimental fiction is *Some Vague Wife* (2002). She is also he author of two chapbooks: *Genealogy* (1999) and *Re Dress* (1994), winner of the Michael Rubin Award. In addition, she is coeditor of the journal *Lipstick Eleven*. Among her scholarly articles are essays in the collections *Rainbow Darkness: An Anthology of African American Poetry* (2005) and *Biting the Error: Writers Explore Narrative* (2004). Schultz received her MFA in creative writing from San Francisco State University. She then went on to complete a PhD in English at the University of Pennsylvania, where her research focused on Afro-Modernist poetry and she was a dissertation fellow at the Center for Africana Studies. She is an assistant professor of English at the University of Memphis.

MAUREEN SEATON is a graduate of the College of New Rochelle and received an MFA in creative writing from Vermont College. She is the author of several collections of poetry, including *Venus Examines Her Breast* (2004), *Little Ice Age* (2001), and *Furious Cooking* (1996), winner of the Iowa Poetry Prize and the Lambda Literary Award. She is a coeditor, with Denise Duhamel and David Trinidad, of *Saints of Hysteria: A Half-Century of Collaborative American Poetry* and a cocollaborator, with Niki Nolin, on "Literal Drift," "Chaosity," and the forthcoming "Cave of the Time-Stream," Web-based hypermedia collages. The recipient of an NEA fellowship, an Illinois Arts Council grant, and two Pushcarts, she directs the creative writing program at the University of Miami.

ELENI SIKELIANOS was born in Santa Barbara, California, in 1965 and spent much of her youth hitchhiking across other continents. Her books include *The Monster Lives of Boys & Girls* (2003), winner of the National Poetry Series; *Earliest Worlds* (2001); *The California Poem* (2004); and the nonfiction book *The Book of Jon* (2004). Her awards include a Fulbright Senior Scholar writer's fellowship, a National Endowment for the Arts fellowship, and both a New York Foundation and New York Council for the Arts Award. She received her MFA from Naropa. She has lived in San Francisco, Paris, New York, and Greece. She is currently an associate professor at the University of Denver and lives in Boulder with the novelist Laird Hunt and their daughter, Eva Grace.

TRACY K. SMITH was born in 1972 in Falmouth, Massachusetts, and is the author of *The Body's Question* (2003), winner of the 2002 Cave Canem Poetry Prize, and *Duende* (2007), winner of the 2006 James Laughlin Award of the Academy of American Poets. She was the recipient of a Rona Jaffe Writers' Award in 2004 and a Whiting Writers' Award in 2005. She received her MFA from Columbia University and is currently assistant professor of creative writing at Princeton University. She lives in Brooklyn, New York.

ELIZABETH TREADWELL was born in Oakland, California, in 1967 of Cherokee, English, Irish, and unknown heritage; she lives there now with her family. She is the author of *Eleanor Ramsey: The Queen of Cups* (1997); *Populace* (1999); *Chantry* (2004); *LILYFOIL + 3* (2004); *Cornstarch Figurine* (2006); *Wardolly* (2007); and *Birds & Fancies* (2007). She was also the editor and publisher of *Outlet* magazine and Double Lucy Books from 1997 to 2002. She received an MFA from San Francisco State University and a BA from the University of California–Berkeley. She is the director of Small Press Traffic Literary Arts Center at the California College of the Arts in San Francisco.

ANNE WALDMAN was born in Millville, New Jersey, in 1945 and grew up on MacDougal Street in New York City. She received her BA from Bennington College. From 1966 until 1978 she ran the St. Mark's Poetry Project. Afterward she founded the Jack Kerouac School of Disembodied Poetics at the Naropa Institute in Boulder, Colorado, with Allen Ginsberg. Waldman's honors include the Dylan Thomas Memorial Award and the Shelley Memorial Award for poetry, and she is a two-time winner of the International Poetry Championship Bout in Taos. She has published over forty books of poetry, including *In the Room of Never Grieve: New and Selected Poems, 1985–2003* (2003), *Marriage: A Sentence* (2000), *Kill or Cure* (1994), *Iovis: All is Full of Jove* (1993), *Helping the Dreamer: New and Selected Poems 1966–1988* (1989), and *Fast Speaking Woman* (1974). Her work can also be found in numerous films, videos, and sound recordings. She is editor of several anthologies including *The Beat Book* (1996) and *The World Anthology: Poems from the St. Mark's Poetry Project* (1969). She has cotranslated *Songs of the Sons & Daughters of Buddha* (1996), a book of traditional Buddhist scripture originally in Sanskrit and Prakrit. Waldman is the director of the MFA writing and poetics program at the Naropa Institute and divides her time between Boulder and Greenwich Village.

SUSAN WHEELER was born in 1955 in Pittsburgh, Pennsylvania. She has a BA from Bennington College and did graduate work at the University of Chicago. Her most recent books are *Ledger*, winner of the Iowa Poetry Prize (2005), and the novel *Record Palace* (2005). Her first book, *Bag o' Diamonds* (1994), won the Norma Farber First Book Award from the Poetry Society of America in 1994. She is also the author of *Smokes* (1998) and *Source Codes* (2001). Her awards include the Grolier Award, a New York Foundation for the Arts fellowship, and a Guggenheim fellowship, and she has been included in many volumes of *Best American Poetry*. She has been an instructor at the School of the Art Institute of Chicago, The New School, Rutgers University, Princeton University, and the University of Iowa Writers' Workshop, among others. She lives in the New York area.

CRYSTAL WILLIAMS was born in 1970 in Detroit. She is the author of *Kin* (2000) and *Lunatic* (2002). She holds an undergraduate degree from New York University and an MFA from Cornell University. She is currently on faculty at Reed College in Portland, Oregon, and lives in Portland and Chicago.

REBECCA WOLFF was born in New York City in 1967. Her two books of poems are *Manderley*, winner of the National Poetry Series (2001), and *Figment*, winner of the Barnard Women Poets Prize (2004). She is the founding editor of the literary magazine *Fence* as well as the press Fence Books and the online poetry review journal *The Constant Critic*. She received her MFA from the University of Iowa Writers' Workshop. Wolff is being paid to edit her press by the University of Albany, in a happy partnership with the New York State Writers Institute. She lives in Athens, New York, with her husband, novelist Ira Sher, and their children Asher Wolff and Margot Sher.

RACHEL ZUCKER was born in 1971 in New York City. She received her BA from Yale and MFA from the University of Iowa Writers' Workshop. She is the author of *The Bad Wife Handbook* (2007), *The Last Clear Narrative* (2004), and *Eating in the Underworld* (2003). She is the recipient of the Barrow Street Prize, the Strousse Award, and the Center for Book Arts Prize. She is the founder and editor of *Boomerang! A Contributors' Journal* and recently served as poet-in-residence at Fordham University. She lives in Manhattan with her husband and three sons.

PERMISSIONS

INDEX

Factor, Jenny, 1–10; aesthetics compared with those of Marilyn Hacker, 5; correspondence with Marilyn Hacker, 4; on mentorship, 4–5; Works included: "Adrift," 9; "Scotch and Soda," 7; "Confidential P.S.," 10; "'Now what can we do for my Pretty?' you ask...," 8–9; "Playing Doctor," 8; "Rubyfruit," 7–8; "Safer Sex?," 9–10

feminism, 172–175, 207–209; and class, 207; Second Wave, 165; theory, 172–173, 208

Fence, 277

Fennelly, Beth Ann, 13–22; on humor, 15; on motherhood, 15; on single-sex vs. coed education, 13; *Tender Hooks*, 15; University of Notre Dame, 14; Woodlands Academy of the Sacred Heart, 13–14, 16; Works included: "Because People Ask What My Daughter Will Think of My Poems When She's 16," 19–20; "First Warm Day in a College Town," 21–22; "The Mommy at the Zoo," 17–19

Fern, Fanny, 99

Field, Miranda, 25–32, 78; childhood in England, 26; on motherhood and writing, 26; on poetic influence, 27; *Swallow*, 26; Works included: "Animal/Vegetable Fable," 30; "Break," 31; "I Do Not Sleep for Sleep Is Like the Wind and Trees Amazed," 31–32

Finch, Annie, 165; "Confessions of a Postmodern Poetess," 165

Flaubert, Gustave, 221

Ford, Katie, 35–42; *Deposition*, 38; at Harvard Divinity School, 35, 37; on Julian of Norwich, 37; on religious belief, 35–36; Works included: "It's Late Here How Light Is Late Once You've Fallen," 42; "Last Breath with Belief in It," 41; "Put Your Hands upon Your Eyes," 40–41

Four Bean Stew, 149

Fraser, Kathleen, 210

Frick Collection, 195–196

Frick, Henry Clay, 196

Frost, Robert, 162, 260

Gatsby, Jay, 69

gender: and American families, 164, 172; bias, 160; and mentorship, 163; and teaching, 163; stereotypes, 171–172; and writing, 159–161

Gernes, Sonia, 14

The Ghost and Mrs. Muir, 276

Ginsberg, Allen, 117

Giovanni, Nikki, 260, 262

Gladman, Renee, 210

Glover, Danny, 259

Glück, Robert, 210

Goia, Dana, 274

Goldbarth, Albert, 56

Goldsworthy, Andy, 58

Gottlieb, Daphne, 45–54; on communal mentorship, 47–48; on feminist community, 48; on rape as a subject, 46; Works included: "Greyhound Rescue," 51–53; "She Makes Me Feel Like," 50; "speed times distance," 54

Graham, Jorie, 35–39, 43–44; *Erosion*, 36; at Harvard University, 35–36; as a teacher, 37–38; Works included: "History," 43–44

graphic novels, 57

Green Mill Poetry Slam, 184

Guest, Barbara, 210

H. D., 4, 76, 131

Hacker, Marilyn, 1–6, 11–12; aesthetics compared with those of Jenny Factor, 5; "Ballad of Ladies Lost and Found," 3; correspondence with Jenny Factor, 4; demi-confessional verse,